D1542940

Making Economic Policy in Congress

Edited by Allen Schick

American Enterprise Institute for Public Policy Research
Washington and London

HC
106.5
·M356
1983

Library of Congress Cataloging in Publication Data

Main entry under title:

Making economic policy in Congress.

    (AEI studies ; 391)
      1. United States—Economic policy. 2. United States
Congress. I. Schick, Allen. II. Series.
HC106.5.M356 1983   338.973   83-15501
ISBN 0-8847-3534-5
ISBN 0-8447-3535-3 (pbk.)

1 3 5 7 9 10 8 6 4 2
AEI Studies 391

Printed in the United States of America

Making
Economic Policy
in Congress

Contents

Foreword

The separation of powers between the branches of government is a cornerstone of the American Constitution. The Framers devoted particular attention to powers involving money, taking care to vest appropriation powers in Congress, to give special revenue authority to the House of Representatives, to place the tariff authority firmly on Capitol Hill. All these powers are shared with the president and divided between the House of Representatives and the Senate. A lot has changed since 1789, of course. The development of the presidential budget in 1921, Congress's formal statement in 1946 of governmental responsibility for economic health, and the congressional budget reforms of 1974 are only a few of the milestones along the way. With all of this, the framework of separate powers has remained crucial to the government's performance. Given these elements of continuity and change, what role does Congress now play in shaping American economic policy?

A careful examination of the economic powers of Congress, the politics of economic policy making on Capitol Hill, the political and policy interactions over economic policy between the White House and Congress, and the state of economic analysis in Congress is particularly appropriate now. The United States faces international economic turmoil, rising protectionist sentiments, and domestic economic uncertainty. Federal budget making is still in flux in the aftermath of major reform of the budget process in 1974. Economic policy powers are shifting after the extraordinary events of the early 1980s: Congress accepted President Reagan's sweeping economic program, including a massive tax cut, in 1981; in the very next year President Reagan accepted Congress's major tax increase. (Just as striking, that tax increase was initiated by the Senate, not by the House of Representatives.)

How these economic and political conditions relate to the institutions and individuals in Congress is at the core of the task of AEI's Congress Project. The Congress Project was set up in 1979 to monitor and analyze Congress as an institution and to relate the institutional characteristics of Congress to the broader public policy process. Given the central attention Congress pays to economic policy and its importance to the country and the world, the Congress Project has devoted considerable time and resources to an examination of the role of Congress in the making of economic policy. Each year, for example, under adjunct scholar Allen Schick's direction, the Congress Project publishes an assessment of the congressional budget process. AEI's *Vital Statistics on Congress, 1982* tracked the performance of Congress in the appropriations and budgeting arenas over the past decade or so.

This volume is the centerpiece of AEI's work in the area of Congress and economic policy. *Making Economic Policy in Congress* examines the role of Congress in each key area of economic affairs, from revenues and expenditures to international economics and economic forecasting. It also addresses broader questions, such as, Can an incremental budget process work in an era of decrementalism? Change in economic policy making in the past decade or so and a look to the future are core elements of the book. AEI's Congress Project will continue in future volumes and studies to assess the role of our government institutions in public policy making and the ways in which institutional structures affect policy.

WILLIAM J. BAROODY, JR.
President
American Enterprise Institute

Making
Economic Policy
in Congress

Introduction

Allen Schick

Congress has been making economic policy since it first convened in 1789. The early congresses grappled with such pressing issues as repayment of the war debt and establishment of a national bank. Taxes and tariffs were recurring concerns, and every Congress had to appropriate funds for government agencies. The federal government was small in relation to the national economy; on the eve of the Great Depression in 1929, federal expenditures amounted to only about 3 percent of the gross national product (GNP). Because the government was small, it did not have a major role in steering the economy.

For most of its first 130 years, the United States was governed by a "fiscal constitution" that required balanced budgets except during emergencies such as war. This fiscal norm was supported by consensus about the government's limited role in economic management. The government had few options, but it also had few responsibilities. Business cycles came and went without causing much of a ripple in the trend line of federal revenues and expenditures. Congress did not rush to legislate whenever the nation experienced economic difficulties.

Although the government's economic role was progressively enlarged during the half-century after the Civil War, it was not until the depression and the New Deal that the national government came to be regarded as responsible for the performance of the economy. The "fiscal revolution" of the 1930s not only enlarged the relative size of the government—the budget has grown during the past fifty years from 3 to 25 percent of GNP—but also legitimized government intervention to sustain economic growth and to ameliorate economic difficulty. No longer could the government remain on the sidelines and allow the economy to zigzag according to its own dynamics. Every president since Herbert Hoover has been judged by the performance of the economy. Although Ronald Reagan came to office in 1981 determined to shrink the federal government and to reestablish free enterprise principles, he has staked his administration on the performance of the economy.

1

If the president cannot disengage himself from economic issues, neither can Congress. During the past half-century a substantial portion of its legislative output has pertained to the economy. Yet Congress rarely makes economic policy directly and explicitly; legislation enacted for other reasons affects the economy. Congress does not have an overall economic framework within which it shapes the many relevant measures it considers during the year. The closest Congress comes to adopting a comprehensive and consistent economic policy is in its budget resolutions, but these highly aggregated measures express policy only in budgetary terms and do not reach to the many economic issues (such as energy and trade) that are not decided through tax and spending decisions.

Congress is a fragmented institution in which power is dispersed among numerous committees and subcommittees. Although it has a Joint Economic Committee and House and Senate Budget committees, it has chosen to withhold legislative jurisdiction from them. But most of the committees that do handle legislation have a role in economic policy. As a result, no one in Congress is in charge of the economy, but the economy is not thereby neglected. Through the specialized perspectives of House and Senate committees, Congress attends to its economic business.

It should not be surprising, therefore, that economic policy is made piecemeal and that a "macro" view is lacking. The great strength of Congress as a political institution is its capacity to give voice, access, and representation to the diversity of interests that operate on the American political scene. No two of the 435 members of the House come from the same district; no more than two senators come from the same state. As districts and states are distinguished by economic and political concerns, so too must Congress, if it is to play the role assigned to it by our constitutional scheme, distinguish among the economic issues and interests that come to it for resolution. Congress satisfies diverse economic interests by fragmenting economic policy among its many committees; it is not always efficient or consistent in handling economic issues, but at least it is open to a variety of perspectives and viewpoints.

This book explores the many ways that Congress makes economic decisions. The first two chapters deal with overall policy, the middle chapters consider how Congress functions in a redistributive environment, and the next chapters address particular economic issues. The book concludes with an assessment of the implications of economic difficulties for Congress.

The first chapter traces the development of economic policy from the Employment Act of 1946 to the Humphrey-Hawkins Act of 1978.

Lance LeLoup shows that despite the expanded role of government, there is no consensus on Capitol Hill about what that role should be. Because of the lack of consensus, both pieces of legislation were seriously diluted as they moved through Congress, and neither conformed to the objectives originally set by their sponsors. The recent economic malaise has sharpened conflict over those objectives and has weakened confidence in the capacity of government to achieve its policy ends. During the growth-oriented postwar decades, it was possible to dampen economic conflict by pursuing a multiplicity of objectives without confronting the contradictions among them. The federal government could promote price stability and high employment; the public sector could expand along with the private sector; guns and butter could both be purchased out of the fiscal dividends provided by an expanding economy. Now that growth is weak and uncertain, Congress (and other policy makers) must face difficult trade-offs. At one time Congress knew what it wanted to accomplish and had confidence in its fiscal tools; now Congress does not know what to do or how to do it.

This floundering is not due to a lack of economic information. Robert Reischauer demonstrates in chapter 2 that Congress has all the economic information it needs. It receives timely forecasts on economic assumptions and in-depth analyses of particular issues. Moreover, Congress obtains its information from a variety of sources and can pick and choose from a number of orientations and assumptions. Its capacity to cope with economic issues has been strengthened by the placement of trained economists on committee and personal staffs. Yet there is a big difference between having and using economic information. Except in the budgetary arena, where there is a direct link between economic assumptions and legislative decisions, Congress often does not adequately exploit the data and analyses available to it. Reischauer reminds us that Congress is a political, not an economic, marketplace and that information must compete with other kinds of congressional intelligence. What may be regarded by some observers as misuse of economic data is seen by members of Congress as a proper and conventional use of material.

The shift in policy making from distributive to redistributive outcomes and from incremental to decremental conditions has led to a mismatch between the institutional norms of Congress and the pressure for cutbacks. Congress excels as an institution that defines legislation in distributive terms. When it appropriates funds, it decides who shall get what, not whose budget is to be cut; when it changes the tax laws, it determines whose burden shall be reduced, not whose shall be raised. This distributive impulse is facilitated by the fragmented environment in which Congress operates. But, as John Ellwood points out in chapter 3, the comprehensive framework established by the Congressional Budget and Impoundment Control Act of 1974 compels Congress to make allocative decisions in redistributive terms. The result has been a significant increase in legislative conflict and a failure to achieve some of the goals of the Budget Act. Thus the failure of Congress to make appropriations or to complete other budgetary actions according to the timetable laid out in the Budget Act is due principally to redistributive tensions, not to legislative incapacity. In dealing with contemporary economic problems, Congress seems to be in a difficult predicament: the more Congress is organized to make redistributive decisions, the less capable it is of doing so.

A similar theme is sounded by Naomi Caiden in chapter 4. Caiden shows how Congress was able to function in an orderly manner during the heyday of incrementalism but that it suffers serious breakdown and disorientation when forced to make decremental decisions. The cornerstone of redistributive budgeting has been the reconciliation process used by Congress since 1980, but Caiden demonstrates that it has bred confusion over budgetary estimates and has contributed to a decline in congressional confidence in its budgetary apparatus.

Although Congress is not effectively organized for redistribution, it sometimes seeks to make redistributions through particular programs. In chapter 5 John Ferejohn links the composition and status of congressional committees with the types of legislation they produce. Consensual committees, such as the House Ways and Means Committee during the Mills era, command broad support in their chamber, are favored by rules that facilitate floor approval of legislation, and tend to distribute program benefits among a wide swath of the population. But ideologically based committees—for example, the House Committee on Education and Labor and the Senate Committee on Labor and Human Resources—tend to produce redistributive legislation, which encounters considerable difficulty on the floor. Ferejohn's analysis explains why social security is popular but not redistributive while food stamps are unpopular and redistributive.

The next chapters examine three areas in which Congress makes economic policy. Robert Pastor argues in chapter 6 that the role of Congress in trade policy is often misunderstood. Congress often appears on the brink of adopting protectionist measures, but the legislation actually enacted endorses the principle of free trade. Pastor suggests that more attention ought to be paid to what Congress does than to what it says. When Congress talks protectionism but votes free trade, it strengthens the hand of the president in dealing with other countries.

The outcome is not so encouraging in the tax field surveyed by Catherine Rudder in chapter 7. Rudder found that the sweeping institutional changes made by Congress during the past decade impaired its capacity to produce responsible tax legislation. Congress, and especially the House Ways and Means Committee, became more open and vulnerable to pressure from interest groups. As a consequence, the process of tax legislation has been bypassed, and ad hoc legislation has become more frequent.

In the regulatory field, Congress has been guided by political opportunities, not by a single, unifying theory of regulation. This finding by Mark Nadel in chapter 8 explains why Congress behaves erratically with respect to regulatory policy. During the 1960s Congress pushed for more vigorous enforcement by regulatory agencies; during the 1970s it complained about the zeal with which agencies were enforcing the laws. The lack of guiding principles makes Congress vulnerable to transitory pressures.

Most of the chapters in this volume consider how Congress has been affected by the redistributive environment in which it now operates. Accordingly, the closing chapter analyzes the capacity of Congress to make redistributive decisions and how the congressional budget process affects that capacity.

1

Congress and the Dilemma of Economic Policy

Lance T. LeLoup

Economic policy has been a dilemma for members of Congress in the postwar period. They face complex problems, fragmented institutional arrangements, competing goals, and uncertain information with their own mixture of political and economic motives. This overview of the role of Congress in making economic policy focuses on attempts to set economic priorities, the organizational arrangements within Congress, and the influence of Congress on fiscal and monetary policy. Although Congress almost never acts alone and is often overshadowed by the president and the executive branch, it has become increasingly concerned with the economy, and its collective actions have had important effects on national policy.

Members of Congress rarely are trained economists, but they respond to the main currents of economic thought, ranging from Keynesian to supply-side ideas, and to the performance of the economy. Senators and representatives have constituency tugs that may lead them to place local concerns ahead of national economic problems. The factors that motivate their policy-making behavior are mediated by the institutional arrangements and processes of Congress. These institutional conditions may enhance or detract from their collective ability to make economic policy.

The 1970s and early 1980s were a period of poor national economic performance, characterized by high unemployment, inflation, unbalanced budgets, and escalating federal outlays. Much of the blame for this situation has been heaped on Congress. Political scientists who take a rational-choice approach, relying on models that assume

Thanks to Patricia Roth for her assistance with the research, Eugene Meehan for helpful comments on an earlier draft, and Terry Stack and Mary Hines for typing the manuscript.

economic rationality on the part of political actors, find fundamental flaws in the way democracies deal with economic decisions. And Congress, as the most "democratic" national institution, is the most flawed. Buchanan and Wagner point a finger at Keynesian economic theory, which, they claim, undermined the "fiscal constitution" of the United States: unwritten but normatively strong support for the principle of a balanced budget.[1] "Once democratically elected politicians, and behind them their constituents in the voting public, were finally convinced that budget balance carried little or no weight, what was there left to restrain the ever-present spending pressures?"[2]

Others carry their arguments further. Morris Fiorina has identified a change in the behavior of members of Congress: he argues that they now concentrate on reelection to the virtual exclusion of other goals.[3] The change has increased pressure to return "pork" to the district and, in his view, has come to dominate congressional behavior. Greater emphasis on service to congressmen's districts, he argues, helps explain why the expansive bureaucracy—the "Washington establishment"—has come about: it provides more benefits for constituents and increases their dependence on their representatives to get those benefits from the bureaucracy.

As public policy comes to be seen from the perspective of the relative geographical distribution of benefits, members of Congress act to increase both their district's or state's share of the pie and the size of the total pie to be divided. Ken Shepsle labels these phenomena the distributive tendency and the growth tendency.[4] To ensure continued service to their constituencies and hence to themselves, representatives have turned to the committee system, especially to subcommittees, to institutionalize their ability to deliver benefits. Jurisdictional jealousies arise from committees' efforts to control particular elements of what there is to distribute.

To provide more advantageous committee positions, Congress has created a proliferation of subcommittees and a selection process that increases the likelihood of members' serving on "useful" (for reelection) committees. Critics charge that these changes make it difficult for Congress to base economic decisions on broad fiscal concerns. The result is a congressional budget process that increases overall spending by simply adding up the inflated requests of the subcommittees and committees.

Rational-choice critics suggest a number of policy consequences of these seemingly inherent defects: an upward bias in spending, a special-interest bias in tax laws, unbalanced budgets and deficits, and a distributional attitude toward most policy decisions. The proposed solutions focus on restraining the spending bias of Congress. Buchanan and Wagner want a constitutional amendment requiring a balanced budget to restore the old fiscal constitution.[5] Aaron Wildavsky, quipping that "governments only know how to add, not subtract," recommends a constitutional amendment to fix expenditures at a certain proportion of GNP.[6] Shepsle recommends strengthening the Appropriations committees to restrain spending and strengthening the president just in case they do not.[7] Has Congress really become institutionally incapable of making economic decisions?

There are several flaws in this kind of analysis of Congress. Much of it is simply conservative prescription in the guise of social science. This is unfortunate because many of the observations about developments on Capital Hill are empirically correct. The predisposition of these critics toward certain theories and policies prevents them from providing a more balanced framework. It is true that advocacy by Appropriations committee members is stronger than when Richard Fenno wrote *The Power of the Purse* two decades ago. Budget resolutions have reflected an adding-machine process and often have not restrained spending. Budgets, bureaucracies, and deficits have all grown. But is the drive by members to secure benefits for their districts so much greater than in the past, or does it now come into greater conflict with national policy "needs" than in earlier years? Is the desire to ensure reelection by securing benefits for constituents a complete explanation of congressional behavior?

Pocket calculators in the hands of legislators during floor debate are insufficient proof that all issues have been localized. Surely this is too simple a view of the world. Congress operates with an extremely complex set of motives and incentives, as the research of Richard Fenno and others clearly demonstrates.[8] Members have a wide variety of political and economic goals about industry, trade, growth, money and credit, stabilization strategies, and the size and shape of the national budget. As the performance of the economy changes, their goals may change.

The following analysis recognizes strong evidence of the localization of issues and the tugs of constituency when tangible, divisible goods are involved. The analysis is predicated on the view that this observation alone is insufficent to explain the difficulties economic policy causes members or the decisions Congress reaches. Four other factors considered here help to explain the record of Congress in making economic policy in the postwar period.

1. Macroeconomic stabilization goals are not separate from allocative goals. Goals related to defense spending and domestic spending interact and are traded off with goals related to inflation, unemploy-

ment, taxes, and the size of the deficit. There is no isolation of goals in the decision-making process, and attempts to isolate them have failed. Nor are there clear distinctions between economic and political objectives.

2. Collective goals change relatively quickly. If the sum of congressional actions reflects a murky but discernible set of relative priorities, one observes a great deal of change in the highest priorities. Although cutting taxes and increasing defense spending may have been the highest priorities in 1981, for example, reducing the deficit seemed to have become an even higher priority in 1982. The performance of the economy is highly salient for members, and there is a record of volatility in what congressional majorities have supported.

3. Imprecision and inaccuracy in economic estimates foster additional conflict in the process and inhibit the formation of clear policies. When errors in estimation create uncertainty, the range of claims about what policy alternatives will accomplish widens. Error also increases political rhetoric and the use of political rather than economic calculations by individual members.

4. Along with or perhaps because of multiple and shifting goals, changing economic conditions, and considerable uncertainty, Congress has failed to establish institutions or processes capable of making clear, consistent policies over the long run. No committee or set of leaders seems to have sufficient authority to overcome the fragmented system of decision making. Yet, given the multitude of economic and political motives among members, organizational arrangements hold a key to congressional policy making.

This chapter begins with a brief review of the main economic ideas that influenced Congress in the immediate postwar period and helped create the Employment Act of 1946. This statute is important both because it attempted to formalize economic goals and because it created new institutions for economic policy making in the executive and legislative branches. The performance of the domestic economy over the next thirty years created a different environment for the Humphrey-Hawkins Act of 1978, the next major attempt to formalize economic goals. These laws are examples of how goals can change despite efforts to fix priorities. The chapter then turns to a consideration of congressional institutions and their performance: oversight of monetary policy, attempts at coordination by the Joint Economic Committee, and fiscal policy making through the budget process. The conclusion suggests ways that Congress may handle the difficulties of making economic policy.

Economic Ideas at the Beginning of the Postwar Period

Economic theory in the United States was revolutionized by the writings of John Maynard Keynes.[9] Keynes's works, beginning with *The Economic Consequences of the Peace* (1919) and culminating in the *General Theory of Employment, Interest, and Money* (1936), constituted a radical departure from existing economic thought and created a new vocabulary to conceptualize basic economic processes. As early as the beginning of the 1920s, Keynes saw the need to supplement monetary policy with direct government investment. According to Keynes, "Government investment will break the vicious circle. If you can do that for a couple of years, it will have the effect . . . of restoring business profits more nearly to normal."[10] An important addition to his developing theory came in 1933 with his first calculation of the multiplier: government spending produces output greater than its original amount, determined by the amount of the initial expenditure that the recipient spends. Keynes provided an answer to critics of deficit spending; deficits produce more income and thereby increase tax receipts and savings.[11]

The *General Theory* elaborated a theory that would make monetary policy largely subservient to fiscal policy. Keynes argued that because it would be impossible to get interest rates below some floor, monetary policy alone could not return the economy to full employment. The notion that equilibrium at less than full employment was possible changed the parameters of what was commonly assumed for monetary policy and left fiscal policy as the most critical government tool for economic stabilization.

In 1946, the year of Keynes's death, the economist Joseph Schumpeter noted that Keynesianism had already become a school: a great man, a sacred text, and a set of interpreters who held the key to solving the economic problems.[12] The government's experiences during World War II had led to several important changes in policy and economic thinking. Beginning in the fourth quarter of 1940 and continuing for four years, rapid increases in expenditures—working through the multiplier that Keynes had identified—led to a rapid rise in income, consumer spending, and investment.[13] By 1943 unemployment was below 2 percent.

These were some of the ideas and experiences that affected the members of Congress by the end of the war.[14] Perhaps most important, there appeared to be an emerging bipartisan consensus on the goal of full employment as a national objective. The business-oriented Committee for Economic Development supported it. Republican presidential candidate Thomas Dewey favored full employment, and it appeared as a goal in both the Republican and the Democratic platforms in 1944 (though in bolder terms in the Democratic platform).[15] Even before the end of the war, there were a number of proposals in Congress to formalize Keynesian economics and mandate full employment as a national policy objective. The Roper poll in 1944 reported that 68 percent of the American people answered yes to the question, "Do you think the federal government should provide jobs for everyone able and willing to work but who cannot get a job in private employment?"[16]

The principle of budget balancing was not dead, however. Part of the consensus was made possible by the notion that the budget would be balanced at full employment. Built-in stabilizers would produce a deficit only during a recession and would generate a surplus in boom times. Yet conservatives in Congress remained leery.

Was there really a consensus? By historical standards the immediate postwar period may appear consensual, but there were both underlying philosophical disagreements and specific policy disputes. What were shared were a concern with reconversion from a wartime to a peacetime economy and a general fear of a depression when military expenditures were cut. The consensus on economic goals did not extend much further than this. The old-time fiscal religion of balanced budgets as sound economic management still thrived in Washington.

Goal Setting: The Employment Act of 1946

Many Republicans and conservative Democrats were deeply suspicious of Keynesian economics and considered full employment legislation an excuse by liberals to engage in unlimited deficit spending. Steven K. Bailey's account of the politics surrounding the Employment Act of 1946 emphasizes the significant toning down of objectives from the original bill to the final version that became law.[17] The original full employment bill introduced in the Senate in 1945 was a product of Senate liberals and their allies in organized labor and farm organizations.[18] Even before it was introduced, its language was modified in anticipation of conservative opposition. The coalition, led by Senator James E. Murray (Democrat, Montana), wanted to establish the basic "right" of Americans to a job and make it the responsibility of the federal government to use all possible means to secure this right.[19]

The original version had a number of interesting features not included in the final bill. It declared that "all Americans able to work and seeking work have the right to useful, remunerative, regular,

11

and full time employment, and it is the policy of the United States to assure the existence at all times of sufficient employment opportunities to enable all Americans . . . to exercise the right."[20] The bill went on to declare that to the extent that full employment cannot otherwise be achieved, "it is the further responsibility of the Federal Government to provide such volume of Federal investment and expenditure as may be needed."[21] Besides the clear establishment of full employment as the first among equally desirable economic goals, the Senate bill provided for the submission of a National Production and Employment Budget. It mandated that the president provide for any deficiency in projected employment with specific legislation relating to "banking and currency, monopoly and competition, wages and working conditions, foreign trade and investment, agriculture, taxation, social security . . . and other such matters as may . . . affect the level of non-Federal investment and expenditure."[22] If this was still inadequate, the bill called for the creation of federal jobs.

The proposed National Production and Employment Budget expanded considerably on the existing federal budget. The bill would have created a Joint Committee on the National Budget in Congress to review the president's proposals. This committee would have reported a joint resolution by March 1, to guide other congressional committees.[23] The makeup of this proposed committee differed considerably from that of the Joint Budget Committee established by the 1946 Legislative Reorganization Act.

The full employment bill never became law. Conservative pressures expressing concern for free enterprise, distrustful of the "right" to a job, dubious about spending, led the House to reject the strongest provisions of the Senate bill, including the production budget. What emerged from conference was the Employment Act, establishing as a goal of the United States "to use all practicable means consistent with its needs and obligations and other essential considerations of national policy" for the purpose of promoting "maximum employment, production, and purchasing power."[24]

Congress did much less than it might have, but it was never clear, even among proponents of the original bill, just what "full employment" was.[25] With the removal of the provisions calling for the National Production and Employment Budget, the compromise goal of "maximum" employment was not related to any specific means of achieving the objective. The president had his new Council of Economic Advisers, Congress its new Joint Committee on the Economic Report of the President, but policy makers were neither encumbered with nor guided to specific policy actions. As an exercise in national goal setting, the Employment Act was limited. It recognized the importance of employment as one desirable goal among others and legitimized the use of Keynesian compensatory fiscal policy to prevent another depression. But the consensus on employment was a superficial one. Nothing resembling a policy consensus existed, and many of the disputes continued in remarkably similar form through the postwar era.

The Postwar Economy

The 1947–1948 period demonstrates the phenomena of shifting priorities and goal displacement. Although many Republicans had supported the Employment Act, by the time of the 1946 elections cutting taxes had become their highest priority. After their takeover of the Eightieth Congress, the Republican leaders set about to enact a 20 percent across-the-board cut in personal income taxes.[26] President Truman and most congressional Democrats favored the notion of a tax cut but placed it below two other priorities: balancing the budget and preventing an increase in the inflation rate. The administration anticipated a cut in expenditures from $40 billion to about $25 billion but, because a deficit of $1.9 billion was originally anticipated, opposed the Republican plan.[27] Truman vetoed two Republican tax bills in the summer of 1947, forcing proponents to seek additional Democratic supporters for their plan.

Not only did tax cutting displace full employment as the top priority for a majority of Congress, but the various projections of revenue allowed competing claims about what the tax cut would achieve. Republicans claimed that even with a $5 billion tax cut, there would be a budget surplus.[28] Truman disputed this view but was known to be consistently conservative in his revenue estimates. Despite the general acceptance of compensatory fiscal policy, the battles and decisions made in this period revealed the lack of clear guidance for fiscal policy. In the absence of definitive answers from economists, the process became overtly political. Economic goals were in competition with one another in a very partisan context. Estimates were used as weapons of political combat.

The tax cut finally passed by Congress in 1948 proved to be well timed, since the first postwar recession occurred in 1948–1949. Five other recessions occurred before the passage of the Humphrey-Hawkins Act in 1978. How did the U.S. economy perform between 1946 and the mid-1970s? Figure 1-1 shows the severity and length of five recessions; figure 1-2 shows inflation and unemployment over this period. Although compensatory fiscal policy smoothed out some

FIGURE 1-1
POSTWAR RECESSION AND RECOVERY PATHS, 1953–1975

Index of real GNP
(previous peak = 100)

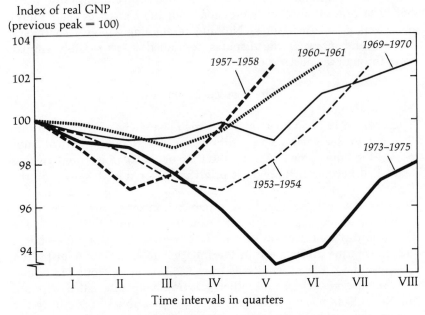

Time intervals in quarters

SOURCE: U.S. Congress, Joint Economic Committee, *1976 Joint Economic Report,* 94th Congress, 2d session, Senate Rept. 94–690, March 10, 1976.

of the bumps in the business cycle, it did not eliminate fluctuations in the economy.

The Eisenhower administration experienced three recessions, but none was deep or long lasting. Under Kennedy and Johnson during the 1961–1968 period, the economy performed well. One of the notable enactments was the 1964 tax cut, championed at the time as a model of Keynesian stabilization policy. First developed in the Kennedy administration, the Revenue Act of 1964 included both personal and corporate tax reduction at a time of relatively high unemployment (for the period). Real output rose substantially, and with it government revenues, without noticeably aggravating inflation. Most economists agree that the Keynesian prescription of increased expenditures and reduced taxes helped spur growth and a decrease in unemployment to below 4 percent from 1966 to 1969.[29] But escalation of expenditures for the Vietnam War initiated high inflation that persisted throughout the next decade. In 1968 the Johnson administration turned to restrictive tax legislation for the first time in a decade. Congress and the president went through a protracted

FIGURE 1-2
UNEMPLOYMENT AND INFLATION, 1948-1979

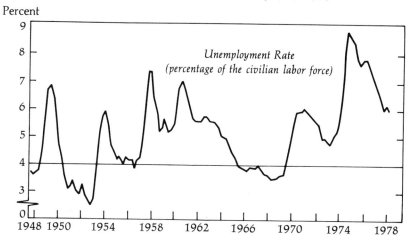

Unemployment Rate
(percentage of the civilian labor force)

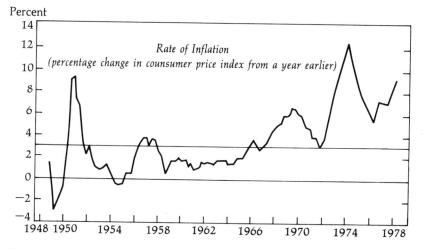

Rate of Inflation
(percentage change in counsumer price index from a year earlier)

SOURCE: U.S. Department of Labor, Bureau of Labor Statistics.

period of negotiations in linking a spending limit with a tax surcharge. Despite the tax increase, economic activity and inflation continued to grow.[30] Goal displacement occurred again in a relatively short time as increasing military spending and fighting inflation became more salient than full employment and increased domestic spending for social programs. Economic estimates for budget planning proved unreliable, outlays consistently exceeding projections. There were

15

growing signs of discontent and frustration and increased conflict within Congress over economic policy.

Increasing inflation led the Nixon administration—with congressional authorization—to impose direct wage and price controls in 1971. Although the controls restrained inflation in the short run, their removal helped fuel an inflationary surge in 1973. Keynesian economics and the notion of a trade-off between inflation and unemployment were coming under increased attack. Even during the 1960s the influence of fiscal conservatism was never far below the surface. Milton Friedman, the foremost critic of reliance on fiscal policy to stabilize the economy, called for monetary policy to be used instead.[31] In Friedman's words, "Inflation is always and everywhere a monetary phenomenon."[32] In 1968 he warned that there was an equilibrium unemployment rate not tied to inflation and beyond the scope of any fiscal policies to affect. Below this "natural" unemployment rate, inflation would continue to accelerate.[33] He was one of the first to suggest that the Phillips curve (which depicts the trade-off between unemployment and inflation) was unstable in the short run and would not make accurate predictions in long periods of excess demand. These ideas became more important in the 1970s as stagflation—simultaneously high unemployment and inflation—plagued the U.S. economy.

Inflation was shown to be vulnerable to external pressures and not simply a function of excess demand in relation to the productive capacity of the economy. Reductions in supplies of oil because of the OPEC boycott and of food because of poor harvests abroad triggered massive price increases that moved rapidly through all sectors of the economy. Food and energy prices accounted for 62 percent of the increase in the consumer price index in 1973.[34] Through the 1960s the sum of unemployment and inflation was in the range of 6 to 8 percent. By 1974–1975 the sum was 20 percent as both measures hovered around the double-digit range.

At the same time federal outlays continued to grow rapidly, both absolutely and as a percentage of GNP. Deficits continued to mount, and so did congressional concern. Figure 1-3 shows receipts and outlays as a percentage of GNP since the early 1950s. Although the budget was out of balance in most of those years, the deficits have grown most noticeably since the mid-1970s. Concern with monetary policy and the supply side (as opposed to Keynes's emphasis on the demand side) grew in the 1970s and early 1980s. Interest rates reached new highs, and real growth of GNP was lower than in either the 1950s or the 1960s. As the nation's economy languished, there was another concerted effort to establish full employment as the highest priority of Congress and the national government.

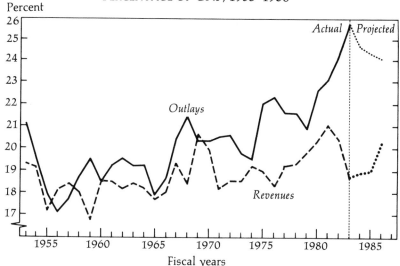

FIGURE 1–3
FEDERAL REVENUES AND OUTLAYS AS A
PERCENTAGE OF GNP, 1953–1986

NOTE: Outlays include off-budget outlays.
SOURCE: *Budget of the United States Government*, 1982.

Goal Setting: The Humphrey-Hawkins Act of 1978

Attempts to revive the old full employment concept were a result both of the relatively high unemployment of the 1970s and of a desire by congressional liberals to renew the commitment of the 1960s to civil rights and social justice. They also reflected a desire for more coherent economic planning and coordination of fiscal and monetary policy. The economic situation of the 1970s was a far different climate for setting economic goals than had existed thirty years earlier. In some ways the Humphrey-Hawkins Act was an anomaly in a historical period that emphasized fiscal restraint and budget cutbacks. California's tax limitation Proposition 13 was more reflective of the national mood of 1978 than was Humphrey-Hawkins, which was passed in the same year. The incongruity of this legislation with broader trends may help explain its failings and its rapid abandonment.

When Hubert H. Humphrey, former vice president and 1968 Democratic presidential nominee, returned to the U.S. Senate, he turned his attention to the national policy objective of full employment. In October 1974 he introduced a full employment bill in the

17

Senate. An ambitious bill, it called for achievement of a 3 percent unemployment rate within eighteen months of passage.[35] A similar bill was introduced in the House by Representative Augustus Hawkins (Democrat, California), from the Watts area of Los Angeles. Little happened in the Ninety-third Congress, but extensive hearings were held across the country by Humphrey as chairman of the Joint Economic Committee.

Serious legislative efforts were launched in 1976 with a coalition of labor and civil rights groups. A version of the Humphrey-Hawkins bill cleared the House Education and Labor Committee in May, and a revised version was reported in September.[36] The Full Employment and Balanced Growth Act declared it the right of every adult American to obtain employment at fair rates of compensation. Like the production budget of the full employment bill thirty years earlier, the legislation called for the submission of a Full Employment and Balanced Growth Plan. Unlike its predecessor, the president's plan would be targeted to concrete, quantifiable employment goals: 3 percent unemployment within four years of passage. The bill declared that inflation was "a major national problem" and that price increases should be held to "levels consistent with reasonable price stability."[37]

No further action was taken in the Ninety-fourth Congress, and the bill languished in the first session of the Ninety-fifth. President Carter endorsed the bill in late 1977 after its supporters made modifications that increased the discretion of the president.[38] Carter's major economic advisers were hostile to the bill, but the president was under pressure from the congressional Black Caucus and organized labor. The House took up the bill in March 1978 after the Education and Labor Committee had substantially altered it. A series of continuing concessions to conservative and moderate opponents reduced the elements of national planning in the bill but kept the notion that national economic decisions should be more coordinated and specific. Conservatives focused opposition on the inflationary effect of the bill and on the provisions calling for direct creation of public jobs by the federal government.[39]

The House Rules Committee attached an important amendment to the bill before it went to the floor that would have changed the congressional budget process. The amendment proposed that the Joint Economic Committee would report a concurrent resolution setting numerical goals for economic indicators (except inflation) and would establish economic aggregates. Most members of the House and Senate Budget committees opposed this amendment on the grounds that it would undermine the budget process.[40]

By this time many observers considered the bill a shell of the original legislation, more symbolic than substantive. As in the process that increasingly characterized the budget resolutions in the late 1970s, the bill was subjected to a barrage of floor amendments to achieve anything from the removal of barriers for handicapped persons to encouraging light capital technology. Despite this "Christmas tree" aspect, gone from the House-passed bill were the automatic triggering devices to create jobs. Gone was the president's full employment plan. Gone was the Joint Economic Committee's increased role. Proponents in the House successfully fought off attempts to include in the bill a specific inflation goal, a balanced budget requirement, and a tax cut.

Despite charges that the bill had been emasculated, it was still a matter of high priority to its supporters. Senate Banking Committee hearings in May 1978 included testimony from an impressive array of economists and public officials who supported the general thrust of the bill. Leon Keyserling, New Deal veteran, former chairman of the Council of Economic Advisers, and one of the architects of the 1946 Employment Act, stressed the need for more comprehensive management of policies and the legitimacy of congressional targets for unemployment:

> This central purpose is to bring more discipline and effectiveness into national economic policy by substituting longer-range analysis and action for a series of disconnected fits and starts in response to the seeming problems of yesterday, today, or the next few months; to provide more effective use of past experience as a guide to current decisions; to substitute greater consistency of action . . .; to develop a closer connection between the goals sought and the means used, with the means continuously evaluated in terms of progress toward the goals; and, in relations between the Executive and Legislative Branches, to accent processes . . . so that excessive resort to the checks does not result in stalemate and frustration.[41]

Humphrey-Hawkins was attractive because it included two irresistible ideas: full employment and better national economic management to achieve it. But, as in the House, the multitude of other desirable economic (and many noneconomic) goals threatened to scuttle the legislation. The bill went nowhere during the summer of 1978 and appeared doomed until a last-minute push from the White House (after angry threats from the Black Caucus) and additional concessions by proponents led to a compromise version.[42] The bill cleared Congress on October 15 and was signed by President Carter two weeks later, just before the 1978 midterm elections.

The final version of the legislation listed congressional goals for the economy. Humphrey-Hawkins declared a national policy of promoting full employment, increased real income, balanced growth, a balanced budget, growth in productivity, and price stability. Was anything omitted? It declared primary reliance on the private sector and the desirability of lowering federal expenditures as a percentage of GNP and set goals of 3 percent unemployment and 3 percent inflation in five years, 0 percent inflation in ten years. It required the president to include statements in the budget and economic report on how these goals were being met. It directed the Joint Economic Committee to report to the Congress on progress and gave the Budget committees the option of including economic goals in the first concurrent resolution.[43] Had Congress come closer to achieving the clarification of economic priorities or improving national economic management?

It is easy to be cynical about congressional efforts in the Humphrey-Hawkins Act. Only three months after it was enacted, the Congressional Budget Office (CBO) in carefully chosen language stated that achieving both its unemployment and its inflation targets would be "difficult."[44] Using only monetary and fiscal policy—even acknowledging questions about the trade-off between inflation and unemployment—the goals would be impossible. A hypothesized high growth path by CBO estimates could lower unemployment to nearly 4 percent in 1983 but with inflation of over 8 percent.[45] Inflation, conversely, might be brought down to 4 percent by 1983 but with unemployment no lower than 7 percent. In December 1982, one year before the target date, unemployment in the United States was at 10.8 percent. Inflation was running in the 5 to 6 percent range. The employment goal had been completely abandoned.

The Employment Act and the Humphrey-Hawkins Act attempted to increase Congress's responsibility for the economy, but neither significantly increased Congress's power to exercise that responsibility. The Employment Act legitimized actions the government had already taken. Humphrey-Hawkins did little more than restate the many elements of the economy for which the government is responsible, even though solutions were to come through the private sector. Although the original versions of both bills attempted to make full employment the primary economic goal, the final versions stated multiple economic wishes. Given the lack of clarity, the Employment Act appropriately left the question of means vague. The authors of Humphrey-Hawkins made the mistake of quantifying goals without providing useful guidance on how the multiple objectives could be achieved simultaneously.

The postwar era began with a pervasive fear of another great depression. The Employment Act was in some ways a policy imperative to avoid a relapse and tame the business cycle. Public policy did just that in the following decades, but by the 1970s new problems were apparent. Humphrey-Hawkins was a less serious, less urgent legislative effort. By 1978 more members of Congress were concerned with taxes and inflation than with full employment, but the legislation was approved as a statement of good purposes.

We have seen examples of the multiplicity of economic goals that exist at any time and of how economic events and political calculations shift priorities. It is clear that agreement on abstract statements of goals has little meaning, particularly when the uncertainty of economic predictions offers policy makers little confidence or guidance. The inconsistency in goals and policies is exacerbated by the institutions and processes within Congress. Although Congress has attempted in various ways to establish institutions that would enhance the ability to manage the economy, the maintenance of a fragmented system increases the tendency to try to do everything at once. The next sections examine attempts to oversee monetary policy, efforts at coordinating economic policy by the Joint Economic Committee, and actions to make fiscal policy through the budget process.

Oversight of Monetary Policy

Fifty years after Congress passed the Federal Reserve Act, the political scientists Harvey Mansfield and Myron Hale made the following observations about Congress and monetary policy:

> Congressional controls rest lightly on the [Federal Reserve] System. In law the Congress can abolish the System or alter it in any way. In practice the System can safely disregard these contingencies. . . . In the past the Board has had sufficient friends on both sides of the aisles in both Houses to prevent floor consideration of unwanted changes in its Statute.
>
> System officials appearing as congressional witnesses are regularly asked, and cheerfully agree, to repeat the time worn formula that the Federal Reserve is an "agent of Congress" or a "creature of Congress" and as such "responsible to Congress." . . . System members can readily acknowledge the existence of a power they can be confident will not be exercised, while refusing to take direction from the power they actually confront.[46]

The national goals articulated in the Employment Act presumably also became the goals of monetary policy, but nothing specific was included about the Federal Reserve Board. The main complaint against the board on Capitol Hill has been that its independent actions have often blunted the thrust of other economic policies. Advocates of greater political accountability of the Federal Reserve, such as Michael Regan, offered the following views:

> The System continues to be organized as though its responsibilities were solely to bankers and to the business community. In fact, its responsibilities are to the Nation, its policies affect the whole Nation, and its structure should therefore provide for accountability to the whole Nation. It is not enough that the Chairman of the Fed should make verbal obeisance to the Employment Act; the President and Congress should be in a position to insist that the Fed not undercut policies determined by themselves as politically responsible officers of Government.[47]

During the 1960s and 1970s Congress made a number of efforts to increase its influence over monetary policy. In 1964 the House Banking Committee proposed that the president set forth guidelines for the growth of the money supply in his economic report and that it be targeted to achieve the goals of the Employment Act.[48] In 1968 the committee published a report with broad academic support recommending the establishment of fixed guidelines for monetary growth.[49] At the time of the writing of the 1974 Congressional Budget and Impoundment Control Act, proposals were made to treat monetary policy in the same way that fiscal policy was to be treated: Congress would have to approve an annual plan for the growth of M1 and its implications for key economic indicators.[50] The proposals were not seriously considered.

In 1975 Senators William Proxmire (Democrat, Wisconsin), James Buckley (Republican, New York), and Humphrey cosponsored a resolution that passed the Senate stating that the Federal Reserve should "maintain long run growth of the monetary and credit aggregates commensurate with the economy's long run potential to increase production, so as to promote effectively the goals of maximum employment and stable prices."[51] In 1977 Congress approved legislation to amend the Federal Reserve Act, requiring the Federal Reserve to "consult with Congress at semiannual hearings . . . with respect to the ranges of growth or diminution of monetary and credit aggregates for the upcoming twelve months, taking account of past and prospective developments in production, employment and prices."[52]

These actions might appear to have substantially increased the amount and precision of congressional oversight. As Robert Wein-traub points out, however, by allowing the Federal Reserve the freedom to set targets for multiple aggregates, Congress made it possible for it always to hit one of the targets.[53] The Humphrey-Hawkins Act in 1978 required the Federal Reserve Board to report to the Joint Economic Committee twice a year on its monetary policies and their relation to the goals of the act.[54] The board was also required to include annually its predictions for the economy. The effect of this provision appears to have been much the same as that of other attempts to make the board more responsive to Congress. Did the changes in the 1970s have any effect on oversight? James Pierce concluded:

> No revolution has occurred. Monetary policy continues to be pursued and executed in its customary fashion. Congress has seen fit to exert little or no influence on monetary policy and the Fed has not shifted its actual policies in a manner consistent with controlling monetary aggregates. The Federal Reserve has succeeded in sidestepping the intent of congressional resolution and public law alike and conducts its business in virtually the same way it always has. Congress has salved its conscience by passing a resolution and then a law but it has showed little interest in providing meaningful oversight of monetary policy.[55]

In 1981, when interest rates reached historic highs, many legislators again blamed the Federal Reserve Board. One House member introduced a resolution to impeach Chairman Paul Volcker and the seven-member board of governors.[56] In July 1981 the House approved a resolution condemning interest rates as "needlessly and destructively high."[57] Scores of bills to restructure the Federal Reserve System were introduced, but little serious action was taken. In 1982 Democrats in both houses introduced the Balanced Monetary Policy Act to force the Federal Reserve to abandon its policy of controlling the money supply and to establish long-term targets for interest rates. The House-passed version of a continuing resolution for fiscal 1983 instructed the Federal Reserve to set targets for interest rates. Although there is more disgruntlement from Capitol Hill, no revolution of the Federal Reserve is yet in sight. Cause and effect are hard to determine, but the lowering of interest rates in late 1982 may have been partially influenced by the complaints from Congress and the administration. Congressional control over monetary policy remains weak, but if the Federal Reserve moves too far out of step with Congress, tighter controls may yet be imposed.

The Joint Economic Committee

The Employment Act put into law what had been practice during the last half of the Roosevelt administration; it formalized the government's responsibility to promote employment, stable prices, and economic growth.[58] There is evidence of at least some legislative ambivalence about delegating power to the president; several members saw the Employment Act as a restoration of the economic powers of Congress. Senator Joseph C. O'Mahoney (Democrat, Wyoming) commented in the floor debate, "This is a bill to vest in Congress the power and responsibility of meeting the issue instead of continuing delegating the power to the executive branch."[59] This does not appear to be what actually happened. Instead, Congress created a process in which the president and his Council of Economic Advisers have primary responsibility. Congress wanted the executive branch to take the lead, but members also wanted an opportunity for input and consultation. This had not occurred during the war, when the National Resources Planning Board (NRPB) acted unilaterally. The Employment Act created in Congress a Joint Committee on the Economic Report of the President (renamed in 1954 the Joint Economic Committee) to (1) study the economic report, (2) study means of coordinating programs to foster the economic goals of the act, and (3) make recommendations to the legislative committees. The committee was given no legislative power or responsibilities, only an oversight mission. The final version of the Humphrey-Hawkins Act did not include provisions for an economic resolution reported by the committee to precede the budget resolution but did include enhanced oversight of monetary policy. What has been the effect of the Joint Economic Committee on economic policy making in Congress?

The Joint Committee on the Economic Report of the President was originally composed of seven members each from the House and the Senate, the chairmanship alternating between the two houses. It began operations after the 1946 elections, which produced a Republican Congress highly critical of President Truman. Its job was to review the president's economic report, attempt to coordinate programs to further the goals of the act, and make other reports and recommendations that it deemed advisable. This left the committee with considerable flexibility to define its own activities but precluded it from having much more than an advisory or educational role.

These are the functions the Joint Economic Committee has played in the last four decades. Ralph Huitt called it a congressional anomaly: "a planning and theory group in a culture fiercely devoted to the short-run and practical."[60] The committee became a haven for congressional intellectuals; it conducted business more like a college seminar than a congressional committee. Another observer called it "the world's largest economics class."[61] It has generally had strong representation from the banking committees. It is a committee that is of interest to some members, is perceived as useful to others, but is generally not seen either as powerful or as a desirable assignment. The committee has usually pursued a variety of interests of concern to the chairman. Senator Paul Douglas (Democrat, Illinois), a professional economist, took over the committee in 1955 and alternated with Representative Wright Patman (Democrat, Texas) until 1966. Before Douglas, the committee issued a single report, but after 1955 majority and minority views were issued.[62] When Senator Proxmire became chairman in 1966, the committee expanded into other areas. Perhaps the most controversial was the supersonic transport controversy, bringing the committee far afield of oversight of economic policy. Humphrey used the committee in 1974 as a platform for his hearings on full employment legislation.

The Joint Economic Committee played a unique role in Congress until 1975. It was the only forum for discussion of certain economic issues, for it had the luxury of considering rather esoteric, technical topics. The creation of the Congressional Budget Office and the Budget committees in 1974 was a step toward making the committee redundant. The CBO had a larger staff, a more prominent director, and more concrete responsibilities. As Congress geared up to take a more active role in budgeting and fiscal policy, the committee was left with its original tasks. The failure to gain a new economic role in the 1978 Humphrey-Hawkins Act sealed its fate as a relatively minor player.

The work of the Joint Economic Committee has generally been evaluated as positive but extremely limited. The committee has served an educational function, but the budget process in the late 1970s probably educated more members of Congress on the complexities of macroeconomics in a year than the committee did in thirty. It published a number of studies, some of which, such as Employment, Growth, and Price Levels (1960), gained prominence; critical of Eisenhower's economic politics, the report influenced the Kennedy campaign.[63] But critics claim that even given its limited responsibilities, the committee has failed to capture congressional attention, to dramatize itself, or to have much influence.[64] The relative impotence of the committee is primarily a result of its lack of any real power in the legislative process. The most influential congressional tool in making economic policy is in approving taxes and spending through the budget process. It is on this process that we now focus.

Fiscal Policy Making through the Budget Process

The authorization-appropriations process evolved in Congress as a method of reviewing agency operations and making individual funding and program decisions. It was not a means of making fiscal policy. Similarly, the revenue process was designed to raise sufficient revenues to finance essential functions. The Ways and Means and Finance committees were not concerned with changes in the tax laws for purposes of economic stabilization until the postwar period. Congress recognized as early as 1946 the limitations of these traditional processes for making fiscal policy. Although the provisions for a production and employment budget were deleted from the Employment Act, Congress attempted to institute a legislative budget in that same year.

A Joint Committee on the Budget was established through the Legislative Reorganization Act of 1946.[65] The committee was composed of all members of the Ways and Means, Finance, and House and Senate Appropriations committees. By February 15 of each year this committee of over 100 members was to report a legislative budget to both houses.[66] The concurrent resolution containing the budget was to include a ceiling on spending and an estimate of the surplus or deficit. This attempt at a legislative budget failed and was abandoned by 1950. Louis Fisher argues that it failed because the committee was too large, there was inadequate time to deliberate, there were no provisions to amend the ceiling, and the resolution was not binding.[67] The institutional arrangements created by Congress failed to alter the traditional system.

When the performance of the economy began to deteriorate in the late 1960s, dissatisfaction with congressional procedures increased rapidly. The president knew whom he had to deal with in Congress when tax proposals went to the Hill, but when fiscal policy objectives focused on expenditures, he seemingly had no one to bargain with. As upward pressure on spending mounted in the late 1960s, both Congress and the president struggled to find some way to limit spending. In 1967 President Johnson requested a tax surcharge to help shrink the deficit. Ways and Means Chairman Wilbur Mills (Democrat, Arkansas) held the surcharge request hostage until a spending lid was adopted. Both became part of the tax bill of 1968, but increases in entitlements pushed outlays above the ceiling.[68]

In each of the next two years, Congress passed statutory limits on spending, but outlays again exceeded the ceilings. Congress tried a continuing resolution, a tax bill, and a supplemental appropriations bill to limit expenditures, and all failed. By 1972 President Nixon was threatening Congress with impoundments and criticized Congress for its lack of control over spending.[69] Congress agreed on the desirability of reducing outlays but was reluctant to delegate any more power to the president.

When one examines the roots and causes of the Congressional Budget and Impoundment Control Act of 1974, many factors are apparent. The inability of Congress to take an overview of the budget, and hence of national fiscal policy, was cited by the Joint Study Committee on Budget Control in 1973 as one of the major weaknesses of congressional procedures.[70] The committee believed that members lacked a responsible way to balance the whole with the parts. It was possible for members to vote for their own pet spending projects while decrying the spending excesses of others. Since there was no mechanism for reviewing the budget as a whole, fiscal policy became the domain of the executive by default. There was no forum within Congress to consider the president's economic assumptions, no effective ways of deciding how much fiscal stimulus or restraint to provide, especially if it disagreed with the policies of the president. Finally, proponents argued that there was no means of establishing national priorities without the constraints of the budget.

Improving congressional ability to make fiscal policy was only one of a number of objectives implicit in the Budget Act. Highly contentious issues of inflation and unemployment could be dealt with in a Humphrey-Hawkins Act where specific policy actions were absent. But the budget process makes real choices and operates at a level of controversy that threatens its very existence. Therefore, the Budget committees have not attempted to accentuate fiscal policy issues. As Allen Schick has observed:

> Fiscal policy has been a derivative concern, and the talk has centered on budget numbers rather than jobs, economic growth, and prices. At no time do the members of the Budget Committees vote on economic policy directly; nor do such votes occur when the budget is debated in the House or Senate.[71]

House Budget Committee Democrats have warded off Republican attempts to divide the process into stages in which the economic aggregates would be decided first, the functional allocations second. This position was reversed when the Rules Committee attempted to amend the Humphrey-Hawkins Act in 1978. As noted earlier, it wished to give the Joint Economic Committee responsibility for an additional resolution setting economic totals before the allocation decisions. The switch in positions—the Democrats defending the fiscal role of the Budget Committee and the Republicans opposing the new procedure—can be attributed to their overall position on the Humphrey-Hawkins Act.[72]

Despite attempts to deemphasize some macroeconomic aspects of the budget resolutions, the fiscal elements of policy seemed to grow in dominance through the late 1970s and early 1980s. Lacking any separate process for establishing fiscal policy aggregates, Congress finds in the budget process, specifically the first resolution, its main opportunity to make its mark on fiscal policy.[73]

In the first year of the budget process, unemployment jumped almost three percentage points to 7.8 percent, a postwar record. Since each percentage point of unemployment automatically adds many billions to the deficit, there was an immediate problem with the fiscal year 1976 budget totals. While the Democrats wanted to do something about unemployment, President Ford attempted to cut domestic spending to prevent the largest deficit in history. Congress demonstrated the independence of its new budget procedures under Ford, approving outlays greater than the president's requests by 7.1 percent in fiscal year 1976 and 4.8 percent in fiscal year 1977.[74] The Democratic House and Senate were willing to accommodate President Carter in 1977 by passing a third concurrent resolution to allow for a jobs program and a tax rebate. Members were disgruntled when Carter attempted to amend a budget resolution on the floor and then suddenly withdrew the tax rebate proposal. Nonetheless, during the Carter administration Congress approved revenue and outlay totals within 3 percent of what the president requested.

The debates over budget resolutions, which took an ever-growing share of legislative time, revealed the more explicit competition among priorities. The needs to increase defense, reduce the deficit, increase employment, and cut inflation were argued and bargained. Since there was no single set of numbers that really satisfied a majority, leaders, particularly in the House, emphasized the need to maintain the process and tried to deemphasize the many policy disputes.[75] The budget process survived and even met most of the deadlines in the first few years, but most observers agreed that no major policy changes in economic stabilization strategies or budget allocations were made.

Nonetheless, members of Congress were operating more nearly at a level of parity with the president and the executive branch. The Congressional Budget Office and the staffs of the Budget committees provided members with independent information and base-line projections as a basis for decision making. The Senate used the CBO's current policy projections as a starting point for markup of the budget resolution, and the House used the president's requests. Both now use current policy base lines.

The existence of independent CBO economic assumptions highlighted the problems of uncertainty in projections. When the CBO's assumptions differed from the president's, members were confronted with the problem of which assumptions to use. Although the members of the Budget committees usually resisted the temptation to use the most favorable assumptions, there were still many occasions when House-Senate conference committees had to begin their negotiations by choosing between divergent estimates. On several occasions the conference could not resolve the difference and simply "agreed to disagree" on the economic assumptions.

The high margin of error in economic and budget assumptions confounds the question of how effectively Congress makes fiscal policy or how "independent" it is of the president. In the first five years, although there were substantial differences with the president on several major issues, differences in estimation were greater than those resulting from policy changes by Congress. This became even more of a problem in the first year of the Reagan administration, when very optimistic estimates were presented to Congress. These increased conflict and uncertainty and also created a problem of credibility for the administration as the economic situation rapidly worsened in 1981 and 1982.

The budget process itself deteriorated badly after 1979. A combination of economic conditions, the presidential election, another recession, and partisan changes within Congress brought about a situation that in some ways resembled the pre-1975 days: appropriations bills not passed on time, increased use of continuing resolutions, delayed passage of budget resolutions, and the demise of the second resolution as a meaningful part of the process. The first year of the Reagan administration, however, demonstrated a potential for the budget process that had not previously been seen. Using the overlooked reconciliation provisions of the act, the administration was able to implement the first stages of a dramatically different economic program, which included major cuts in domestic outlays, increases in defense, and a three-year tax cut.[76] Both the substantive policies and the use of reconciliation were highly controversial, but major changes were made.

Although the long-term economic effect of the Reagan administration's fiscal policies is yet to be seen, the recession in 1981–1982 with its rapid increase in unemployment to nearly 11 percent threatened to scuttle the long-term plan. Only one year after the impressive series of victories on Capitol Hill, concern about the exploding federal

TABLE 1–1
Major Committee Economic Staff, 1950–1978

	1950	1960	1970	1978
House				
Appropriations	39	59	77	128
Banking	6	14	50	110
Budget	—	—	—	77
Ways and Means	13	22	24	93
Senate				
Appropriations	18	31	42	78
Banking	28	22	23	48
Budget	—	—	—	93
Finance	8	6	16	45
Congressional Budget Office	—	—	—	203
Joint Economic Committee	—	—	20	42

Sources: Kozak and Macartney, *Congress and Public Policy* (Homewood, Ill.: Dorsey Press, 1982), pp. 58–62; and *Congressional Staff Directory*, various years.

deficit required the president to support a tax increase in the summer of 1982. Once again priorities shifted in a very short time.

Despite its weaknesses and defects, in several important ways the budget process has enhanced Congress's ability to make fiscal policy. Congressional information has improved tremendously: CBO data and information have helped in a number of ways. The use of five-year projections has given members a longer-term perspective on their taxing and spending actions. Despite the fact that until 1981 the Budget committees acted primarily as "adding machines" in aggregating the requests of the standing committees, Congress does decide on totals that have economic consequences. Even if the aggregates are not set separately, the economic implications of decisions are more explicit.

Staff support for economic policy making has increased substantially since 1945. Table 1-1 shows the increase in the four main House and Senate economic committees, the CBO, and the Joint Economic Committee. Increases in staff mean little per se but along with other evidence make it clear that economic issues have more prominence and members greater staff support to deal with them. In general, the budget process has helped educate members in some of the basics of macroeconomics and economic stabilization even if it has not yet given Congress the ability to set fiscal policy.

Conclusions

Many of the economic problems that currently plague Congress are endemic to all decision makers in national government. Difficulties are related to the structure of federal taxation and outlays. Taxes are more subject to variations in economic performance in the United States than in most developed countries.[77] Outlays dominated by uncontrollables, entitlements, off-budget items, and a growing defense share exert direct constraints on the actions of economic policy makers. More seriously, there is inadequate economic theory to link actions to outcomes with any reliability. Both Congress and the president are vulnerable to shallow and expedient advice of dubious validity. This review of the institutions and processes within Congress has revealed a complex, fragmented, highly differentiated, but overlapping system for dealing with economic issues.

Congressional economic actions reflect a nominal ranking of competing "goods." There is a blending of fiscal and allocative priorities, in which defense spending, inflation, and deficit reduction compete against one another in the process of arriving at a collective decision. Outcomes may or may not reflect the economic priorities of the president, but it appears that more often than not they do. Despite the strong constituency incentives of members, priorities shift. The process we observe in the 1980s, despite the decline of marginal seats, the growth of deficits, and other changes, reflects conflict among priorities that resemble those of the 1940s and successive decades. Priorities shift for a number of reasons, especially election results. But the performance of the domestic economy remains essentially the main factor that changes how members behave with regard to relative economic priorities.

Congressional efforts at setting economic goals have not been notably successful. They have failed because they try to establish one goal as the highest economic priority without clear political support for doing so. There is a tendency to draw up an economic wish list and ignore what is still a reality about how Congress makes economic decisions: that various fiscal and allocative goals compete with and displace one another in response to economic and political stimuli. The Employment Act with its unquantified goals was a more useful exercise than Humphrey-Hawkins with its unachievable specific targets. Both were more symbolic than substantive. Congress has become more individualistic, and this may be related to the increased tendency for members to promote their reelection by procuring tangible benefits for their constituencies. But a strong case can be made that members do have other incentives, including economic policy concerns. The problem is that the legislative process tends to facilitate the achievement of individual goals at the expense of collective policy making.

Congress has failed to create an institution or process capable of making economic policy or responding to the president's proposals coherently and consistently. The Joint Economic Committee may have the perspective to do so but does not have the power. The oversight of monetary policy remains limited, and Congress does little more than express displeasure over policies of the Federal Reserve. The House and Senate Budget committees are in a position to have the most influence on the shape of fiscal policy, but their subservience to other standing committees has kept them from playing a leading role in economic policy making.

Can Congress do anything to make national economic policy more coherent and consistent? The experience of the past four decades suggests some directions, if not solutions, that are more likely than others to improve the ability of Congress to help manage the economy. Procedural reforms need to focus on developing processes that will make it easier to achieve policy goals. If reforms are needed, they are changes that will foster lawmaking and majority rule over representation. These are quite different from statutory or constitutional straitjackets that would institutionalize the economic policy goals of conservatives. Rather, legislative leaders should look, to the extent possible, to policy-neutral procedures that could be used equally by majorities of the right or left. It should be possible to translate the macroeconomic objectives of individuals into collective policy actions. If a conservative majority dominates, the process should allow programs and budgets to be cut. If a new majority emerges with full employment as a higher priority, the procedures should facilitate actions that could achieve that end.

The use of reconciliation, closed rules, continuing appropriations, and omnibus bills has alarmed many observers.[78] It may be a bad way to govern, as Representative Barber Conable (Republican, New York) has said, but the alternative is not to govern at all. Certainly there are costs; to the committee system, to the ability to scrutinize legislation carefully, to the pet projects of individuals. But there are benefits as well.

Without presenting a long list and an elaborate justification, let me suggest procedures that might be made permanent if Congress is to remain a relevant participant in economic policy making. The Budget committees and the budget process should be strengthened. The first resolution should be strengthened; the second might be dropped. Reconciliation should be institutionalized as a regular part of the first resolution. Omnibus appropriations bills could become the rule, not the exception. As it is, continuing resolutions may become the norm anyway. All these measures should be considered under a closed or modified-closed rule in the House and under as close an approximation as the Senate can muster.

These changes would still allow for competition between economic objectives. Once some relative ordering has been arrived at, however, they would allow congressional decisions to be made. Individuals would not be able to subvert the decision-making process. The changes would facilitate leadership by the president if he had the support of a majority in Congress and would allow a congressional majority to negotiate with a hostile president who did not.

As the economic debate in Congress becomes more rhetorical, members attend to the symbolic implications of their actions rather than the real economic effects. Changes that further majority rule will do nothing to improve the quality of forecasting, to facilitate economic planning, or to prevent presidents from claiming that they can increase defense, cut taxes, and balance the budget all at the same time. They might only make it possible to have somewhat more durable priorities, at least for the life of a Congress.

Congressional oversight of economic policy making could be more effective, but it is unlikely ever to have a major coordinating or planning effect. Efforts by the banking committees to make the Federal Reserve more accountable should proceed, and some statutory changes may be appropriate. The Joint Economic Committee should concentrate on planning and coordination rather than on extraneous and tangential issues. Particularly important would be efforts to compare the efficacy of fiscal and monetary policies with alternatives such as industrial, employment, or incomes policies. It is probably not necessary to separate votes on the economic aggregates from budget allocations. Sound policy can be made with the blending of these concerns. There will be times when spending priorities take precedence over macroeconomic goals.

The indictment against Congress is only half right. Attempts to change procedures must recognize the operative incentives of individual members. Yet recognizing and building on the existence of members' broader policy incentives, Congress should develop procedures that permit a majority to work its will. This could be achieved without eliminating the ability of members to serve their reelection needs and without locking in conservative economic policies.

Notes

1. James Buchanan and Richard Wagner, *Democracy in Deficit* (New York: Academic Press, 1977).

2. Ibid., p. 50.

3. Morris Fiorina, *Congress: Keystone of the Washington Establishment* (New Haven, Conn.: Yale University Press, 1977).

4. Kenneth Shepsle, "Geography, Jurisdiction, and the Congressional Budget Process: A Memo to the Chairman of the House Budget Committee," Center for the Study of American Business, Washington University, St. Louis, Mo., April 1982.

5. Buchanan and Wagner, *Democracy in Deficit*, pp. 175–79.

6. Aaron Wildavsky, "Constitutional Expenditure Limitation and Congressional Budget Reform," in Rudolph G. Penner, ed., *The Congressional Budget Process after Five Years* (Washington, D.C.: American Enterprise Institute, 1981), pp. 87–100.

7. Shepsle, "Geography," p. 27.

8. Richard Fenno, *Congressmen in Committees* (Boston: Little, Brown, 1973); and idem, *Home Style* (Boston: Little, Brown, 1978).

9. Herbert Stein, *The Fiscal Revolution in America* (Chicago: University of Chicago Press, 1969).

10. Roy F. Harrod, *The Life of John Maynard Keynes* (London: Macmillan, 1951), p. 417.

11. Stein, *Fiscal Revolution*, p. 153.

12. Joseph Schumpeter, "John Maynard Keynes, 1883–1946," *American Economic Review*, vol. 36 (1946), p. 515.

13. Robert Gordon, *Economic Stability and Growth* (New York: Harper and Row, 1974), p. 82.

14. See Stein, *Fiscal Revolution*, pp. 170–96, for lessons of World War II.

15. Steven K. Bailey, *Congress Makes a Law* (New York: Columbia University Press, 1950).

16. Elmo Roper, *You and Your Leaders*, (New York: William Morris, 1957), p. 56, quoted in Stein, *Fiscal Revolution*, p. 174.

17. Bailey, *Congress*, pp. 41–42.

18. Ibid., chap. 5.

19. Ibid., pp. 57–58.

20. S. 380, 79th Congress, 1st session; app. A in Bailey, *Congress*, p. 243.

21. Bailey, *Congress*, p. 244.

22. Ibid., p. 245.

23. Ibid., section 5 of the act, pp. 246–48.

24. Ibid., p. 228.

25. Stein, *Fiscal Revolution*, p. 200.

26. Ibid., p. 208.

27. Ibid., 207.

28. Ibid., p. 211.

29. See Arthur Okun, "Measuring the Impact of the 1964 Tax Reduction," in Warren Smith and Ronald Teigen, eds., *Readings in Money, National Income, and Stabilization Policy* (Homewood, Ill.: Richard D. Irwin, 1970), pp. 345–58; and Lawrence R. Klein, "Econometric Analysis of the Tax Cut of 1964," in J. S. Duesenberry et al., eds., *The Brookings Model: Some Further Results* (Chicago: Rand McNally, 1969), pp. 459–72.

30. See Arthur Okun, "The Personal Tax Surcharge and Consumer Demand, 1968–70," *Brookings Papers on Economic Activity*, no. 1 (1971), pp. 167–217; William L. Springer, "Did the 1968 Surcharge Really Work?" *American Economic Review*, vol. 65 (September 1975), pp. 644–59; and Lawrence R. Klein, "An Econometric Analysis of the Revenue and Expenditure Control Act of 1968–69," in Warren Smith and John Colbertson, eds., *Public Finance and Stabilization Policy* (Amsterdam: North-Holland, 1974), pp. 333–55.

31. Milton Friedman, "Monetary and Fiscal Framework for Economic Stability," *American Economic Review*, vol. 38 (1948), pp. 245–64; and Robert Gordon, "Postwar Macroeconomics: The Evolution of Events and Ideas," in Martin Feldstein, ed., *The American Economy in Transition* (Chicago: University of Chicago Press, 1980), p. 102.

32. Milton Friedman, quoted in Gordon, "Postwar Macroeconomics," p. 102.

33. Milton Friedman, "The Role of Monetary Policy," *American Economic Review*, vol. 58 (1968), pp. 1–17.

34. U.S. Senate, Committee on the Budget, *Hearings, First Concurrent Resolution on the Budget, FY77*, vol. 4, February 26, 1976, p. 10.

35. *Congressional Quarterly Almanac*, 1976, p. 371.

36. Ibid., p. 372.

37. *Congressional Quarterly Almanac*, 1977, pp. 175–76.

38. *Congressional Quarterly Almanac*, 1978, pp. 273–74.

39. Ibid., pp. 275–76.

40. Allen Schick, *Congress and Money* (Washington, D.C.: Urban Institute, 1980), p. 113.

41. U.S. Senate, Committee on Banking, Housing, and Urban Affairs, *Hearings, Full Employment and Balanced Growth Act of 1978*, 95th Congress, 2d session, May 8–10, 1978.

42. "It's Not Over Till It's Over," *National Journal*, October 21, 1978, p. 1688.

43. *Congressional Quarterly Almanac*, 1978, p. 273.

44. Congressional Budget Office, *The Fiscal Policy Response to Inflation*, January 1979, pp. 55–68.

45. Ibid., pp. 62–63.

46. U.S. House of Representatives, Committee on Banking and Currency, *Hearings, the Federal Reserve System after Fifty Years*, 88th Congress, 2d session, vol. 3, April 1964, pp. 1971–75.

47. Ibid., statement by Michael Regan, pp. 1576–77.

48. U.S. House of Representatives, Committee on Banking and Currency, *Proposals for the Improvement of the Federal Reserve System and Staff Report*, 88th Congress, 2d session, 1964.

49. Robert E. Weintraub, "Congressional Supervision of Monetary Policy," *Journal of Monetary Economics*, vol. 4 (1978), p. 34.

50. Ibid., p. 344.

51. James L. Pierce, "The Myth of Congressional Supervision of Monetary Policy," *Journal of Monetary Economics*, vol. 4 (1978), pp. 363–70.

52. Public Law 95-188, section 202, 2A.

53. Weintraub, "Congressional Supervision," p. 347.

54. *Congressional Quarterly Almanac*, 1978, p. 273.

55. Pierce, "The Myth," p. 364.

56. *Congressional Quarterly Weekly Report*, November 7, 1981, p. 2159.

57. Ibid.

58. Bailey, *Congress*.

59. *Congressional Record,* September 27, 1945, p. 9204.

60. Ralph K. Huitt, "Congressional Organization and Operation in the Field of Money and Credit," in Commission on Money and Credit, *Fiscal and Debt Management Policies* (Englewood Cliffs, N.J.: Prentice-Hall, 1963), p. 477.

61. John W. Lehrman, "Administration of the Employment Act," *Twentieth Anniversary Symposium, Joint Economic Committee*, U.S. Congress, February 23, 1966, p. 89.

62. Hugh S. Norton, *The Employment Act and the Council of Economic Advisers, 1946–76* (Columbia: University of South Carolina Press, 1977), p. 253.

63. Ibid., p. 247.

64. Huitt, "Congressional Organization," p. 482.

65. Jesse Burkhead, "Federal Budgetary Developments, 1947–48," *Public Administration Review*, vol. 8 (Autumn 1948), pp. 267–74.

66. Louis Fisher, "Experience with a Legislative Budget," in Committee on Government Operations, *Improving Congressional Control over the Budget: A Compendium of Materials*, March 27, 1973, pp. 250–51.

67. Ibid., p. 249.

68. Allen Schick, "Congressional Control of Expenditures," U.S. House of Representatives, Committee on the Budget, 95th Congress, 1st session, January 1977, pp. 49–59.

69. Ibid., p. 52.

70. Report of the Joint Study Committee on Budget Control, *Recommendations for Improving Congressional Control over Budgetary Outlay and Receipt Totals*, 93d Congress, 1st session, April 18, 1973, p. 8.

71. Schick, *Congress and Money*, p. 112.

72. Ibid., p. 113.

73. On the congressional budget process, see Lance T. LeLoup, *The Fiscal Congress: Legislative Control of the Budget* (Westport, Conn.: Greenwood

Press, 1980); Schick, *Congress and Money*; and Dennis Ippolito, *Congressional Spending* (Ithaca, N.Y.: Cornell University Press, 1981).

74. LeLoup, *Fiscal Congress*, p. 161.

75. Lance T. LeLoup, "Process versus Policy: The U.S. House Budget Committee," *Legislative Studies Quarterly* (May 1979).

76. Lance T. LeLoup, "After the Blitz: Reagan and the U.S. Congressional Budget Process," *Legislative Studies Quarterly* (August 1982).

77. U.S. House of Representatives, Committee on Ways and Means, "New Tax Directions in the U.S.," December 15, 1975.

78. *Congressional Quarterly Weekly Report*, September 25, 1982, pp. 2379–83.

2

Getting, Using, and Misusing Economic Information

Robert D. Reischauer

The importance of economic information to Congress has grown tremendously during the past decade. This growth has been accompanied by a proliferation of sources of economic expertise, an expansion of the capacity of Congress to assimilate economic advice, and an increased sophistication in its ability to use and misuse economic data and arguments effectively. But the increased importance of economic information has brought with it a new source of confusion, frustration, and disagreement on Capitol Hill.

This chapter analyzes the ways in which Congress gets and uses economic information. The first section describes the basic types of economic information that Congress uses and the various roles played by that information. The second section catalogs the several sources on which Congress relies for its economic information and the key congressional institutions and mechanisms for gathering and assimilating such advice. The third section explores the problems, tensions, and temptations that have been generated by the growing importance of economic information. A final section evaluates some of the proposals that have been put forward to rationalize and improve congressional use of economic information. The remainder of this introductory section examines the reasons for the growing attention Congress has paid to economic information.

Congressional decisions have always affected and been affected by economic conditions. Nevertheless, the preoccupation of Congress with economic matters is recent. Four factors are responsible for it. The first is the increased extent to which economic problems have come to dominate the public policy agenda. Issues such as war

The views expressed in this chapter are those of the author and do not reflect positions of the Urban Institute, its employees, trustees, or sponsors.

(Korea and Vietnam), poverty, pollution, civil rights, urban riots, inadequate health care, poor interstate highways, and educational deprivation consumed the attention of lawmakers during the 1950s and 1960s; economic matters became the focus of their attention after the oil price shock of 1973. After this shock and the subsequent sharp recession, most major policy initiatives were aimed at dealing with unemployment, inflation, slow economic growth, and lagging productivity. Even policy initiatives that were directed at other problems were evaluated, in part, by their potential effect on the economy.

The second factor is the growth in the degree to which budget outcomes have been affected by the economy. The persistence of large and growing deficits has been attributed to the weak state of the economy. The proliferation of entitlement programs with indexed or quasi-indexed benefits means that an increasing fraction of federal outlays is tied inextricably to inflation. The percentage of federal outlays linked directly or indirectly to inflation, which was 9.3 percent in 1967, had risen to 48.5 percent by 1983.[1] The sensitivity of the federal budget to changes in real growth and unemployment also increased until enactment of the tax and spending cuts of 1981. Currently, a one-percentage-point increase in unemployment reduces federal revenues by 4.4 percent and increases spending by 1.2 percent.[2] With the deficit strongly affected by the condition of the economy and the economy subject to seemingly wild gyrations, congressional interest in economic information has intensified.

The third and most important cause has been the Congressional Budget and Impoundment Control Act of 1974. The congressional budget process established by this act elevated the role of Congress in economic policy making. Before 1974 Congress was content to criticize the administration's economic outlook and to review, modify, and vote on the administration's policy proposals affecting the economy. To perform these tasks Congress needed little expertise and few formal mechanisms. The skeletal economic forecasts provided by the administration were evaluated by the Joint Economic Committee, a committee with no legislative authority and no role in the appropriations or tax legislation processes. While its expertise kept the executive branch from straying too far down the path of unbridled optimism, the committee did not provide an alternative economic forecast upon which subsequent actions by Congress could be based. Rather, the appropriating, authorizing, and taxing committees were content to leave the responsibility for economic assumptions and estimates entirely with the executive branch. None of these committees had the expertise needed to understand the effects of economic assumptions or to make independent forecasts. Although the relevant authorizing committees debated, marked up, and voted on the administration's countercyclical tax and spending initiatives, Congress was hesitant to take the lead by proposing fiscal policies of its own.

The Budget Act changed this. The requirement that it pass two budget resolutions each year forced Congress to specify the economic assumptions on which its budget actions were predicated. Under the act Congress could have opted to base its budgets on the administration's economic assumptions, but it chose to debate and adopt its own assumptions. The task of putting its imprimatur on what has often been a gloomy economic forecast, together with the necessity of approving the outlines of a comprehensive budget, pushed Congress to become an active formulator of economic policy and a voracious consumer of economic information.

The final source of Congress's growing need for economic information is the challenge posed by the Reagan administration's bold "program for economic recovery." For a number of years before Reagan's election, a debate raged within the economics profession over macroeconomic theory. Few public policy decision makers were aware of this debate; most accepted explicitly or implicitly the models and policy prescriptions of the Keynesian school without much questioning. But Keynesian fine-tuning, which proved moderately successful in the 1960s, failed to cope with the problems of the 1970s. Rival theories—some old, such as monetarism; others quite new, such as rational expectations and supply-side theory—grew in strength. Each suggested radically different conclusions about the efficacy of various macroeconomic policies to solve the problems of the 1970s. The Reagan program was grounded on a mixture of monetarism and supply-side theories. When it was placed on the congressional agenda in February 1981, the theoretical debate burst out of the halls of academe and into those of Capitol Hill. The need for economic expertise and information grew because Congress was asked to judge the appropriateness of competing economic theories.

Economic Information: Types and Roles

Congress makes use of three basic types of economic information. The most important of these is information concerning the likely state of the economy over the next few years. Such information is needed so that Congress can settle on the short-run economic assumptions that underlie its budget decisions.[3] With revenues, expenditures, and the deficit highly responsive to the rate of economic growth, inflation, and unemployment, the economic forecasts assumed in the budget resolutions are among the most important budgetary decisions made by Congress.[4] These forecasts are also used by the Congressional Budget Office to estimate the cost of proposed legislation and to inform Congress of the progress of its spending and revenue decisions.

The Budget Act's requirement that the Congressional Budget Office issue five-year budget projections also created a need for economic assumptions extending beyond those of a short-run forecast.[5] This need was intensified when Congress, realizing that the scope of the process would have to be multiyear if spending were to be brought under control, incorporated multiyear targets in its budget resolution. The House began to include brief discussions of the five-year implications of its budget resolution in its reports in 1977, the Senate started to provide multiyear projections in its reports in 1978, and the budget resolutions adopted by Congress began to incorporate multiyear targets in 1980.

The long-range economic assumptions, or projections, extend for three years beyond the two years generally covered by the short-run forecasts. Both the executive branch and Congress have treated these long-range assumptions not as extended forecasts of probable economic conditions but as attainable, noncyclical paths from the economic conditions of the short-run forecast toward the national goals of full employment and low inflation. In other words, inflation is assumed to decline gradually, the unemployment rate to fall steadily until full employment is attained, and real economic growth to slow down to the rate of growth of potential GNP as the economy reaches full employment. There is no attempt, as there is for the short-run economic forecasts, to make these longer-run economic projections consistent with the long-run budget estimates. The fiscal policy inherent in the budget estimates may or may not conflict with the economic projections.

The second type of economic information used by Congress is analysis of the likely effects of various macroeconomic and regulatory policy initiatives. During the past decade many major pieces of legislation have been designed to reduce unemployment, curb inflation, enhance economic growth, or stimulate savings and investment. The Kemp-Roth tax cut proposal, the public works and CETA expansion bills of the mid-1970s, and the hospital cost containment and countercyclical revenue sharing initiatives are examples. Analysis of the effects of these policies on employment, economic growth, and inflation has been crucial to their political viability.

Finally, Congress uses analysis of the economic ramifications of policies whose main objectives are not economic stabilization. Most issues before Congress are not designed primarily to affect the economy but are aimed at other objectives, such as boosting farm income, providing health care for the aged, or improving access to higher education. Nevertheless, some of these proposals have significant economic repercussions. When the economy is weak or is beset by inflation and high interest rates, the political importance of these secondary economic repercussions increases. In recent years Congress has sought information on the effects of dairy price supports and natural gas deregulation on inflation, of increased defense spending on employment, of acid rain on the economy, and of banking deregulation on interest rates.

The uses of economic information, advice, and data reflect the functions performed by the legislature and its members. Congress uses them to formulate a budget for the government, to establish the priority of new programs, to justify positions, to make legislative decisions, and to embarrass the opposition political party.

Each year Congress is besieged with pressures to enact new programs, revise tax laws, and establish new regulatory policies. Only a limited number of items can be taken up in each legislative session. With the state of the economy the central issue facing the nation, economic information has helped in setting priorities. The economic ramifications of competing programs have been important in determining which initiatives are moved onto center stage. The alacrity with which Congress took up the administration's Surface Transportation Act of 1982 in the lame-duck session of the Ninety-seventh Congress is a testament to this. The measure provided long-term capital outlays for roads and transit systems, an issue that had failed to get the attention of Congress earlier in 1982 or the year before when some of the highway programs were up for reauthorization. The rapid rise in the unemployment rate during the summer and fall of 1982, however, combined with the perception that this was a jobs bill, spurred Congress to divert its attention from the regular appropriations bills and to enact this proposal.

Economic information also assists in making and justifying decisions. Congressmen take positions for a variety of reasons. Objectively determining whether a policy is in the national interest is certainly important, but so too are personal and party loyalties, effects on local constituencies, and philosophical convictions. Economic information may vitally influence a legislator's decision to support or oppose a piece of legislation. It may also be used to rationalize a position. If economic arguments can be marshaled to buttress a position taken for other reasons, most members will exploit those arguments.

Economic information also plays a purely partisan role in Congress. The state of the economy, rightly or wrongly, is generally held to be the responsibility of the party in control of the White House. Those in Congress from the other party will, therefore, try to highlight bad economic news through congressional hearings and floor speeches. Similarly, good economic news will be hailed by those sympathetic to the president. When the White House and both houses of Congress are held by the same party—as during the Carter years (1976–1980)—attention to bad news is muted because the opposition has limited forums for its views. But during times of split party control, partisan economic debate can dominate Capitol Hill.

Sources of Information and the Assimilation Process

Congress is an open institution, a condition that is reflected in the way it obtains economic information. Although there are loci of responsibility for the initial decisions on economic assumptions and economic policy, jurisdictions are not absolutely defined. Moreover, because the full House and Senate debate and vote on budget resolutions and economic stimulus and tax cut bills reported by legislative committees, every member has a right to an opinion and a voice on these matters. With over 300 committees and subcommittees and various leadership groups and functional and party caucuses, there are numerous forums where members can focus on economic issues.

On complex or technical issues congressmen often turn for advice to members who have become expert because of committee assignments, previous experience, or hard work. This is not true with respect to the economy and economic policy. When the topic is front-page news and so clearly affects every constituency, the incentive for members to become "expert" (that is, to be informed and to speak out) on the economy is overwhelming.

The economic information and advice received by Congress flow in both formal and informal channels. The relative importance of the two is impossible to judge, but most of the macroeconomic information used by members who do not serve on the Joint Economic Committee, the Budget committees, the banking committees, or the tax-writing committees probably is obtained through informal channels.

Newspapers and business weeklies are the main informal sources of economic information for the average congressman. Because of their accessibility and their extensive economic coverage, the *Wall Street Journal*, the *Washington Post*, and the *New York Times* dominate this source of information. Reports and analyses prepared by affected interest groups and public interest lobbies are also important informal sources of information.

Congressmen spend a great deal of time interacting with constituents, representatives of interest groups, and experts. Therefore, it should not be surprising that they obtain considerable economic information and advice from personal contacts. Bankers, businessmen, farmers, home builders, and car dealers in their districts may provide members with much of their insight into the state of the economy and the need for government action. These politically loaded interpretations of the nation's economic health affect a member's job tenure more than the dispassioned projections of economic forecasting firms. Some committee and subcommittee chairmen may rely on Wall Street contacts, conversations with nationally known economists, and speeches and meetings with trade and business associations for informal advice of this sort.

Formal channels of economic information have multiplied considerably in recent years. These consist of the regular reports that the executive branch, the Federal Reserve Board, and the Congressional Budget Office must submit to Congress. The Budget and Accounting Act of 1921, the Employment Act of 1946, the Congressional Budget and Impoundment Control Act of 1974, and the Full Employment and Balanced Growth Act of 1978 (Humphrey-Hawkins Act) contain the legal prescription for most of these formal reports. Other formal mechanisms for gathering economic information include hearings and intermittent reports that Congress requests from its support agencies (the CBO, the General Accounting Office, and the Congressional Research Service).

Each year the administration provides Congress with a short-run economic forecast on which its budget proposal is based together with a set of longer-run numerical goals for several key economic indicators (employment, unemployment, GNP, real income, productivity, and prices). This information is conveyed in the budget document and the *Economic Report of the President*.

Since the passage of the Budget Act there has been an astonishing increase in the detail of the economic information provided by the administration. Before 1975 the budget document included in its chapter on receipts a one-paragraph section labeled "economic assumptions," which gave estimates of nominal GNP, personal income, and corporate profits for the current and following calendar years. In those years the *Economic Report of the President* contained a description of the expected growth of GNP and its components (personal consumption expenditures, business fixed investment, net exports, government purchases, residential construction, and inventory investment) and an analysis of the current economic situation. Rough estimates of the rate of price increases and unemployment for the coming year were also included.

The economic forecasts and projections currently provided by the administration not only cover five years but also are more detailed. Estimates are given for two broad measures of inflation (the GNP deflator and the consumer price index), real GNP and its components, compensation per hour, housing starts, the unemployment rate, and interest rates. Although the information conveyed to Congress does not constitute a detailed macroeconomic forecast, it is sufficient for assessing the realism and internal consistency of the administration's assumptions. These assumptions are updated or reaffirmed during the year—most notably when the administration submits its midsession (July 15) review of the budget.

Since 1978 the Federal Reserve Board has been required by the Humphrey-Hawkins Act to report to Congress twice a year. These reports—in February and in July—contain a review of current economic conditions, ranges for the monetary policy that the Federal Reserve Board expects to follow during the year, and an analysis of the relationship of the policies of the board to the goals laid out by the administration in the *Economic Report of the President*. In recent years the Federal Reserve Board's reports to Congress have also specified forecast ranges for such key economic variables as nominal GNP, real GNP, the GNP deflator, and the unemployment rate. These ranges encompass the various projections of the members of the Federal Reserve's Open Market Committee. This information enables Congress to sense how reasonable the Federal Reserve Board considers the administration and CBO forecasts.

The CBO's periodic reports on the economic outlook contain information similar to that presented by the administration. These reports include an economic forecast covering the current and the next years, economic projections for the following three years, and an analysis of recent economic events. Unlike the administration's analysis, CBO reports usually contain estimates of the effects of alternative fiscal and monetary policies on the economy and of changes in spending and taxing policies.

The principal CBO economic report is presented to Congress at about the time the president submits his budget. If the economy changes rapidly in the early months of the year, the Budget committees may ask the CBO for an updated outlook in March for their formulation of the first budget resolution.

The CBO economic forecasts and projections are important

because they offer alternatives to those of the administration and because the CBO uses them in its five-year base-line projections of congressional budget action and its analysis of the president's budget. The base-line budget shows the revenues, expenditures, and deficits that would result if existing congressional policies continued unchanged for the ensuing five years. The CBO reestimates the president's budget proposal by applying its economic and technical assumptions to the budget policies proposed by the president. In recent years the CBO's more pessimistic economic assumptions have led to forecasts of considerably higher deficits than those implied by the president's budgets—$4.0 billion for fiscal year 1983, $13.5 billion for fiscal year 1982, and $7.8 billion for fiscal year 1980.

The CBO's short-run economic forecasts tend to be close to the consensus or average view of the forecasting profession. In the preparation of its forecasts, the agency uses several commercially available macroeconomic models.[6] The assumptions the CBO makes are intended to be as neutral and noncontroversial as possible. The fiscal policy assumptions are those that would flow from a continuation of current congressional policies, and the monetary policy conforms to the Federal Reserve Board's most recent pronouncements. Other assumptions, such as sharp changes in energy prices, are spelled out in great detail. The preliminary CBO forecast that emerges from this procedure is reviewed by a panel of distinguished economic advisers who reflect the diverse views within the profession. The panel not only provides useful advice but also helps to shield the CBO from charges of bias. Using the panel's insight and the judgments of the CBO staff, the CBO prepares an official forecast. The entire process guarantees that the final product will not deviate much from the consensus forecast and that accusations of political manipulation will be minimized. For further protection and to underline the uncertainty inherent in economic forecasts, the CBO also prepares a pessimistic and an optimistic alternative to its base-line forecasts.

The media's interpretation and accounts of the various reports constitute a major channel of economic information, and hearings built around these reports are an equally significant source of information. Administration witnesses—usually the chairman of the Council of Economic Advisers, the secretary of the Treasury, and the director of the Office of Management and Budget—testify on the economic outlook before the Budget committees, the banking committees, the Appropriations committees, and the Joint Economic Committee. The Joint Economic Committee is required by the Employment Act of 1946 to furnish Congress with an analysis of the major recommendations contained in the *Economic Report of the President* by March 1.

The chairman of the Federal Reserve Board testifies first before the banking committees and then before the Joint Economic Committee and the Budget committees. The director of the Congressional Budget Office explains the CBO forecast to the Budget committees, the Appropriations committees, and the Joint Economic Committee. At all these hearings the various economic forecasts are described, examined, and defended, questions are asked, and additional detail is provided.

The formal hearings on the state of the economy also gather the forecasts of outside experts. The Budget committees generally call upon representatives of economic forecasting firms and economists from universities, corporations, think tanks, and financial institutions. These experts offer their own views of the economy and appraise the forecasts of the administration and the CBO. In short, the formal system for gathering information about the likely state of the economy is extremely open.

Congress's sources of information on the economic effects of macroeconomic policies and of other proposed legislation are similar to those for the overall economic outlook. Administration witnesses play a key role in describing the economic effects of proposals that emanate from the executive branch. At the request of a committee the Congressional Budget Office will provide a report on a specific proposal. In 1978, for example, the CBO published an analysis of the economic effects of the Kemp-Roth tax cut proposal.[7] The CBO also analyzes the effects of various economic policy options in its regular economic reports. Its July 1977 report discussed alternative policies for curbing inflation; its February 1983 report described policy options for reducing unemployment.

In addition to the many analyses provided by the Congressional Budget Office, information is supplied by other legislative support agencies. The Congressional Research Service (CRS) provides Congress with briefings, materials, and analyses on issues such as the economic effects of gas deregulation, world oil prices, and business tax cuts. The General Accounting Office (GAO) provides some economic information, although most of its work deals with individual federal programs or activities. Interest groups, trade associations, and university- and business-based economists testify and furnish analyses of the economic effects of specific legislative proposals.

On occasion congressional committees contract with economic consulting firms for special analyses. This was done in 1978 when the House Budget Committee and the Joint Economic Committee requested Data Resources Incorporated (DRI) and Wharton Econometric Forecasting Associates to simulate the effects of countercyclical policy.[8]

In 1979 the Senate Budget Committee asked DRI to analyze the economic effect of increased defense spending with and without an accommodative monetary policy.

A committee may be willing to pay for outside economic advice for various reasons. Congressional staff agencies may lack specific expertise, may not be able to do the job in the required time, or the committee may feel it has greater control over the results of the investigation if an outside contractor does it. Although the requester has the right to withhold results of CBO, CRS, and GAO studies, that right is rarely exercised, and nothing can stop another committee or congressman from asking for a similar study.

The task of sifting, translating, and assimilating the economic information that inundates Capitol Hill falls mainly to the staffs of committees and members. With the increasing importance of economic information, the economic expertise of congressional staff has grown considerably. In 1970 the Joint Economic Committee was the only committee employing a significant group of professional economists; today the Budget committees, the Joint Committee on Taxation (which provides staff services to the Senate Finance Committee and the House Ways and Means Committee), and the Ways and Means Committee also have strong staffs of economists. Numerous other committees, such as the banking committees, usually have one or two professional economists on their staffs.

Some members, particularly those who serve on committees dealing with economic matters or have a keen interest in economic problems or harbor presidential ambitions, have placed economists on their personal staffs. It is interesting to note that the Senate and House leaderships have not built up any professional economic expertise of their own despite the growing importance of economic matters during the past decade. They have been content to rely on outside assistance, consultants, and committee staffs.

The work of many staff economists consists of writing committee reports, speeches, and position memorandums based on economic information and data that flow to the Hill. By and large, information provided by economists, even by those working for congressional agencies, does not arrive in a form that fits easily into political or legislative debates. For this reason economists on committee and personal staffs are often translators and winnowers of such information.

Some committee staffs are sources of original information and analyses. The staffs of the Joint Economic Committee and the Joint Committee on Taxation are noted for the economic analyses they generate, as are the staffs of the Budget committees. In the early years of the budget process the House Budget Committee economists constructed their own economic forecasts using commercially available forecasting models, but the Senate Budget Committee relied heavily on the forecasts prepared by the CBO. This dependence was dictated by the commitment of the committee's chairman, Senator Edmund Muskie (Democrat, Maine), and its ranking minority member, Senator Henry Bellmon (Republican, Oklahoma), to a bipartisan approach. Relying on CBO forecasts, they reasoned, would keep the choice of economic assumptions from becoming a partisan issue and would reduce squabbles between the majority and minority staffs. Neither committee now does its own full-fledged forecast, but both do make adjustments in the forecasts prepared by the CBO and commercial forecasting firms.

Before settling on the assumptions that underlie their recommended resolutions, the Budget committees examine the administration and CBO forecasts and those of a number of commercial firms. The particular forecasts examined have been influenced by the prevailing political climate. In the early years the major firms (DRI, Wharton, and Chase Econometrics) were most frequently consulted. After some congressmen protested that the views of business and supply-oriented models were being ignored, the committees included forecasts from IBM (U.S. Economic Research and Forecasting), Merrill-Lynch Economics, and Evans Economics. The task of formulating the economic forecasts that underlie each budget resolution has been left entirely to the Budget committees. Despite the importance of these assumptions, the leadership in the House and Senate has not interfered or even shown substantial interest in this process.

Although Congress has its own institutions for providing economic information and analysis, the assistance of these agencies is not always requested or desired. Freedom to remain ignorant of the economic consequences of legislative action is important to Congress and underscores another role of Hill staff. Sometimes politically important legislation may have adverse economic consequences or may not be likely to achieve the spectacular economic results claimed for it. In such cases Congress may find it easier to support the legislation if the economic effects are not explicitly addressed in expert testimony, a CBO report, or an administration study. Instead, the information will be conveyed unofficially in memorandums from committee staffs, the CBO, the CRS, and the administration. None of this information becomes part of the public record, but it enables members to judge whether the noneconomic benefits of the legislation are compelling enough to overcome its adverse economic consequences.

The All Savers Certificate proposal, which was added by Congress to the Reagan administration tax cut proposal of 1981, illustrates how official information and analysis might make the passage of legislation more difficult. Supporters claimed that this legislation, which exempted from federal income tax the first $1,000 ($2,000 for joint returns) of interest on special accounts, would help the ailing savings and loan industry, revive housing by lowering mortgage interest rates, and increase aggregate savings. Staff memorandums from the CBO, the Treasury Department, and the Joint Tax Committee clearly informed members that these salutary economic effects would be marginal at best, that the bill would provide a significant windfall to banks and existing savers, and that the Treasury would experience a substantial ($5–7 billion) revenue loss. Without official evidence to the contrary and using the optimistic claims of representatives of the banking and housing industries, Congress quickly approved the proposal.

The failure of the Ninety-eighth Congress to ask for analyses of the economic effects of the social security legislation it passed early in 1983 offers another example. Although the tax increases, benefit cuts, and general revenue financing proposed by the National Commission on Social Security Reform should have adverse macroeconomic effects in the short run, the urgency of passing this legislation quickly caused Congress to avoid sources of potential contention. Therefore, Congress deliberately refrained from asking any agency to examine these possible effects.

Congress has purposely distanced itself from the agencies that provide it with economic advice to increase its freedom in economic policy making and to insulate the agencies from political bias. Nowhere is this more evident than in CBO economic forecasts. Between February 1976 and December 1982 the CBO furnished Congress with fourteen economic forecasts that could have been used as assumptions underlying the budget resolutions. The forecasts were used eight times as the basis for resolutions offered by the Senate Budget Committee and modified or rejected by the committee six times. They were used for the resolutions drafted by the House Budget Committee five times and modified or rejected nine times. The resolutions ultimately approved by Congress relied on CBO forecasts six times and on other economic assumptions eight times.[9]

It might seem strange that Congress would establish its own sources of economic information and then reject their best judgment. Yet this behavior is quite rational and can be explained by three factors. The first is the conflict between the nonpartisan, objective approach adhered to by the congressional support agencies and the political environment in which the information is used. To its credit Congress chose to establish support agencies free from partisan control and charged them with providing objective information and analysis. This means that the information may turn out to be embarrassing or politically unacceptable to the majority of Congress.

A second reason for the failure of Congress to accept information and advice from its own agencies unquestioningly has been the concern of some members that the information is biased. This has been a particular problem for the CBO, which bases much of its analysis on commercial forecasting models. The most frequently used models have a short-run focus and tend to be demand oriented. They give relatively little weight to the relationships that supply-side, rational expectations, and monetary theories of economics emphasize. Members of Congress who support these views have frequently argued that information and analysis provided by the CBO favor Keynesian —or active short-run stabilization—solutions to economic problems and fail to reflect adequately the long-run, growth-oriented needs of the nation.

Moreover, some critics have pointed out that the CBO's analysis of fiscal policy options such as tax cuts and jobs programs lends support to a policy of intervention. This bias, it is argued, occurs because the CBO focuses on short-run effects—such as increased employment—and gives scant attention to the possible long-run consequences for economic growth of enlarged deficits and reduced work incentives.

Several academic economists were the first to criticize the CBO's use of demand-oriented economic models.[10] The CBO's methods became an issue of great importance when the Reagan administration took office. Although previous administrations had used models and methods similar to those of the CBO to generate their forecasts, the new administration sought advice from the Claremont Economic Institute, a small forecasting firm that gave heavy emphasis to supply-side theories. The administration's forecast was considerably more optimistic than the CBO's, and supporters of the administration took steps to discredit the agency's methods. At an earlier time Senator Orrin Hatch (Republican, Utah) expressed these views:

> The econometric model used by the CBO is simplistic and has come under intense criticism within the economics profession. The CBO model gives results which are biased in favor of higher spending and taxes and against savings. Its analysis emphasizes the short-run and ignores the long-run implications of its economic policies. Since CBO's policies designed to stimulate short-run growth are inconsistent with long-run growth, the CBO analysis leads us down a path of long-run economic decay.[11]

The CBO has responded to these criticisms by adding supply-oriented models to those that it examines when formulating its forecast and by incorporating such models into the methodology used to evaluate the effects of alternative fiscal policies. Its recent reports have also contained expanded discussions of the possible long-run repercussions of various short-run stimulative policies. Nevertheless, as long as the methodological framework used by the CBO is one that can engender contention, Congress is unlikely to accept its economic advice routinely.

Flexibility is a third factor that reinforces the reluctance of Congress to embrace the economic analyses or forecasts offered by the CBO or the other support agencies. With the outlays, revenue, and deficit of the budget resolutions affected by the economic forecasts, small adjustments in the economic assumptions offer an appealing way to reconcile differences between conflicting positions within the Budget committees and between the House and the Senate.

In the first few years of the budget process, the Budget committees adjusted the economic assumptions for many of the fiscal policy changes that were adopted during the markup of the resolutions. The CBO would be asked to provide estimates of the effect of an extra $5 billion in revenue sharing or CETA money on the unemployment rate, inflation, and federal revenues. In recent years this practice has diminished as the inability of economists to forecast the economy with precision has become more apparent and as the committees have come to recognize the importance of monetary policy to short-run economic conditions.

The practice of "playing" with or fine-tuning the economic assumptions for political advantage has been criticized and has led to some small inconsistencies. The changes made by this practice, however, have usually been well within the range of forecasting uncertainty. If the CBO forecast were automatically accepted, some valuable flexibility would be lost.

Problems, Tensions, and Temptations

Economic information creates problems, tensions, and frustrations in an open legislative body. Moreover, such information can be manipulated for political advantage.

From the standpoint of Congress, expert advice and information are most useful if they are easy to understand and noncontentious. In economic matters, however, this condition rarely prevails. The economy is complex, highly interdependent, and conditional. When one factor in the economy changes, everything else changes, at times in counterintuitive ways. The first-round or short-term effects of a policy may be negated or enhanced in the long run. Economic answers tend to be conditional. When the economy is slack, economists tell Congress that increased government deficits will not appreciably drive up prices or crowd out private investment; when the economy is strong, economists warn of the inflationary effects of deficits and their harmful effect on private capital formation. Shifting advice sows confusion and generates frustration among legislators who cannot devote much time to understanding such complexities.

If economic systems were predictable, their complexity, interdependence, and conditionality would not be an insurmountable problem for Congress; but they are not. There is a good deal of controversy concerning how the economy works, that is, how much weight to give to Keynesian, monetarist, supply-side, and rational expectations theories. Therefore, Congress often finds itself receiving conflicting economic advice from prestigious experts.

The uncertainty of economic forecasts and advice has led economists to hedge their predictions and to give information in ranges. From 1975 through 1982 the forecasts provided by the Council of Economic Advisers in the *Economic Report of the President* were given in ranges, although point estimates were supplied in the budget. The CBO has either presented its forecasts as ranges or supplied optimistic and pessimistic alternatives to its base-line forecast. At times the ranges have been large enough to encompass both an improvement and a worsening of the economy. The CBO's September 1982 forecast, for example, predicted that real GNP would grow between -0.3 and 1.7 percent from the fourth quarter of 1981 to the fourth quarter of 1982. Since Congress is required to make decisions that depend on point estimates of economic conditions, the efforts of economists to hedge their forecasts has led to confusion. Some members have regarded the use of ranges as waffling. If economists are unwilling to provide point estimates, how can legislators have better insight?

Uncertainty has given Congress a good deal of flexibility, which has sometimes been politically useful. The Budget committees can make their job easier by adopting a forecast near the optimistic end of the CBO range, while retaining their credibility by accepting a forecast within that range.

Congressional confusion also arises from a failure to understand the importance of assumptions in economic analysis. The advice Congress receives often stems as much from the initial assumptions of the adviser as from any derived analysis. The importance of assumptions is most obvious with respect to forecasts. No matter what model is used, assumptions must be made about fiscal policy, monetary policy, the price of OPEC oil, the weather and its effect on crop yields, the tendency of state and local governments to substitute federal grants for their own revenues, and the probability that a prolonged strike will occur in a major industry.

Each forecast presented to Congress is based on a different fiscal policy assumption. The administration naturally assumes that its budget proposals will be enacted completely and speedily; the Congressional Budget Office assumes a continuation of current congressional policies; and the forecasts of private firms are based on educated guesses about spending and taxing legislation that Congress will enact over the next few years.

In many years differences in assumptions have only a minor effect on the forecast and hence on the spending, revenue, and deficit estimates of the various budget proposals. When large policy shifts are likely to occur, however, the effect can be substantial and can lead to confusion or frustration. An example of this occurred in the spring of 1981 when the Reagan administration submitted its revisions of the Carter budget for fiscal 1982. These revisions included substantial multiyear tax reductions and spending cuts. The new administration predicted that these budget changes would have a dramatic stimulative effect on the economy, and its forecast was considerably more optimistic than that prepared by the previous administration or by the CBO. The latter's forecast assumed no tax or spending reductions; the Carter forecast was based on smaller changes in fiscal policy.

The ephemeral nature of economic information has also caused problems for Congress. From Congress's perspective good information is information that remains constant at least through a legislative cycle. There is a well-defined cycle for the acceptance and use of economic information on Capitol Hill. This cycle starts with the presentation of the president's budget in January. Budget resolutions are then formulated by the Budget committees in March or April and passed by the House and Senate in May or June. Reconciliation, appropriations, and tax bills, tied in a general way to the budget resolution, are then the order of business. Until 1981 another cycle began in the summer with the presidential budget reestimates and the formulation and passage of a second congressional budget resolution. In 1981 and 1982, however, Congress did not adopt a second resolution, choosing instead to operate under the resolution it passed in the spring.

If the economic assumptions on which budget resolutions are based appear to be unrealistic before the resolutions are passed, then the credibility and discipline of the budget process deteriorate. In recent years economic conditions have often changed sharply and unpredictably in the middle of the budget cycle. Sharp unexpected drops in real GNP occurred during the second quarters of 1979, 1980, and 1981, the unemployment rate jumped by 1.3 percentage points between February and May 1980, and the consumer price index rose by more than a point per month during the first half of 1980. A sense of futility and frustration permeates congressional budget discussions when there are unpredicted fluctuations in the economy.

Such shifts have both galvanized Congress into action and led it to avoid reality. The first of these responses was evident in 1982. At the beginning of the year economists in and outside government predicted a modest recovery beginning during the first or second quarter of the year. This expectation was incorporated in the forecast used by the Budget committees in marking up the first budget resolution for fiscal 1983. As the year progressed, the economy not only failed to recover but declined precipitously in the first and fourth quarters. The unemployment rate continued to increase, reaching double digits by September. Rather than the $104 billion deficit envisioned in the first resolution, the CBO predicted a deficit of approximately $155 billion, due in large part to the weakening of the economy. The frustration over the weakness of the economy added impetus to efforts to cut spending and raise taxes and led to the enactment of most of the deficit-reducing measures assumed in the first budget resolution. Ironically, Congress ended up almost exactly where it had started—while tax increases and spending cuts lowered the estimated deficit for fiscal 1983 by $54 billion, the deterioration in the economy and certain technical factors raised it by $51 billion.

A different response occurred in 1981. In that year Congress reacted like an ostrich when faced with worsening economic news. The first budget resolution for fiscal 1982, which was passed in June 1981, incorporated the proposals of the new Reagan administration. The House adopted the Gramm-Latta substitute for the resolution proposed by the Budget Committee. This substitute contained a significantly more optimistic economic forecast and deeper cuts in domestic spending and taxes than the House Budget Committee had proposed. After a speedy but painful process, virtually all the tax and spending cuts outlined in the budget resolution were enacted through the Omnibus Reconciliation Act of 1981 and the Economic Recovery Tax Act of 1981. Rather than springing to life as projected, however, the economy deteriorated, offsetting the effect of the spending cuts on the deficit. Coming to grips with this bad economic and political news was so painful that Congress chose to ignore it and to forgo a second budget resolution for fiscal 1982. The CBO's cost and budget estimates in late 1981 continued to be based on the rosy economic assumptions underlying the first resolution, although those assumptions bore little resemblance to reality. Realizing this, the Budget committees and many authorizing committees asked the CBO for unofficial cost and scorekeeping estimates based on more realistic economic assumptions. The CBO was forced to keep two sets of books. In September 1981 the president acknowledged the lack of an economic recovery and asked for more spending cuts, a request that was greeted with nearly unanimous opposition. Not until 1982, when the president's budget for 1983 acknowledged that the economy had deteriorated, did Congress withdraw its head from the sand.

Uncertainty, lack of consensus, variability, and fallibility of economic advice have given Congress a good deal of leeway in using the information given to it. As mentioned before, Congress has felt no compunction about accepting either the administration's or the CBO's forecasts or economic analyses. This situation creates a temptation. Acceptance of an optimistic economic outlook makes Congress's budget task easier because a stronger economy means higher revenues, lower outlays, and a reduced deficit.

To its credit Congress has generally resisted the temptation of assuming wildly optimistic economic conditions even when this has meant projecting a deficit larger than that in the president's budget proposal. It has generally adopted more pessimistic economic assumptions than those contained in the president's budget and the mid-session review.[12] Table 2–1 provides a comparison of components of the recent economic assumptions of the administration, the CBO, the Budget committees, and the conference report on the budget resolution. In the 1979–1983 cycles Congress has usually assumed higher unemployment rates than those contained in the administration's forecast. Higher unemployment increases spending, reduces revenues, and expands the deficit. The congressional assumptions about nominal GNP, which affects federal revenues, have exceeded those of the administration slightly more often than the reverse has been the case.

During the first years of the congressional budget process this situation existed because the Republicans controlled the executive branch and the Democrats controlled both houses of Congress. Partisan political advantage could be gained by arguing that the president had overstated the strength of the economy. But the persistence of this behavior during the Carter years and now into the Reagan presidency must be explained by the commitment of the leadership of the Budget committees to realism and discipline in budgetary policy.

This is not to suggest that Congress has avoided temptation altogether. The economic assumptions in the budget resolutions have been generally more optimistic than the forecasts provided by the CBO eight times and never significantly more pessimistic; the resolutions have assumed a more favorable economy than a consensus of private forecasts eight times, a weaker economy three times, and roughly equal economic conditions once.[13]

The tendency to accept unrealistically optimistic forecasts is most notable in the long-run projections accepted by Congress. Congress is not alone in this. The administration's and the CBO's long-run projections have been similarly unrealistic. For the most part this situation arises from the nature of these projections, which assume steady progress toward the national economic goals of full employment and low inflation. There are no cycles in these projections; a political dilemma would be created if there were. If a recession or a sudden rise in inflation were predicted, the public would put pressure on Congress for remedial action.

The optimism of these projections has created an unrealistic long-run budget outlook. Inevitably the future deficits implied by current budget policy are underestimated, and progress toward balancing the budget is overstated.

The temptation to ignore or reject economic information extends beyond the issue of economic forecasts. When compelling pressure builds for a proposal, economic information is rendered powerless. The Surface Transportation Act of 1982 offers a recent example of this phenomenon. This act moved speedily through the legislative process during the lame-duck session in 1982 because of its alleged effect on jobs. This claim was contradicted in a widely reported memorandum of the chairman of the Council of Economic Advisers, the analyses of several of the major economic forecasting firms, and the testimony of the director of the Congressional Budget Office, all of which suggested that the result of the program could range from a small net job gain to a small net job loss.

Improving the Use of Economic Information by Congress

Whether Congress needs to reform the way it gets, assimilates, and uses economic information is debatable. A decade ago Congress gathered little economic information, lacked economic expertise, was not fully aware of the economic ramifications of its actions, and did not focus on the effects of changing economic conditions on its

TABLE 2–1

ECONOMIC ASSUMPTIONS MADE BY THE ADMINISTRATION,
CONGRESSIONAL BUDGET OFFICE, HOUSE BUDGET COMMITTEE,
SENATE BUDGET COMMITTEE, AND CONGRESSIONAL BUDGET RESOLUTION

Resolution for Which Forecast Was Prepared[a]	Adminis-tration	Congres-sional Budget Office	House Budget Com-mittee	Senate Budget Com-mittee	Congres-sional Budget Resolution
1983—first resolution					
GNP (billions of dollars)	3,524	3,515	3,493	3,493	3,493
GNP deflator (percent)	6.0	7.3	7.3	7.3	7.3
Unemployment (percent)	7.9	8.0	8.4	8.4	8.4
1982—first resolution					
GNP (billions of dollars)	3,293	3,289[b]	3,324	3,293	3,323
GNP deflator (percent)	8.3	9.2[b]	9.2	8.3	8.3
Unemployment (percent)	7.2	7.9[b]	7.3	7.2	7.2
1981—second resolution					
GNP (billions of dollars)	2,821	2,799	2,832	2,874	2,841
GNP deflator (percent)	10.0	8.8	9.0	9.7	9.4
Unemployment (percent)	8.5	9.0	8.0	8.5[c]	8.0
1981—first resolution					
GNP (billions of dollars)	2,842	2,875[d]	2,875	2,875	2,875
GNP deflator (percent)	8.8	9.7[d]	9.7	9.7	9.7
Unemployment (percent)	7.4	7.5[d]	7.5	7.5	7.5
1980—second resolution					
GNP (billions of dollars)	2,572	2,571	2,571	2,571	2,571
GNP deflator (percent)	8.9	9.0	9.0	9.3	9.0
Unemployment (percent)	6.8	7.2	7.2	7.2	7.2
1980—first resolution					
GNP (billions of dollars)	2,565	2,585	2,585	2,585	2,594
GNP deflator (percent)	6.8	7.7	7.2	7.6[e]	7.2
Unemployment (percent)	6.2	6.8	6.2	6.8	6.5
1979—second resolution					
GNP (billions of dollars)	2,330	2,316	2,316	2,316	2,313
GNP deflator (percent)	6.6	6.5	6.9	6.7	6.5
Unemployment (percent)	5.7	5.7	5.7	5.7	5.7

a. Values are the nominal GNP, the annual increase in the GNP deflator, and the annual unemployment rate. Unless otherwise noted all are for the calendar year corresponding to the fiscal year for which the resolution applied.

(Notes continue on facing page.)

budgetary decisions. This certainly is not the case today. One could argue that Congress is now too concerned with the economic dimension of its policy initiatives.

Congress is receiving sufficient economic information for its needs. This information is not consistently biased in any direction and reflects the diverse views of the economic community. Congress has shown itself capable of assimilating and using this information constructively when it wants to, yet capable of ignoring the information when it contradicts powerful political forces. Whether Congress chooses to use information or not is a political question. The answer reflects the strengths and weaknesses of Congress as an institution, not the limitations of the advice or of the information-gathering system.

There are a number of areas in which Congress's use of economic information could be improved. One problem is unnecessary confusion arising from the proliferation of economic forecasts, a second is the optimistic bias of the long-run economic projections, and a third is the politicalization of economic information.

Much of the confusion surrounding economic forecasts reflects the recent turbulence of the economy, the unsettled state of economic theory, and the limitations of macroeconomic forecasting tools. Some confusion could be eliminated if alternative budget proposals relied on the same economic assumptions, a situation that would highlight the true policy differences between competing proposals. One approach would be to encourage or mandate closer coordination between the executive branch and Congress, possibly even establishing a mechanism through which the executive branch and the Budget committees could agree on a common forecast.[14] Such an approach would probably be unrealistic without more fundamental integration of policy making than now exists. Because an economic forecast depends on the fiscal policy initiatives proposed in the budget, it would be difficult for Congress and the executive to agree on common sets of assumptions. Agreement about the economic assumptions might be interpreted as capitulation to the president's fiscal policy.

Furthermore, the current budget process is sequential, a situation that gives Congress added freedom that it would be reluctant to

---

b. CBO forecast assuming President Reagan's budget policies.
c. Fiscal year value.
d. CBO March 1980 updated forecast.
e. Fourth-quarter-over-fourth-quarter increase.
SOURCES: Various years of Office of Management and Budget, *The Budget of the United States Government*, CBO economic reports, House and Senate Budget committee reports on the budget resolutions, conference reports on the budget resolutions, and author's estimates based on unpublished materials.

relinquish. The executive must settle on an economic forecast for its budget proposal fully three months before Congress must set forth the economic assumptions that underlie its budget plan. When economic conditions are changing rapidly, it is unreasonable to expect Congress to adhere to a forecast that may be clearly out of date.

Another approach would be to require that the president resubmit his budget and construct his midsession review using the economic assumptions adopted by Congress for its latest budget resolution.[15] Although this approach would not eliminate inconsistencies between the forecast and the proposed fiscal policy, it would keep the budget process sequential.

The tendency of Congress to adopt unrealistically optimistic economic assumptions for its budget resolution is a second area in which there could be improvement. Optimism is not a serious problem in Congress's short-run forecasts. The forecasts underlying the congressional budget resolutions tend to be slightly more optimistic than those of the CBO and the Blue Chip consensus forecast but on average are marginally less optimistic than the forecasts of the administration. Some components of these forecasts for recent years are compared in table 2–2. The deviation from actual economic conditions has been small, and the errors of the congressional forecasts are similar to those of independent forecasters.

The situation with respect to the long-run economic projections is quite different. The five-year projections of Congress, like those of the administration and the CBO, have proved far too optimistic. In part this stems from the nature of these projections, which are attainable, noncyclical paths from the short-run forecast toward the nation's long-term goals of full employment and low inflation. It also stems from the political imperative to show steady economic improvement. The unrealistic long-run economic assumptions present the future budget outlook in too favorable a light, reducing the pressure to lower the deficit.

Several proposals have been made to correct this situation. One is to substitute a mechanistic procedure for the current quasi-political process of setting long-run economic assumptions.[16] The average economic performance of the preceding five years, for example, could be the basis for economic assumptions for the three years following the forecast years. Unrealistic discontinuities and anomalies could arise, however, from splicing mechanically derived averages onto these forecasts.[17] If this technique were used for the first resolution of 1983—the economic assumptions of which were jointly constructed by the Congress and the executive branch—there would be a sharp jump in inflation from 6.9 percent to 8.9 per-

TABLE 2–2

COMPONENTS OF THE ECONOMIC ASSUMPTIONS OF THE ADMINISTRATION,
CONGRESSIONAL BUDGET OFFICE, HOUSE BUDGET COMMITTEE,
SENATE BUDGET COMMITTEE, AND CONGRESSIONAL BUDGET RESOLUTION
(percent)

Resolution for Which Forecast Was Prepared[a]	Adminis- tration	Congres- sional Budget Office	Congres- sional Budget Resolution	Blue Chip Consensus
1983—first resolution (1982)				
GNP	8.1	7.5	6.6	9.2
GNP deflator	7.9	7.5	7.4	7.7
Unemployment	8.9	8.9	9.1	8.0
Treasury bill	11.7	12.0	12.0	11.7
1982—first resolution (1981)				
GNP	11.1	11.6	12.0	12.2
GNP deflator	9.9	10.0	9.8	10.4
Unemployment	7.8	7.7	7.5	7.2[b]
Treasury bill	11.1	12.7	13.5	11.5[b]
1981—second resolution (1981)				
GNP	10.3	9.9	10.5	11.1
GNP deflator	10.0	8.8	9.4	9.5
Unemployment	8.5	9.0	8.0	7.0[b]
Treasury bill	9.0	8.7	10.6	7.3[b]
1981—first resolution (1980)				
GNP	8.3	9.3[c]	9.3	8.0
GNP deflator	8.9	9.3[c]	9.3	9.1
Unemployment	7.0	6.8[c]	6.8	7.4
Treasury bill	10.5	10.9[c]	12.4	10.4
1980—second resolution (1980)				
GNP	10.0	10.0	10.0	9.0
GNP deflator	8.9	9.0	9.0	8.4
Unemployment	6.8	7.2	7.2	7.3
Treasury bill	8.2	8.4	8.4	8.5
1980—first resolution (1979)				
GNP	11.3	11.6	12.1	10.0
GNP deflator	7.7	8.2	8.5	7.8
Unemployment	6.0	6.2	6.0	6.7
Treasury bill	8.8	9.2	9.2	9.7

(Table continues)

61

TABLE 2–2 (continued)

Resolution for Which Forecast Was Prepared[a]	Adminis- tration	Congres- sional Budget Office	Congres- sional Budget Resolution	Blue Chip Consensus
1979—second resolution (1979)				
GNP	11.2	10.7	10.6	10.1
GNP deflator	6.6	6.5	6.5	6.8
Unemployment	5.7	5.7	5.7	6.4
Treasury bill	6.6	7.4	7.4	7.3
1979—first resolution (1978)				
GNP	11.0	10.9	11.0	10.7
GNP deflator	6.1	6.1	5.8	6.2
Unemployment	6.3	6.3	6.3	6.4
Treasury bill	6.1	6.7	6.6	7.0

a. Values are the annual increase in nominal GNP, the annual increase in the GNP deflator, the annual unemployment rate, and the three-month Treasury bill rate for the year in parentheses.

b. Fourth-quarter-over-fourth-quarter increase.

c. CBO March 1980 updated forecast.

SOURCES: Various years of Office of Management and Budget, *The Budget of the United States Government*, CBO economic reports, conference committee reports on the budget resolutions, *Blue Chip Economic Indicators* (Eggert Economic Enterprises, Inc.), and author's estimates based on unpublished materials.

cent between 1984 and 1985 while estimated real growth would drop from 4.1 percent to 1.8 percent. Such discontinuities could undermine the credibility of the budget process. It is difficult to imagine Congress accepting these anomalies if they would adversely affect the budget picture.

Another possibility would be to change the procedure for making the long-run economic assumptions used by Congress. Rather than reflecting steady progress toward full employment and low inflation, the economic conditions expected to exist in the final quarter of the short-run forecast could be extended for the ensuing three years. Although this alternative would reduce the optimism inherent in the current procedure and eliminate the possibility of discontinuities, it has some weaknesses. It might exert pressure to make the short-run forecast more optimistic since the long-run budget outlook would be determined by the short-run situation.

A third alternative would be to tie the long-run economic as- sumptions to the average outlook of private forecasters. While many firms and individuals provide short-run economic forecasts, only a few generate serious long-run projections. The average outlook of some of the most respected of these firms could be used as Congress's long-run economic assumptions. Discontinuities could still exist between the short- and long-run assumptions of Congress, but the tendency toward optimism would be reduced. The economic assumptions for 1985 that underlie the first budget resolution for 1983, for example, are slightly more optimistic in all dimensions than the average of four private forecasting firms (see table 2–3).

A third area of concern is the tendency for Congress to politicize economic information. In most years this has not been a serious problem. While Congress on occasion may fail to solicit economic information that is detrimental to a favored proposal, this does not mean that the information is unavailable. Congress did not request a CBO report on the expected economic effects of the All Savers Certificate or expert testimony on the number of jobs likely to be created by the Surface Transportation Act, but analyses of these issues were widely available. A private forecasting firm analyzed the potential for job creation of the Surface Transportation Act as part of its regular report to clients. Interest groups whose cause would be aided by such information do their best to disseminate it to Congress, as do the media.

The short-run forecast underlying the fiscal 1982 budget resolution clearly was a political issue. In 1981 President Reagan claimed that his tax and spending policies would generate robust economic growth and reduce the inflation rate. The administration argued that its economic recovery program should be accepted to achieve these salutary economic results. The program and the economic forecast were inextricably intertwined.

Several mechanisms have been suggested for reducing the possibility that Congress's short-run forecasts will become politically charged. One approach would be to have some neutral body, like the Congressional Budget Office, private forecasting firms, or a council of distinguished economists, prepare the forecasts. This approach would raise some fresh problems. The CBO might be unable to withstand the political pressure that would be exerted on it; the private forecasts might all be based on fiscal policy assumptions quite different from those that would result from implementation of the policies in the budget resolution.

Another approach would be to eliminate forecasts as they are currently used in the congressional budget process. Budgets could be estimated using a constant unemployment assumption and some modestly declining inflation rate. This could reduce confusion, high-

TABLE 2–3

COMPARISON OF THE AVERAGE PRIVATE FORECAST FOR 1985 WITH
THE ECONOMIC ASSUMPTIONS IN THE FIRST BUDGET RESOLUTION
FOR FISCAL 1983

	First Budget Resolution	Private Forecast[a]
Gross national product (constant 1972 dollars, percent change)	3.7	3.2
GNP deflator (percent change, year over year)	6.0	6.15
Consumer price index (percent change, year over year)	6.4	6.6
Unemployment rate (annual average, percent)	7.2	7.25
Interest rate, three-month Treasury bills (annual average, percent)	6.9	10.0

a. The private forecasts are Data Resources Incorporated (April 1982), Chase Econometrics (April 1982), Wharton Forecasting Associates, Inc. (April 1982), and Townsend-Greenspan (May 1982).
SOURCES: Senate Report 97-478, "First Concurrent Resolution on the Budget—Fiscal Year 1983, Conference Report," June 18, 1982, p. 20; and House of Representatives, Report No. 97-521, "First Concurrent Resolution on the Budget—Fiscal Year 1983, Report of the Committee on the Budget to Accompany H. Con. Res. 345," May 17, 1982, pp. 63–65.

light the policy differences between the various budget proposals, and allow for meaningful comparisons of the competing budgets. Worthy as these objectives are, a forecast is needed if the deficit (as opposed to the constant employment deficit), revenues, and outlays of the resolution are to be estimated as required by the Budget Act. New confusion would result if the constant employment budget aggregates bore little relation to the actual results. As long as the president or Congress makes the state of the economy a political issue, it is probably unrealistic to try to insulate congressional economic assumptions from political pressures.

A final concern that has been expressed with respect to the use of economic information by Congress is that such information creates a bias to action. Because Congress adopts economic assumptions for its budget resolutions, it must acknowledge the state of the economy and thereby take responsibility for economic conditions. This situation has forced Congress to play a more active role in economic policy making than it did before 1975, when the president dominated economic and budget policy making. This pressure becomes especially strong when the economy is weak.

The policies that result from pressure for action may do little good and might do harm. Congressional inaction may be the most efficacious policy. Even when fiscal policy responses do not result from this situation, Congress may feel a need to shift the blame to some other actor. Doing so could have adverse consequences for the stability of the financial community. In addition to the president, the chairman of the Federal Reserve Board has been singled out for such blame.

Any solution to this problem must insulate Congress from the pressure to act. As long as a majority in Congress believes that fiscal policy affects economic conditions and Congress retains a major role in determining spending and taxing levels, there is little likelihood that these pressures can be brought under control. Measures that shift the responsibility for economic conditions to the executive branch might help. Meaningful moves in this direction, however—such as giving the president authority to impound budget authority, to impose positive or negative surtaxes, or to set monetary policy—would constitute fundamental changes in the nation's governmental process. They should be pursued only after thoroughly weighing their other costs and benefits.

Conclusion

To sum up, in the past decade Congress has greatly increased the amount of economic information it needs and uses. On the whole it has gathered, assimilated, and used this information effectively and responsibly. Although confusion, frustration, and political manipulation have accompanied this proliferation of economic advice, the sources of these problems lie largely in the nature of the nation's economic problems, the limitations of economics as a science, and the nature of a legislative body. Therefore, reforms of one sort or another are unlikely to make things significantly better.

The proliferation of economic information and advice on Capitol Hill has significantly affected congressional behavior. The condition of the economy has framed the debates on the budget, debates that have consumed the legislative calendar of recent years. The relative priority accorded to new initiatives has also been affected by economic analysis as concerns over inflation and the weak condition of the economy have intensified.

Economic information and analysis have acted to constrain the legislative process. Questions are now asked about the short- and long-run costs of a proposal and about its effect on the deficit. Attention is focused on the effects of legislative and regulatory initiatives on inflation and on economic efficiency. Such concerns were rarely, if ever, raised a decade ago. Although Congress can always ignore the answers or accept unrealistic assumptions, it is undeniable that the policy-making environment has been constrained by the recent explosion of economic information and concerns.

Notes

1. The 1983 estimate is derived from information contained in Congressional Budget Office, *Baseline Budget Projections for Fiscal Years 1984–1988*, February 1983. The 1967 estimate is derived from information contained in Executive Office of the President, Council of Economic Advisers, Office of Management and Budget, *Report on Indexing Federal Programs*, January 1981.

2. Calculated from figures contained in Congressional Budget Office, *The Economic and Budget Outlook: An Update*, September 1982, and *Baseline Budget Projections*. The calculations are for fiscal 1984 and assume an increase in unemployment of one percentage point beginning January 1, 1983. The tax cuts of 1981 and the spending cuts in food stamps, unemployment benefits, and other means-tested programs have reduced this sensitivity somewhat over the past two years.

3. Section 301(d) of P.L. 93-344 requires that the reports accompanying the concurrent resolution include "(5) the economic assumptions and objectives which underlie each of the matters set forth in such concurrent resolutions and alternative economic assumptions and objectives which the committee considered."

4. The following table provides CBO estimates (in billions of dollars) of the sensitivity of the fiscal 1984 budget to changes in several economic conditions beginning in January 1983:

	Unemployment One Percentage Point Higher	Inflation One Percentage Point Higher	Real Growth One Percentage Point Lower
Outlays	10	1	5
Revenues	−29	15	−23
Deficit	39	−14	28

SOURCE: Congressional Budget Office, *Economic and Budget Outlook*, table B-1.

5. See section 308(c) of P.L. 93-344.

6. During 1982 the CBO used the models of Data Resources Incorporated (DRI), Wharton Econometric Forecasting Associates, Incorporated, Townsend-Greenspan and Company, Inc., and Evans Economics, Incorporated. The choice of forecasting firms used by the CBO and various committees is influenced by ease of use, flexibility, and accessibility and by the theoretical orientation of the model—does the forecasting firm claim to have captured supply-side effects?

7. Congressional Budget Office, *An Analysis of the Roth-Kemp Tax Cut Proposal,* October 1978, background paper.

8. U.S. House of Representatives, Committee on the Budget and Joint Economic Committee, *Economic Stabilization Policies: The Historical Record, 1962–1976,* November 1978.

9. These figures cover the period from the second budget resolution for fiscal 1976 through the first budget resolution for fiscal 1983. There was no second budget resolution for fiscal 1983 or fiscal 1982. There was a third budget resolution for fiscal 1977. The cases in which it was determined that a CBO forecast was used include instances in which the Budget committees accepted a revised CBO forecast that was prepared at the committee's request after the publication of the CBO economic report. In some instances the refusal to accept the CBO forecast was related to rapid changes in the economy between the time the CBO made its forecast and the time the resolution was formulated. In other instances the CBO forecast was rejected because the "current policy" fiscal policy underlying the forecast was significantly different from that implied by the budget resolution.

10. See David I. Meiselman and Paul Craig Roberts, "The Political Economy of the Congressional Budget Office" (Paper prepared for the Carnegie-Rochester Public Policy Conference, University of Rochester, April 28, 1978); and Preston J. Miller and Arthur J. Rolnick, "The CBO's Policy Analysis: An Unquestionable Misuse of a Questionable Theory," in Rudolph G. Penner, ed., *The Congressional Budget Process after Five Years* (Washington, D.C.: American Enterprise Institute, 1981).

11. Minority views of Senator Orrin G. Hatch, in "Report of the Committee on the Budget, Second Concurrent Resolution on the Budget, FY 1980," August 24, 1979.

12. In the period between the adoption of the first budget resolution for fiscal 1977 and the passage of the first budget resolution for fiscal 1983, the economic assumptions underlying the final resolutions adopted by Congress were generally more optimistic than those proposed by the administration in two instances, more pessimistic nine times, and virtually identical twice. The optimistic-pessimistic classification entails a good degree of judgment. The form in which the economic assumptions are provided is not always identical, making comparisons difficult. In addition, forecasts have a number of dimensions (nominal GNP growth, real GNP growth, inflation, and unemployment) that must be compared. A forecast may be

more optimistic on one dimension and less optimistic on another. Furthermore, the forecasts generally extend for two years. One forecast may be less optimistic than another in the first year but more optimistic in the second.

13. The comparison with private forecasts covers the period from the second budget resolution for fiscal 1977 through the first budget resolution for fiscal 1983. For a description of some of the difficulties inherent in comparing forecasts, see note 12. The significance of these differences should not be overemphasized. Some are attributable to different fiscal policy assumptions, some to the fact that the Congress may set its forecast several months after CBO has prepared its forecast. The private consensus refers to the *Blue Chip Economic Indicators* consensus for the same month as the publication of the CBO report. This series is published by Eggert Economic Enterprises, Inc.

14. This has been proposed by Rudolph G. Penner in "Budget Assumptions and Budget Outcomes," *The AEI Economist* (August 1981).

15. For a description of this proposal, see the statement of Robert D. Reischauer in *Budget Process Review*, "Hearing before the Committee on the Budget," U.S. House of Representatives, September 14, 1982.

16. This has been proposed by Penner in "Budget Assumptions and Budget Outcomes."

17. This point was made by Charles L. Schultze in comments on Rudolph G. Penner's "Forecasting Budget Targets: Why Can't We Get It Right?" (Presented at the symposium "The Fate and Future of the Congressional Budget Process," convened by the Committee for a Responsible Federal Budget and the Garfield Foundation, June 11–13, 1982, Princeton, New Jersey).

3

Budget Control in a Redistributive Environment

John W. Ellwood

The congressional budget process is no longer new. Since its implementation in 1975, the process has been used during nine budget cycles. With the passage of time, it has become increasingly difficult to hold the view that it is too early to judge the effects of the process. It is time to make some judgments.

To reach these judgments, this chapter begins with a description of how the process has evolved since its implementation. The chapter then considers whether the Congressional Budget and Impoundment Control Act has achieved the goals of its authors. The body of the chapter seeks to explain the present unhappiness with the budget process by pointing out that at the same time that a slower-growing economy limited Congress's policy options, the new process made it difficult for Congress to treat redistributive policies as if they were distributive.

The Congressional Budget Process

The budget procedures enacted in 1974 were aimed at providing Congress with a mechanism to relate the parts of the budget to its whole. The centerpiece of the procedure is the concurrent resolution on the budget. This resolution is approved by Congress in the same manner as a statute, but because the president does not have the option of signing or vetoing it, the resolution does not have legal effect.

The Budget Act requires that by May 15 of each year Congress adopt a concurrent resolution on the budget (generally referred to as the first budget resolution). This resolution sets targets for five aggregates: (1) total budget authority, (2) total budget outlays, (3) total budget revenues, (4) total budget surplus or deficit, and (5) total public debt. The resolution also contains targets for budget authority and outlays for the various budget functions. Currently, the federal budget is divided into nineteen categories of the major purposes of federal activity (such as national defense, energy, health, income security).

Once the first resolution is adopted, its targets are allocated to the various committees of the House and Senate on the basis of their jurisdiction over budget authority (these are referred to as Section 302 allocations). For the fiscal 1983 budget, budget authority was provided through 1,257 budget accounts. Two hundred and two of these are for negative outlays—called offsetting receipts—and are not allocated to committees. Of the remaining accounts, 812 (77 percent) are funded through an annual appropriation contained in one of the thirteen regular appropriations bills. These accounts reflect the normal way that federal programs are established and funded—first with the passage of an authorization setting up the program and then with an annual appropriation to fund it.

Although the overwhelming majority of budget accounts are funded through annual appropriations, only 39.6 percent of fiscal 1983 outlays resulted from budget authority funded in this manner. Almost half the outlays—49.5 percent—resulted from budget authority granted in authorizing statutes. These authorizations fund the major entitlements that have been the fastest-growing component of the federal budget during the past twenty years. The annual appropriations process cannot control the funding levels of these accounts because persons are entitled to payments if they meet the tests established in the authorizing statute. Moreover, in many entitlements, the payment is automatically adjusted to the rate of inflation. Thus, for many of these accounts, the authorization provides an open-ended grant of budget authority.

A few accounts are "appropriated entitlements"; their funding is provided in annual appropriations. In practice, however, the authorization determines the funding; the Appropriations committees must provide sufficient funds to finance these entitlements.

Once the targets of the first budget resolution are allocated, the various committees with jurisdiction over spending and revenue legislation bring their bills to the House and Senate. The Budget Act contains a deadline of seven calendar days after Labor Day, by which time Congress is supposed to have enacted all the spending and revenue bills for the coming fiscal year.

Under the original provisions of the act, Congress was required to pass a second budget resolution by September 15. This resolution contains ceilings for total budget authority and total outlays and a floor for total revenues. Once the fiscal year begins, any bill that would cause total budget authority or total outlays to rise above the ceilings or total revenues to fall below the floor is subject to a point of order. Congress can, however, pass another budget resolution modifying the aggregates.

The Budget Act specifies a procedure to reconcile the aggregates in the second resolution with spending and revenue legislation passed during the year. Reconciliation consists of two stages: instructions and a bill. In the instructions Congress notifies committees of the dollar amounts of budget authority, outlays, and revenues that are to be reduced or increased. These committees then recommend changes, which are grouped into a reconciliation bill. The Budget Act provides for the reconciliation bill to be enacted by September 25.

Innovations under the Elastic Clauses. The Budget committees have enlarged the scope of the congressional budget process under two "elastic" clauses in the Budget Act, which allow budget resolutions to contain "such other matters relating to the budget as may be appropriate to carry out the purposes of this Act" and to require "any other procedure which is considered appropriate to carry out the purposes of this Act." The Budget committees have used these provisions to adapt the process to changing political and budgetary conditions. The following are the major changes made under the elastic clauses.

First, Congress shifted from two to a single mandatory resolution. It became increasingly evident that the second budget resolution did little but ratify previous congressional actions. The real decisions were made in the first resolution or in optional third and sometimes fourth budget resolutions. Accordingly, in 1981 Congress set the precedent that the first resolution would automatically set a ceiling on spending and a floor on revenues on October 1 unless a second resolution had been adopted.

Second, the content of budget resolutions has been expanded. Since fiscal 1980 the resolutions have had multiyear targets—for the coming fiscal year and for two additional fiscal years. In the fiscal 1981 cycle, targets for aggregate credit activity (direct and guaranteed loans) were included in the budget resolutions. In the following year, functional targets were added, and in the fiscal 1983 resolution the credit targets were allocated to the various congressional committees (following the Section 302 allocation procedures for direct spending). This resolution also provided that all newly authorized credit activity must be subject to an appropriation.

The third and most important use of the elastic clauses has been to shift the reconciliation process from the second to the first budget resolution. In the fall of 1979 the Senate's version of the second resolution included reconciliation instructions to seven Senate committees. But the House Budget Committee refused to go along with the Senate's position because it had entered into understandings with various House committees under which they would report legislation to achieve "legislative savings." Although some of these understandings were implemented, the House approved legislation saving only about $200 million of the $6 billion that had been targeted. As a result of this experience both Budget committees turned to the reconciliation process in 1980 as the best way to achieve expenditure reductions and tax increases.[1] The Omnibus Reconciliation Act of 1980 (P.L. 96-499) reduced estimated fiscal 1981 budget authority by $3.1 billion and outlays by $4.6 billion. The act also made changes in the tax laws that raised an estimated $3.6 billion in additional revenues.

The reconciliation procedure, invoked for the first time in 1980, was the instrument by which President Reagan and his congressional allies enacted the largest peacetime reductions in domestic spending in American history. The 1981 reconciliation process was dramatic and controversial because of the magnitude of its reductions in nondefense spending and its violation of several congressional norms. The Omnibus Reconciliation Act of 1981 (P.L. 97-35) contained modifications of authorization statutes affecting 232 budget accounts. The Congressional Budget Office (CBO) estimated that these changes would reduce fiscal 1982 budget authority by $53.2 billion and outlays by $35.2 billion. To ensure multiyear savings, the committees were instructed to meet reconciliation targets for each of three fiscal years. In contrast to 1980, when the reconciliation bill packaged tax and spending changes together, in 1981 President Reagan's massive tax reductions were enacted outside the reconciliation process.

The 1982 reconciliation returned to the more moderate savings that had been established in 1980. The CBO estimated that it lowered fiscal 1983 budget authority by $2.2 billion and fiscal 1983 outlays by $6.6 billion. Once again various committees were required to meet savings targets for three fiscal years. The CBO estimated that the act would lower the current policy projection for fiscal 1985 by $5.1 billion in budget authority and $11.3 billion in outlays.

It would appear, therefore, that Congress has a procedure that can be used to achieve steady and significant changes in spending and revenues. One might assume, therefore, that the budget process would receive praise from all sides.

Just the opposite is true. Liberals increasingly identify the process with reductions in funding of programs for poor people.

Conservatives point to the failure of the process to eliminate federal deficits or curb the rate of expenditure growth. In Congress authorizing committees see the process—particularly the reconciliation procedures when invoked with the first budget resolution—as a threat to their autonomy and power. It is useful, therefore, to see how the new procedures have measured up against the goals of the Budget Act.

Goals of the Budget Act of 1974

Students of the Congressional Budget and Impoundment Control Act of 1974 differ about its main goals. The goals of the act can be determined in two ways. First, one can try to determine the motives of its framers. The difficulty of such an approach is that any statute enacted by the overwhelming majorities of 75–0 in the Senate and 401–6 in the House must either reflect divine wisdom or be a bundle of compromises reflecting many different perspectives.

Still, some scholars have assumed that the motives of the prime movers of the 1974 reform can be defined as the goals of the act. Louis Fisher has written:

> It is true that Members of Congress disagreed on the objectives of budget reform in 1974. Some wanted reduced spending and a balanced budget; others wanted the budget used to stimulate the economy; still others thought that the Act would strengthen congressional control over federal spending priorities. But the overwhelming sentiment behind the Act was to create a procedure capable of restraining the growth of federal spending.[2]

A second approach—taken by Allen Schick in the most comprehensive study of the new process—is to argue that the Budget Act reflected such a bundle of compromises that it would be absurd to posit that it reflected a consistent point of view.[3] Because of the complexity of the motives for the act's adoption, Schick recommends that the provisions be judged on what they say; on this basis he comes to the conclusion that the act is not biased toward a particular policy outcome but is "neutral on its face."

The second approach is more useful. It is almost impossible to determine the true sentiments of the members of Congress in 1974. Even if it were possible to identify the original motives, there would be great disagreement over whether some opinions should be weighed more heavily than others.

Although there is no agreement on the aims of the Budget Act, the following expectations of what the act would accomplish were often applauded during the debate over its adoption:

- allow Congress to recapture its historic role of "the power of the purse"
- curb the growth of federal spending and the frequency and size of federal budget deficits[4]
- enable Congress to meet its budgetary deadlines by enacting taxing and spending legislation before the beginning of the fiscal year
- help Congress manage its internal conflict over budgetary questions

There is general agreement that the Budget Act has been successful in restoring congressional initiative and authority on budget and fiscal policy questions.[5] In the nine fiscal years since the act's implementation, Congress has successfully enacted budget resolutions. In several cases, moreover, the resolutions differed significantly from the president's budget recommendation. But the act's ability to bring about the three other goals has been widely questioned.

Controlling Expenditure Growth and Limiting Deficits. Those who assumed that the procedures of the Budget Act would lead to a reduction in the rate of growth of federal budget expenditures and in the frequency and size of federal deficits have been disappointed.

Because federal expenditures are sensitive to changes in the economy, they have to be "normalized" if their true growth rate is to be analyzed. One way to achieve such normalization is to create a time series of what federal outlays would have been if the economy had been operating at its potential. Such an economy would have no cyclical unemployment. The unemployment that would exist—about 4.5 to 5 percent—would be frictional and structural.

Because about half of federal outlays are either directly or indirectly indexed to inflation—most often to the consumer price index (CPI)—it is also necessary to present the "full" or "high-employment" outlay time series in constant dollars. This is done in the first column of table 3–1 for the seven years before the Budget Act and for an equivalent period since its implementation. The second column of the table gives these high-employment outlays in constant 1972 dollars as percentages of what the gross national product (GNP) would have been if the economy had been operating at its potential (potential GNP).

During the seven years before the Budget Act, high-employment federal outlays in constant dollars (both on-budget and off-budget outlays) grew at an average annual rate of 2.8 percent. During the

TABLE 3–1
HIGH-EMPLOYMENT ESTIMATES OF FEDERAL OUTLAYS AND DEFICITS
BEFORE AND AFTER THE BUDGET ACT OF 1974, 1969–1982
(in billions of constant 1972 dollars)

Fiscal Year	High-Employment Total Outlays	High-Employment Outlays as a Percentage of Potential GNP	High-Employment Deficit	High-Employment Deficit as a Percentage of Potential GNP
Before the Budget Act				
1969	221.4	21.0	0.7	0.1
1970	221.6	20.3	−1.5	−0.1
1971	220.6	19.5	10.0	0.9
1972	227.1	19.4	10.5	0.9
1973	231.4	19.1	13.5	0.9
1974	236.9	18.9	5.3	0.4
1975	261.3	20.4	18.3	1.4
After implementation of the Budget Act				
1976	271.8	20.5	21.4	1.6
1977	279.7	20.0	19.7	1.4
1978	296.8	20.6	20.7	1.4
1979	302.7	20.3	8.9	0.6
1980	321.2	21.0	18.2	1.2
1981	330.7	21.0	14.6	0.9
1982	335.6	20.6	17.6	1.1

NOTE: Columns two and four understate the growth of the ratios in recent years for two reasons. First, the OMB uses a series of indexes to deflate its expenditure time series. These have been rising faster than the GNP deflator. This has caused real expenditures as a percentage of potential GNP to be understated in recent years. Second, because of the changing structure of the economy, the measure of potential GNP probably includes capacity that is not economically viable.

SOURCES: High-employment estimates from Frank de Leeuw and Thomas M. Holloway, "The High-Employment Budget: Revised Estimates and Automatic Inflation Effects," *Survey of Current Business*, April 1982, pp. 21–33, August 1982, p. 10, and from Dr. Holloway. High-employment estimates in 1972 dollars calculated by the author using the de Leeuw and Holloway data, OMB budget data, and method described in John Palmer and Isabel Sawhill, *The Reagan Experiment* (Washington, D.C.: Urban Institute, 1982), p. 485. The estimates for high-employment deficits and potential GNP were deflated using the GNP deflator.

next seven years, under the new budget procedures, they grew 29 percent faster, rising at an annual average rate of 3.6 percent. Between fiscal years 1969 and 1975, high-employment outlays in 1972 dollars averaged 19.8 percent of constant-dollar potential GNP. During the next seven years, under the provisions of the Budget Act, this ratio rose to an average of 20.6 percent.

Table 3–1 also contains estimates of what the total federal deficit (the on-budget plus the off-budget deficit) would have been if the economy had been operating at its potential throughout the fourteen-year period. To account for a growing economy, column four presents these deficits as a percentage of potential GNP.

Once again the evidence is disappointing for those who assumed that the Budget Act would reduce federal deficits. In the period from fiscal 1969 to fiscal 1975, the high-employment federal deficit averaged 0.6 percent of potential GNP. During the first seven fiscal years under the provisions of the Budget Act, this measure rose to 1.2 percent of potential GNP.

The prospect for the immediate future is also quite discouraging. The actions of the Ninety-seventh Congress have created a structural deficit that will persist even if the economy recovers. The very large tax reductions of the Economic Recovery Tax Act of 1981 (ERTA)— especially the scheduled indexing of the personal income tax in 1985 and the accelerated depreciation provisions—coupled with increased spending for the procurement of major weapons systems, have created a situation in which, if current policies continue in effect, the budget deficit in current dollars is likely to get larger through fiscal 1988.

A future of increasing deficits would occur even if the economy operated at its potential through fiscal 1988. The Congressional Budget Office estimated in February 1983 that if current funding levels were modified only for already legislated changes and for inflation and if the economy were operating at its potential, the unified budget deficit as a percentage of potential GNP would grow as follows:

	1983	1984	1985	1986	1987	1988
High-employment deficit as a percentage of potential GNP	1.5	2.0	2.7	3.2	3.6	4.0

The debate over whether the new procedures have resulted in higher or lower spending and larger or smaller deficits will always be inconclusive. Too many factors have to be held constant for an accurate explanation; even the higher growth rates for spending in the period after implementation are not conclusive, for, it can be argued, without the new procedures spending might have been even higher. But the expectation that the act would cause a decline in the growth rate of federal expenditures and in the size of federal deficits has not been realized.

Creating a More Efficient Process. A major goal that reappears throughout the history of budget reform in the United States is to make public sector budgeting more "businesslike." In the years immediately preceding the Budget Act, a good deal of criticism was directed at the inability of Congress to pass the thirteen regular appropriations bills before the beginning of the fiscal year.

The Budget Act contained two types of provisions aimed at correcting this problem. First, a series of congressional deadlines was established. Authorizing committees were required to report bills authorizing new budget authority for the coming fiscal year by May 15. The purpose of this provision was to ensure more timely action by the Appropriations committees.

The first budget resolution had to be agreed to by both chambers by May 15. To encourage Congress to meet this deadline, the act provided that appropriations bills could not be brought to the floor until the first resolution had been passed. Since the targets for budget authority in the first resolution were allocated to committees, its prompt passage would provide guidance for the appropriations process.

The act also required that all spending and taxing legislation affecting the coming fiscal year be passed by seven calendar days after Labor Day. No enforcing mechanism, however, was provided for this deadline. It was assumed that the passage of all spending legislation would enable Congress to meet the deadlines of September 15 for the adoption of the second budget resolution and September 25 for an optional reconciliation bill. These two deadlines were to be enforced by the provision that Congress could not adjourn until it adopted a second budget resolution. To give Congress more time to work on appropriations bills, the Budget Act shifted the start of the fiscal year from July 1 to October 1.

Initially, the deadlines and the shift of the fiscal year had the desired effect. As indicated in table 3–2, in fiscal 1977—the first time the Budget Act was fully implemented—Congress enacted all the annual appropriations bills before October 1. During the following budget cycle, ten of the thirteen bills were passed before the beginning of the fiscal year.

But Congress soon returned to its old ways. In the fiscal 1981 budget cycle, only one of the regular bills was enacted before October 1. The following year none of the thirteen appropriations bills was passed before the beginning of the fiscal year. A new,

TABLE 3–2

Number of Regular Appropriations Bills Enacted before the Beginning of the Fiscal Year, 1968–1983

Fiscal Year	Passed before Beginning of Fiscal Year	Passed after Beginning of Fiscal Year	Under Continuing Resolution throughout Fiscal Year
Fiscal year beginning July 1			
Before Budget Act			
1968	2	11	0
1969	1	12	0
1970	0	13	0
1971	0	13	0
1972	3	10	0
1973	3	8	2
1974	0	13	0
1975	0	13	0
Implementation of Budget Act			
1976	0	10	3
Fiscal year beginning October 1			
1977	13	0	0
1978	10	2	1
1979	5	7	1
1980	3	7	3
1981	1	7	5
1982	0	9	4
1983	1	5	7

Source: Computed by the author from *Congressional Quarterly Almanac*, various years, 1968–1982.

and to some a disturbing, trend developed: Congress increasingly relied on continuing resolutions to fund accounts throughout the fiscal year. Three of the regular appropriations bills were funded throughout fiscal 1980 under continuing resolutions. In fiscal 1981 five bills, and in fiscal 1982 four bills, were funded in this manner. An all-time high of seven regular appropriations bills were funded throughout fiscal 1983 under continuing resolutions.

The deadlines of the Budget Act were also aimed at curtailing supplemental appropriations. This aim has been only partially achieved.[6] In fiscal years 1970 through 1975, budget authority granted through supplemental appropriations averaged 7.6 percent of the total budget authority granted through the annual appropriations process. During the next five fiscal years, under the budget process, this percentage declined to 7.5 percent. (Even if fiscal 1977 is excluded under the rationale that the new Carter administration carried out its modification of the last Ford budget through supplemental appropriations, the figure declines only to 6.0 percent of all budget authority.)

The number of items contained in supplemental appropriations bills has not declined since the Budget Act. Excluding fiscal 1977, the average number of items in supplemental appropriations bills in the five fiscal years after the Budget Act was about 30 percent higher than the average number in the first six fiscal years of the 1970s.

Although these data do not support the notion that the Budget Act caused an increase in the size and number of supplemental appropriations, they do refute the expectation that the new procedures would lead to a reduction in supplemental appropriations.

Managing Internal Conflict. Allen Schick refers to the Budget Act as the "Congressional Budget Treaty of 1974." But Schick points out:

> The Congressional Budget Act did not put an end to budgetary strife any more than the introduction of presidential budgeting brought perfect peace a half-century ago. The Budget Act was a respite and a redirection. While it could not assure budgetary tranquility, it at least provided new conditions under which future battles would be fought.[7]

It appears that the respite was brief and the redirection did little to lower the intensity of conflict over budgetary matters. Conflict associated with the making of fiscal and budgetary policy has, if anything, increased in recent years.

One measure of this conflict is the already mentioned difficulty of enacting spending bills before the beginning of the fiscal year. As Schick points out, the movement toward congressional budget reform began after a series of battles among congressional committees and between Congress and President Nixon. These battles reached their peak in the early 1970s. The data in table 3–3 confirm this pattern. Congress took longer to adopt its spending bills in the years with the greatest amount of conflict.

The data in table 3–3 appear to support the hypothesis that Congress does not respond to artificial deadlines. The only deadline that can motivate Congress to action on appropriations bills is the beginning of the fiscal year. When measured against this starting

TABLE 3–3

Average Number of Days Required to Adopt Regular Appropriations Bills before and after the Budget Act, 1968–1983

Fiscal Year	Measured from January 1	Measured from the Beginning of the Fiscal Year
Before Budget Act		
1968	275	94
1969	230	46
1970	353	172
1971	315	131
1972	256	75
1973	276	96
1974	276	95
1975	278	97
After implementation of the Budget Act		
1976	364	183
1977	231	−43
1978	260	−14
1979	309	36
1980	364	91
1981	445	172
1982	442	169
1983	497	224
Annual average before the Budget Act	282	101
Annual average after the Budget Act	364	102

NOTE: It is assumed that continuing resolutions are adopted at the close of the fiscal year. If it is assumed that continuing resolutions are major appropriations bills and thus that the appropriation bill they fund was adopted on the date that the continuing resolution was passed, the average number of days required to adopt all thirteen appropriations bills when measured from January 1 would be 275 before the Budget Act and 302 after the act. When measured from the beginning of the fiscal year, the average number of days would be 94 before the Budget Act and 41 after the act.

SOURCE: Computed by the author from *Congressional Quarterly Almanac*, various years, 1968–1982.

point, Congress has taken just as long, on the average, to adopt the thirteen regular appropriations bills since the Budget Act (102 days) as it did under the prior process (101 days).

The data in table 3–3 also indicate that conflict has been increasing since the fiscal 1980 budget cycle, which was dominated by

President Carter's futile attempt to balance the budget. Since that time fiscal and budgetary policy has been dominated by two severe recessions and the Reagan administration's attempt to revise federal budgetary priorities.

The impression of an increase in conflict is also supported by the rising tide of complaints by congressmen about the budget process. Members complain that the Budget committees have become too powerful. They point to the tendency of the budget process—which was supposed to stay away from specific programs—to mandate line-item changes.

The implementation of reconciliation in conjunction with the first budget resolution—especially in 1981—has caused a great deal of resentment. Some congressmen complain that budgeting has become an all-consuming activity at the expense of congressional oversight and reauthorization of programs. Many charge that the deadlines of the Budget Act—which, as we have seen, have not been effective in ensuring the timely enactment of appropriations—have forced committees to act before they have thoroughly studied the various policy options.

Some congressmen charge that the new layers of budget activity increase the difficulty of positive action and create the opportunity for symbolic voting. Members can endorse policies that will have to be voted on several more times before they actually become law.[8]

Why the Goals Have Not Been Achieved

The aim of this section is to make two points. First, the substance of policy and the character of politics have been more important than procedural arrangements in explaining the shortcomings of congressional actions since the implementation of the Budget Act.

Second, the Budget Act's replacement of a fragmented decision-making system that relied on bargaining with a more comprehensive decision-making procedure that relies on aggregate budget constraints has expanded the arena of dispute and made it more difficult for Congress to treat redistributive issues as if they were distributive.

Economic and Political Factors. The budget wars that led to the passage of the Budget Act resulted from political disagreements over the proper role and size of the federal sector. These political disagreements were exacerbated by the decline in the growth rate of the economy. As the rate of real GNP growth declined, the degree that the federal sector could grow without increasing its proportion of GNP also declined. The decline in real economic growth also

81

TABLE 3–4

PERFORMANCE OF THE ECONOMY, 1950–1982

	1950–1959	1960–1969	1970–1975	1976–1982
Growth (annual percentage increase in real GNP)	3.4	4.4	2.6	2.2
Productivity (annual percentage increase in output per hour in private business sector)	2.7	3.1	1.9	0.6
Inflation (annual percentage increase in the CPI)	2.1	2.4	6.7	9.2
Unemployment (average rate for all workers)	4.5	4.8	5.9	7.3
Unemployment (average rate for adult males)	3.9	3.6	4.3	5.8
Standard of living (annual percentage increase in per capita real disposable personal income)	1.4	3.1	2.0	1.5

SOURCES: Table adapted from table 2–1 in John Palmer and Isabel Sawhill, *The Reagan Experiment* (Washington, D.C.: Urban Institute, 1982), p. 34. Data from *Economic Report of the President* (1983), tables B-2 (p. 164), B-40 (p. 208), B-52 (p. 221), B-31 (p. 199), B-24 (p. 191).

put greater pressure on the trade-off between defense and nondefense spending. The limited growth in federal revenues forced Congress to accept higher taxation, larger federal deficits, or both.

Since the Budget Act was passed, the performance of the economy has been weak. Six measures of economic performance are set out in table 3–4. The average annual increase in real GNP declined from 4.4 percent during the 1960s to 2.6 percent in the six years preceding the Budget Act. Since the act's implementation, the rate of economic growth has declined further—to a 2.2 percent average for the 1976–1982 period.

The same pattern of deterioration exists for the annual rate of increase in productivity, the annual rate of inflation as measured by the consumer price index (CPI), the average annual rate of unemployment of all workers and of adult male workers, and the annual increase in per capita real disposable personal income. Given this pattern, it is not surprising that conflict within Congress has increased rather than declined since the enactment of the Budget Act.

Of particular importance have been the increase in the average annual rate of inflation and the decline in the average annual increase in the standard of living. Under rapid inflation, increasing numbers of individuals believe that they are becoming poorer. The data in table 3–4 indicate that, in the aggregate, this was not true. During the 1976–1982 period, per capita real disposable income increased at a yearly rate of 1.5 percent—a higher rate of growth than occurred during the 1950s.[9]

The decline in the performance of the economy has created a sense of relative deprivation. After several decades of steadily improving economic performance, increases in one's standard of living become taken for granted. It is not surprising that in the late 1970s, for the first time since scientific public opinion polling began in the 1930s, the national government was perceived as the problem rather than the solution to the nation's economic troubles.

The rise in the rate of inflation has been another factor in the public's unhappiness with the results of the budget process. Almost every individual, group, and firm believes that it was made worse off by the rising rate of inflation during the 1970s. In reality this was not true. A number of studies have shown that inflation is primarily a progressive tax, striking upper-income owners of stocks and bonds harder than others whose income is derived from wages and whose wealth is primarily in real estate.[10]

The main reason that the perception of the effects of inflation differs from its reality is that individuals and firms do not associate increases in their wages and profits with increases in the goods and services that they purchase. Higher wages and profits are earned; higher prices and costs are evidence of theft.[11]

Individuals, groups, and firms in the United States responded to perceived and real losses of income exactly as one would expect— each tried to use its economic and political power to guarantee that it would not bear the burden of the losses.[12] To avoid bearing that burden, groups increasingly came to Congress for relief. Unfortunately, we do not have very good measures of the degree to which they petition Congress for relief from their ills. But we do know:

• An ever-increasing number of trade associations have moved their national headquarters to the Washington, D.C., metropolitan area. In 1971, 26 percent of the headquarters were located in New York City, 19 percent in Washington, and 15 percent in Chicago. By 1975, 26 percent were located around the nation's capital, 24 percent in New York City, and 16 percent in the Chicago area. During the last half of the 1970s this pattern continued. In 1983, 30 percent of the headquarters were located in the Washington area, 19 percent in New York City and its suburbs, and 14 percent in the Chicago area.[13]

• The number of lobbyists registering with the clerks of the House and Senate rose dramatically in the 1970s. During the 1960s an annual average of 282 individuals, groups, and firms registered as lobbyists; from 1970 through 1974 that average rose to 430. In 1981, 1,507 registered.[14]

• Since 1970 the tax code has increasingly been used to grant narrow subsidies to individuals and firms. Of the 104 tax expenditures that were part of the tax code in 1982, sixty-nine were enacted into law from 1909 through 1969. Although these subsidies made up 66 percent of 1982 tax expenditure provisions, they accounted for 95 percent of the revenues lost to the Treasury through tax expenditures. Thirty-five tax expenditures—or 34 percent of all 1982 tax expenditures—have been enacted since 1970. But these provisions accounted for only 5 percent of the lost revenues in 1982.[15]

• The number and influence of political action committees (PACs) have increased dramatically since the 1974 Federal Election Campaign Act and the November 24, 1975, SunPac decision of the Federal Election Commission. There were 608 PACs at the end of 1974 and 2,551 by the end of 1980; during the next two years the number of PACs grew by 32 percent, to 3,371 in January 1983.[16]

Internal Factors. Some students of Congress argue that what has changed is not the desire for access but the ease with which that access can be achieved. They point out that although Congress has always been an accessible institution, the decline of the power of congressional leadership, limits on the seniority rule, the explosion of congressional staff, and other reforms of the early 1970s have dramatically increased access. In the 1970s Congress became an institution with many more players for each issue. The greater freedom provided by increased staff and the declining power of specialists and party leaders have allowed junior members to become active on issues that in the past would have been directed and dominated by a small number of senior congressmen and senators.[17]

We cannot separate the effects of the external pressures for relief and the internal reforms allowing greater access. Clearly the reforms of the 1970s increased access. Members who came to Congress before the 1970s often point to increases in the number of special-interest groups and lobbyists. Whether these increases would have occurred if the seniority system had not been modified, if the powers of party leaders and committee chairmen had not been weakened, or if the strength of political parties in the members' districts had not declined cannot be ascertained. But from the viewpoint of a congressman or a senator, the situation was made more painful by the procedures of the Congressional Budget Act. It is to the effects of this internal change that we now turn.

Distributive versus Redistributive Politics. The first imperative for Congressmen is to be reelected.[18] The best way to be reelected is to create the impression of helping a maximum number of voters and hurting a minimum number.[19] A member who wants to be reelected would like to handle issues so that the winners are grateful for their benefits while any losers are unaware of their losses. This is the environment of distributive politics.

The alternative is redistributive politics. In this environment winners and losers are aware of their status. A major goal of congressional politics—at least since the New Deal—has been to take policy issues that on an economic basis are clearly redistributive and treat them as if they were distributive.

The declining performance of the American economy during the 1970s made it increasingly difficult for congressmen to behave distributively. As pressures for relief from inflation, unemployment, and foreign competition rose, the declining rate of growth gave elected officials less to distribute. One alternative was to allow the rapid pace of inflation to generate more revenues by pushing individuals into higher tax brackets. Although this strategy was followed by the Carter administration, the tax revolts of the late 1970s and the election results of 1980 indicate that the electorate, which already perceived that it was losing ground to inflation, would not approve a visible increase in its tax burden.[20] Another alternative is to accept large budget deficits. This strategy is apparently being employed by the Reagan administration. Yet it is clear that the changing nature of the American (and world) economy has eliminated most of the discretion that made the life of a congressman or senator so enjoyable before 1970.

Distributive and Redistributive Politics under the Old and New Congressional Budget Processes. The fragmented budget process that allowed issues to be treated distributively was replaced in 1974 with a more comprehensive process that, by using budget aggregates to restrain decisions on the parts, has made redistributive politics almost inevitable. This new process, moreover, has forced members of Congress to go on record not only on individual items (a distributive action) but also on the appropriate size of total spending, total revenues, and the resulting deficit.

The Budget Act reflected a shift from a fragmented to a comprehensive approach to budgeting. Each approach has its adherents among practitioners and academics. The two approaches differ in the period of time for which decisions are made, the treatment of potentially competing decisions, and the optimal decision process to constrain expenditure growth.

The fragmented approach. The pre-1974 process defined budgeting narrowly as the setting of program expenditure levels. Decisions were made for a short time—usually a fiscal year. Decisions on program funding influenced the overall total of public expenditures.

Those who advocate a fragmented approach contend that under it Congress had greater control over the budget than it now has.[21] They argue that a decentralized process leads to restraint in expenditure growth. Because issues are handled one at a time in subcommittee, conflict is limited. The lower level of conflict allows greater freedom of bargaining. Members are more willing to compromise, and the result is more likely to be a moderate shift from past policy. According to Louis Fisher:

> Increasing the size of a legislative vehicle—from an appropriations bill to a budget resolution—magnifies the scope of legislative conflict and encourages additional concessions to Members. It costs more to build a majority.
>
> In the past, the appropriations subcommittees operated with considerable autonomy, specialization, reciprocity, and group norms (including bipartisanship) that called for staying within the President's budget. The subcommittees reported bills with limited conflict and therefore less need for concessions. Of course some bargaining was necessary, but it was constrained by the size and complexity of each appropriations bill. In contrast the budget resolutions are general vehicles. Each member feels qualified to author amendments.
>
> Ironically, it appears the Members could redistribute budgetary priorities more easily under a fragmented system. They could trim the defense appropriations bill and add to the Labor-HEW appropriations bill, without ever taking money away explicitly from one department and giving it to another. . . . Members do not like to vote on amendments that transfer funds between functional categories. They prefer to do this implicitly and by indirection.[22]

Because the pre-1974 process did not establish aggregates that constrained individual actions, it could be contended that the sum of actions was greater than it would have been if a budget constraint had existed. But those who oppose this view argue that the president's budget provided the needed restraint and that the logic of incrementalism minimized change in a single fiscal year. The members of the Appropriations committees began from a base—most frequently last year's base—and then determined the direction in which they wanted to go from that base. Because of the norms of the appropriations process, these committees usually cut the president's request. They moved sequentially from the base until they reached a number that could obtain a minimum winning coalition. Because they approved a spending level when a winning coalition was reached, expenditure increases above the base were minimized.

The comprehensive approach. The budget procedures introduced by the 1974 Budget Act moved toward a centralization of budget making in Congress. The act's procedures reflect a comprehensive approach to budgeting.

The comprehensive approach holds that the task of budgeting involves not only setting program expenditure levels, but also (1) setting the appropriate fiscal policy (fiscal policy in this context means the use of budget policy to bring about the stabilization of economic cycles),[23] (2) determining the appropriate size of the public sector, (3) setting priorities among types of public sector activities, and (4) determining the appropriate level of taxation.

This approach tends to look beyond a single fiscal year to a multiyear horizon. While the fragmented approach tends to build budgets up from separate decisions on individual programs, the comprehensive approach tends to build budgets down by first determining totals within which the individual funding decisions must be made and then using those totals to constrain or control the funding of individual programs.[24]

In the real world, budgets are never wholly built up or built down: an interactive process occurs. But the emphasis can shift over time, depending on the predispositions of budget makers and on whether macro or micro policy issues are deemed more important. Over the past decade those who are more at home with a comprehensive approach (those trained in the various social sciences that stress optimization techniques—economics, policy analysis, and operations research) have become more prominent. During this period, moreover, policy issues centering on budget totals—the appropriate

fiscal policy, the appropriate size of the federal sector, the tax revolt—
have dominated the budget debate.

In contrast to the decentralized bargaining pattern of decision
making found in the fragmented approach to budgeting, the comprehensive approach strives for rational decision making. As early as
1961 Charles Lindblom pointed out that centralization of congressional budgeting assumes a decision-making process based on the
following principles:

- a comprehensive overview of factors relevant to a decision
- clarity in definition of social objectives
- a means-end approach to policy
- deliberate and explicit choice among policies
- a calculation and minimization of cost
- a unified decision-making process for decisions that are highly
  independent[25]

By increasing the scope of decision making and requiring clear
trade-offs, a rational process is bound to increase conflict. When a
budget plan is before either house, alternatives show the losers as
well as the winners. During the first three years of the budget process
in the House of Representatives, when conservative Republicans
offered a substitute resolution that would achieve a balanced budget,
they were immediately challenged by the Democratic leadership:
"Which programs are you going to cut?" "Whose taxes are you going
to raise?"

As noted above, the implementation of a procedure that made
it difficult to transform redistributive issues into issues perceived to
be distributive came during a period when a slowdown in the
economy decreased the additional revenues that could be distributed
by the budget. Thus since 1975 Congress's freedom of action has
been restrained on both the economic and the political fronts. The
inevitable result has been resentment of the budget process.

The loss of ability to handle issues distributively has led to two
attempts to avoid the constraints of the budget. The first was the
rise in popularity of macroeconomic theories claiming that the stagflation of the 1970s could be overcome without costs. The second,
which is still unfolding, is a revolt against the process that was
triggered when procedures were developed to control expenditure
growth effectively.

Economic Theories to Avoid Redistributive Politics

As illustrated in table 3–4, in the late 1970s the United States faced
a series of economic difficulties. Its rate of economic growth was

declining. Although the average standard of living continued to rise, its rate of increase declined. The average rate of unemployment—even of adult males—rose from economic cycle to economic cycle. Most important to Americans (according to public opinion polls), the rate of inflation reached double digits and appeared to be beyond the government's control.

When elected officials turned to traditional economists for advice, they were told that inflation could be brought under control, but at a price. Although there was disagreement over the magnitude of the price, it was widely agreed that to reduce inflation, increase productivity, and create conditions for more rapid economic growth, some in society would have to suffer. Elected officials were told that they could not avoid the fact that the major economic policies were redistributive.

Keynesians, for example, agreed that a tight fiscal policy would lead to a lower inflation rate, but at the cost of lost output and higher unemployment. Moreover, because of long-term wage contracts and the willingness of many firms and unions to wait out a recession before adjusting their prices or wage demands, Keynesians predicted that a deep and extended recession would be required to bring the inflation rate permanently down.

Some Keynesians suggested that various incomes policies could be adopted to bring inflation down without a deep recession and the resulting high unemployment and lost output. These policies involved many structural changes, each of which might have lowered the inflation rate by a small amount—perhaps 0.1 percentage points. Although these changes might cumulatively have had a significant effect on inflation, Congress was faced with the task of enacting them one at a time. Each change, moreover, would have hurt a significant voting block—farmers, union members, government workers—while barely helping the average citizen. This was a classic recipe for the worst kind of redistributive politics—those who were injured would actively oppose congressmen who voted for the structural reforms, and the average voter would be indifferent.

Monetarists claimed that stable prices could be reestablished if the Federal Reserve followed a policy of a steady, regular, and slow expansion of the money supply. But the monetarists admitted that their policy would not be costless. There would be a transition period of lost output and high unemployment until individuals, unions, and firms realized that the government would not return to the old regime of stop-and-go discretionary fiscal policy. Although monetarists differed on the length and severity of the inevitable recession, there was no question that pain would occur. Thus they also offered elected officials a recipe for redistributive politics.

Macroeconomic Theories for Distributive Politics. By the late 1970s many members of Congress were ready for an economic theory that would promise a return to distributive politics. Two theories were available. One—the extreme form of supply-side economics—claimed that Congress could reduce the inflation rate and spur productivity by lowering marginal tax rates without equivalent reductions in expenditures.

Normally a reduction in taxes without a compensating cut in expenditures will increase the economy's aggregate demand. This, in turn, will lead to an increase in output and a rise in prices. But Arthur Laffer and others claimed that marginal tax rates were so high that individuals were choosing leisure over work and consumption over investment. They believed that a reduction in marginal tax rates would cause an increase in the supply of labor and the amount of investment that would be large enough to lower prices while the output of the economy went up. The shift in aggregate supply would have had to be very large to obtain Laffer's predicted results.

At its heart, then, the argument over supply-side policies centered on a question that could be judged empirically. Would the increase in labor supply induced by a reduction in marginal tax rates be big enough to bring about the required shift in aggregate supply?

Two years before the election of Ronald Reagan, two studies came to the conclusion that supply-side tax reductions could not finance themselves.[26] But these studies did not impede the adoption of the supply-side view by the Reagan administration.

From a political perspective, it is obvious why mainstream economists could not successfully oppose the extreme supply-side theories. They kept telling Congress that any policy would entail costs. But in bad economic times, under a budget process that made explicit the losses that would be suffered, many members welcomed a theory that said: (1) they can cut taxes; but (2) since the tax cut will increase revenues, they can also increase spending; and (3) this budget policy will increase output and lower inflation and unemployment. In short, radical supply-side economics allowed Congress to escape the redistributive effects of the budget process.

A second theory—rational expectations—also promised that price stability could be obtained with little or no cost. Whereas traditional monetarists admitted that to shift from the economic conditions of the late 1970s to an economy with stable prices would cause a good deal of pain, those monetarists who espoused rational expectations claimed that if the government (including the Federal Reserve Board) stated its policy clearly and then refused to shift from that policy, workers and firms would quickly become convinced that the government meant what it said and would restrain their wage and price demands. This would allow the economy to avoid the transition costs anticipated by most monetarists.

From a political perspective, the macroeconomic policies of the Reagan administration's first year were an essential ingredient in its successful budget strategy. Eventually it became clear who the losers would be under the fiscal, monetary, and budget policies of the Reagan administration. Unfortunately free-lunch economic theories cannot be used consistently. Since 1982 Congress has had to live within the constraints of its process. Those constraints are real, and the Budget Act has given Congress the tools to reduce expenditure growth if it wants to do so. But the tools and procedures carry with them redistributive implications. Because of this, the budget process is under the sharpest attack it has experienced since its implementation.

Controlling Expenditure Growth: The Tools and Their Costs

This chapter has pointed out that the rate of expenditure growth and the size of deficits have not been reduced under the procedures of the Budget Act of 1974. Many commentators assume, therefore, that the procedures at best are neutral with respect to the control of expenditures and at worst cause higher expenditures than would have occurred under the old system.

Such a view is flawed, because it assumes that the appropriations process (under either the old or the new budget procedures) is capable of controlling those budget accounts that have caused the growth of spending. But the accounts controlled by annual appropriations have not caused the growth of the federal sector in the past two decades. The growth of the federal budget since 1965 has been largely driven by a few accounts that fund entitlements and provide benefit payments to individuals. Only a process that gives Congress the tools to control spending in those accounts can successfully reduce overall spending. The congressional budget procedures have such a tool—reconciliation associated with the first budget resolution.

The Illusion of Appropriations Control. It is an illusion that Congress controls federal spending through its appropriations process, but it is understandable why many members believe it. As indicated in table 3–5, 77 percent of federal budget accounts are funded through annual appropriations. Moreover, most of the programs that congressmen care most about—the programs that provide visible federal subsidies, such as categorical grants and the various brick-and-mortar

TABLE 3–5

DISTRIBUTION OUTLAYS, BUDGET ACCOUNTS, AND OUTLAY GROWTH BY
TYPE OF HOUSE COMMITTEE BETWEEN FISCAL YEARS 1970 AND 1983
(percent)

Type of House Committee	1983 Outlay Jurisdiction	1983 Budget Accounts	Outlay Growth 1970–1983
Appropriations Committee			
Defense spending	24.5	7.3	19.8
Other spending	21.3	69.7	20.1
Subtotal	45.8	77.0	39.9
Authorizing committees			
Entitlements and fixed costs			
Ways and Means	31.9	2.0	35.2
Other committees	9.8	18.3	11.2
Appropriated entitlements	12.5	2.7	13.7
Subtotal	54.3	23.0	60.1
Gross outlays	100.0	100.0	100.0

NOTE: Interest on public debt excluded. Detail may not add to totals because of rounding.
SOURCES: Columns one and three calculated from data in table B–1 of Congressional Budget Office, *Baseline Budget Projections for Fiscal Years 1984–1988*, February 1983, p. 81. Percentages in column two calculated by the author from a CBO run of fiscal 1983 budget outlays by committee of jurisdiction and type of spending under House rules.

public works programs—are funded through the appropriations process.

In addition, most of the time that members of Congress spend on budget questions pertains to these accounts. Each year Congress must enact the thirteen regular appropriations bills that fund them. Entitlements, on the other hand, are funded through budget authority provided or mandated in their authorization statutes. These authorizations either are permanent (social security) or require reauthorization every few years (food stamps).

It makes political sense for members to spend most of their discretionary time on the appropriations accounts that they can clearly tie to efforts to serve their districts. By doing so, members increase their chances for reelection.

The standard works on congressional control of expenditures remain Richard Fenno's *The Power of the Purse* and Aaron Wildavsky's *The Politics of the Budgetary Process*.[27] The data for both works were collected in the early 1960s before the great expansion of entitlements shifted control of federal expenditure growth from the Appropriations committees to the tax committees and to various authorizing committees.

As late as fiscal 1970, 58.7 percent of all federal outlays were funded through the annual appropriations process. By fiscal 1980 less than half of budget outlays—44.8 percent—were in accounts that went through that process. By fiscal 1983 this figure had been further reduced to 40.7 percent. Even if interest on the public debt were excluded on the ground that it is totally uncontrollable in the short run—as is done in table 3–5—only 45.8 percent of outlays and only 28.2 percent of nondefense outlays are in accounts funded by the annual appropriations process.

The accounts funded by annual appropriations have not been responsible for most of the increase in federal expenditures over the last decade. Only 39.9 percent of the growth in noninterest spending between fiscal 1970 and fiscal 1983 was associated with accounts funded through annual appropriations. If defense expenditures are excluded, the annual appropriations for noninterest accounts caused only 25.1 percent of the outlay growth between 1970 and 1983.

Reversing the picture, we see that only 23 percent of the non-interest budget accounts (the 20.3 percent for entitlements and the 2.7 percent for appropriated entitlements) funded 54.3 percent of the noninterest outlays in the fiscal 1983 budget. If defense spending and interest on the public debt were excluded, these accounts funded 71.8 percent of fiscal 1983 outlays and were responsible for 60.1 percent of the growth in noninterest outlays between fiscal years 1970 and 1983 and for 74.9 percent of the growth in nondefense, noninterest spending over this period. If Congress is to control the growth of nondefense expenditures, it needs a mechanism to control funding in the 23 percent of nonappropriations accounts that really matter.

Reconciliation: The Mechanism for Effective Control. The budget process does provide a means of controlling the spending accounts that are principally responsible for the growth in nondefense, non-interest outlays. Reconciliation gives Congress the mechanism it needs to control domestic spending. It is directed at those accounts that have caused most of the increase in domestic spending over the last two decades. It forces committees that might not want to reduce spending for the entitlements under their jurisdiction to act and report legislation. Finally, when accompanied by a closed or limited rule, it overcomes the potential bias toward higher spending that results from the concentration of benefits in a few recipients while the costs are spread over many taxpayers. A billion-dollar increase in a program, for example, might cost the average taxpayer only an additional $10 per year. In such a situation beneficiaries could be expected to press for the increase, and taxpayers would be unlikely to complain. Only if fifty such incremental increases were enacted would taxpayers realize that their taxes had gone up by $500.

Reconciliation can reverse this bias. By packaging many changes into a single bill and requiring an up-or-down vote on the entire package (or the package and comprehensive substitutes), the debate can be shifted from the losses of the individual programs to the benefits of the whole package.

The 1981 congressional experience with reconciliation created a false impression of its true importance. Many observers see reconciliation as an important tool only if it achieves large savings in the coming fiscal year. But it is not necessary to save $53 billion in budget authority and $35 billion in outlays in one year for reconciliation to control expenditure growth significantly. Changes in entitlements lead to large savings in the future. The 1983 changes in the social security program will save only $8.2 billion in fiscal 1984, but by fiscal 1988 the savings will grow to an estimated $24.4 billion. Thus a series of reconciliation bills that fundamentally change the eligibility and benefit formulas of the major entitlements might save only several billion dollars in the near term but significantly curb nondefense spending in the long run.

Much of the conflict in Congress over the reconciliation process occurred because the advocates of the major entitlements realized that it posed a clear and present danger to their favorite programs. But the experience with reconciliation also illustrates the limits of a budget process that attempts to use aggregate budget totals to restrain expenditure growth in individual programs.

As previously mentioned, under a comprehensive procedure budget aggregates limit the growth of the budget's parts. Such a procedure, however, does not eliminate the pressures for more federal support: it only tries to cap or moderate them by requiring those in favor of a subsidy to do battle with those opposed to it.

Conclusion

This chapter has pointed out that the budget procedures of the Budget Act of 1974 reflect a very different set of assumptions from the procedures they replaced. The new procedures use budget aggregates to force Congress to identify the winners and losers of its budgetary actions. In short, the new procedures have led to a shift from distributive to redistributive politics. This shift occurred at the same time that a poorly performing economy heightened economic conflict in the private sector.

The new procedures give Congress a means of controlling expenditure growth and deficits. Unlike the old system, the new procedures contain a tool—reconciliation—that can be used to limit the expenditure growth of those accounts that have caused the increase in nondefense expenditures.

But in giving Congress more control over the budget, these procedures have increased internal conflict. In the next few years the actions of Congress will answer two basic questions: (1) Can the institution live with the amount of conflict that results from the new procedures, or will members seek to escape from responsibility? (2) Do the American public and Congress really want to cut back on the middle-class entitlements that are principally responsible for the growth of the federal budget?

Notes

1. The best treatment of the procedures of reconciliation is Allen Schick, *Reconciliation and the Congressional Budget Process* (Washington, D.C.: American Enterprise Institute, 1981).

2. Louis Fisher, "The Budget Act of 1974: Its Impact on Spending" (Paper prepared for Conference on the Congressional Budget Process, Carl Albert Congressional Research and Studies Center, University of Oklahoma, Norman, Oklahoma, February 12, 1982), p. 3.

3. Allen Schick, *Congress and Money: Budgeting, Spending, and Taxing* (Washington, D.C.: Urban Institute, 1980), pp. 568–73.

4. Since the growth of federal expenditures cannot be curbed unless Congress controls spending in those budget accounts that cause growth, I include the so-called uncontrollability issue under this goal.

5. Two dissents have been heard from this general agreement. Some have pointed to the failure to enact a second resolution on the fiscal 1982 budget as congressional abdication of its budget responsibility. I would disagree. Congress chose not to change its economic assumptions for political reasons. It simply reaffirmed its spring resolution. In so doing, Congress acted in the same manner as the executive branch, which retained its overoptimistic economic forecast in its midsession review. Yet no one accused the president of abandoning the executive budget process. Congress was under the same pressure as the president and acted in the same manner.

Others have pointed to the acceptance of the Gramm-Latta substitute in 1981 as an example of the failure of this goal. These observers claim that in accepting the substitute, Congress supplanted the work of its committees with a document quickly put together by the Office of Management and Budget (OMB). I do not see how this action differs from other occurrences when the president uses public opinion and other pressures to get Congress to agree rapidly to his program (Franklin Roosevelt's 100 days and Lyndon Johnson's Eighty-eighth Congress come to mind). A majority of the House obviously felt that the OMB substitute was superior to the work of the committees of the House. A true abdication of authority would occur only if this pattern were repeated for several years, but this has not happened.

6. The data on supplemental appropriations are drawn from Congressional Budget Office, *Supplemental Appropriations in the 1970s*, July 1981, pp. 8, 27.

7. Schick, *Congress and Money*, p. 80.

8. Complaints about the current process are extensively covered in U.S. Senate, Committee on the Budget, *Proposed Improvements in the Congressional Budget Act of 1974*, 97th Congress, 2d session, September 14, 16, 21, 23, 1982; and U.S. House of Representatives, Committee on Rules, Task Force on the Budget Process, *Congressional Budget Process*, 97th Congress, 2d session, September 15, 17, 23, 29, 1982. Of particular interest are the statements of senior members of House Appropriations and authorizing committees. In the House hearing see the statements by Representatives Aspin, Brooks, Dingle, Howard, Obey, Perkins, and Rostenkowski.

9. Much of the growth in the standard of living, however, has been achieved through a rise in the percentage of Americans who work. In many families real disposable income would have fallen in recent years if the wife had not gone to work. In 1960, 30.5 percent of married women (in families with the husband present) held jobs. This number had climbed to 40.8 percent by 1970 and to 50.2 percent by 1980. For a hypothetical family of four in which the husband worked at a nonagricultural job and was the only income earner, real spendable weekly earnings in January 1982 ($165.93 in 1977 dollars) were lower than they had been at any time since 1960 ($164.97 in 1977 dollars). See *Economic Report of the President* (1983), table B–39 (p. 207).

10. Joseph J. Minarik, "Who Wins, Who Loses from Inflation?" *Challenge* (January–February 1979), p. 30; and Alan S. Blinder and Howard Y. Esaki, "Macroeconomic Activity and Income Distribution in the United States," *Review of Economics and Statistics* (November 1978), pp. 607–8.

11. Robert M. Solow, "The Intelligent Citizen's Guide to Inflation," *The Public Interest*, no. 38 (Winter 1975), p. 40.

12. James Annable, *The Dual Wage Theory: The Role of Wages in Business Cycles and Economic Growth* (Lexington, Mass.: D. C. Heath, 1983). Annable found that during the 1970s the variation of wage increases granted by the 116 industries used by the Bureau of Labor Statistics to compile its monthly establishment survey increased dramatically as the rate of inflation rose. He also found that larger firms and firms with labor

unions granted larger wage increases than did smaller firms and nonunion firms.

13. Data provided by the research office of the Washington Board of Trade.

14. Figures calculated from *Congressional Quarterly Almanac*, various years.

15. Statistics calculated from data in tables C–1 and C–2 of Congressional Budget Office, *Tax Expenditures: Budget Options and Five-Year Budget Projections for Fiscal Years 1983–1987*, November 1982, pp. 80–89.

16. Data from Federal Election Commission. A number of scholars reject the notion that the rapid growth of PACs implies an increase in the desire of special interests to lobby for federal benefits or relief from federal costs (of regulation, taxes, and so on). In "The Problem of PAC-Journalism," *Public Opinion* (December–January 1983), pp. 15–16, 59, Michael Malbin argues that the growth of PACs has simply shifted the avenues of influence rather than increased the amount of traffic.

17. See Norman J. Ornstein, "The House and Senate in a New Congress," in Thomas E. Mann and Norman J. Ornstein, eds., *The New Congress* (Washington, D.C.: American Enterprise Institute, 1981), pp. 363–83; Norman J. Ornstein, Robert L. Peabody, and David W. Rohde, "The Changing Senate: From the 1950s to the 1970s," in Lawrence C. Dodd and Bruce I. Oppenheimer, eds., *Congress Reconsidered* (New York: Praeger Publishers, 1977), pp. 3–20; Lawrence C. Dodd and Bruce I. Oppenheimer, "The House in Transition," in Dodd and Oppenheimer, *Congress Reconsidered*, pp. 21–53; Norman J. Ornstein and David Rohde, "Resource Usage, Information, and Policymaking in the Senate," in Commission on the Operation of the Senate, *Senators: Offices, Ethics, and Pressures, a Compilation of Papers*, 94th Congress, 2d session, 1977, pp. 37–46; and Allen Schick, "Complex Policymaking in the United States Senate," in Commission on the Operation of the Senate, *Policy Analysis on Major Issues, a Compilation of Papers*, 94th Congress, 2d session, 1977, pp. 4-24.

18. The classic treatment of the implications of this maxim is David R. Mayhew, *Congress: The Electoral Connection* (New Haven, Conn.: Yale University Press, 1974).

The ideas in this section on distributive and redistributive politics benefited from a series of lectures by Douglas Arnold at Princeton University. Arnold is preparing a full treatment of his views on this topic. The notion of distributive and redistributive politics was first suggested by Theodore J. Lowi in his "American Business, Public Policy, Case Studies, and Political Theory," *World Politics*, vol. 16 (July 1964), pp. 677–715. The most useful extension of Lowi's work is Michael T. Hayes, "The Semi-Sovereign Pressure Groups: A Critique of Current Theory and an Alternative Typology," *Journal of Politics*, vol. 40 (1978), pp. 134–61.

19. The implications of the desire of politicians to minimize hurting

others in a legislative setting (the Italian parliament) are outlined in Robert Axelrod, *Conflict of Interest* (Chicago: Markham Publishing Company, 1970). Axelrod points out that a minimum winning coalition will form among those political parties that are closest across the relevant policy spectrums; he posits that the reason for this is the desire to minimize conflict within the coalition. The same theory holds for the minimum winning coalitions that congressmen put together to get reelected.

20. During the first half of the 1970s a series of income tax reductions compensated for the bracket creep induced by inflation. During the second half of the decade the Carter administration carried out the most restrictive fiscal policy of any major nation of the Organization for Economic Cooperation and Development (OECD) except France. This was accomplished by forgoing individual income tax reductions and by legislating increases in the social security wage tax.

Douglas Hibbs and Henrik Madsen have shown that tax revolts in the 1970s in Europe were associated with the visibility of taxes rather than their levels. See Douglas A. Hibbs, Jr., and Henrik J. Madsen, "Public Reaction to the Growth of Taxation and Government Expenditure: Preliminary Comparative Investigation" (Paper prepared for the 1979 annual meeting of the American Political Science Association, Washington, D.C., September 3, 1979). For comparative data on OECD nations' fiscal policies, see Congressional Budget Office, *Balancing the Federal Budget and Limiting Federal Spending: Constitutional and Statutory Approaches*, September 1982, pp. 9–16.

21. The modern statement of this position is found in Fisher, "Budget Act of 1974." The classic argument was by Charles Lindblom, "Decision-Making in Taxation and Expenditure," in *Public Finances: Needs, Sources, Utilization: A Conference of the Universities–National Committee for Economic Research* (Princeton, N.J.: Princeton University Press and National Bureau for Economic Research, 1961), pp. 295–336. Lindblom argues against the rational decision model of budget making implied by the norms and principles of economics and for the disjointed incrementalist model characterized by various forms of partisan mutual adjustment. Lindblom argues for even more decentralization of decision making than existed before the Budget Act.

22. Fisher, "Budget Act of 1974," pp. 19–20.

23. This use of the term "fiscal policy" is not wholly reflected in the public finance literature. Thus Richard and Peggy Musgrave in their standard text—*Public Finance in Theory and Practice*, 3d ed. (New York: McGraw-Hill, 1980)—apply the term "fiscal policy" to three major functions of budget policy: allocation, distribution, and stabilization. I have found, however, that economists and policy analysts in Washington usually apply the fiscal policy rubric to the stablilization function.

24. Barry Bozeman and Jeffrey D. Straussman make the distinction between "top-down" and "bottom-up" budget processes in "Shrinking Bud-

gets and the Shrinkage of Budget Theory," *Public Administration Review* (November/December 1982), pp. 509–15.

25. Lindblom, "Decision-Making in Taxation and Expenditure," pp. 297–98. Lindblom drew these norms from Arthur Smithies, *The Budgetary Process in the United States* (New York: McGraw-Hill, 1955).

26. Congressional Budget Office, *An Analysis of the Roth-Kemp Tax Cut Proposal*, October 1978; and Don Fullerton, "Can Tax Revenues Go Up When Tax Rates Go Down?" Office of Tax Analysis Paper 41 (September 1980), Office of Tax Analysis, U.S. Department of the Treasury. Summarizing the literature, the studies found the elasticity of labor supply in the United States to be about 0.15. At this average elasticity for U.S. workers, the average marginal tax rate would have to be about 80 percent to obtain the revenue response predicted by the extreme supply-side advocates.

27. Richard J. Fenno, Jr., *The Power of the Purse: Appropriations Politics in Congress* (Boston: Little, Brown, 1966); and Aaron Wildavsky, *The Politics of the Budgetary Process*, 2d ed. (Boston: Little, Brown, 1974).

4

The Politics of Subtraction

Naomi Caiden

In the vocabulary of the federal budget process, an assumption of addition has given way to a preoccupation with subtraction. Whereas Congress used to allocate public resources within a context of growth, it now expects to budget in the shadow of scarcity. The change has had a profound effect not only on substantive budget decisions but also on the processes through which those decisions are made. Where once the availability of resources provided incentives to facilitate the passage of the budget through Congress, the need to inflict losses now heightens budget conflicts and strains institutions. The resulting turmoil has provoked serious questioning of the capacity of Congress to control the federal budget and of the ability of the congressional budget process to accommodate pressures to cut the budget.

The progress of the federal budget in recent years has become so complex and hazardous that observers can hardly be blamed for absorbing themselves in the intricacies of congressional procedures, politics, and personalities. But the predicament of Congress is not unique. In most Western industrialized countries, the issue of control of public budgets has moved to the forefront of political concern, and budgeting in an era of limits has turned out to be a complex and difficult matter. Whereas policies of addition act to assuage conflicts, those of subtraction not only are the source of increased conflict but also undercut the accepted means by which it was previously resolved. To understand then why efforts to cut the federal budget have given rise to such turbulence and confusion and why Congress has responded to them in the ways it has, it is necessary to analyze the general problems of institutions faced with demands to cut, instead of increase, the growth of budgets.

Budgeting in an Era of Limits

Concern with the capacity of Western industrialized countries to maintain the level of public expenditures goes back at least a decade and springs from a number of sources. Many believe that the post–World War II momentum of economic growth has come to an end and that the world faces a prolonged period of stagnation in which fewer resources will be available for public and private purposes. Others foresee the beginning of an era of conservation, which will also necessarily affect public consumption. Linked with these is a perception of change to a postindustrial economy requiring a radically revised role for government, which will probably have to adjust patterns of expenditure in reorienting public policy. In contrast, many blame the present economic malaise on the volume of government spending and borrowing and advocate a permanent reduction in public expenditures and taxation as a precondition for a resurgence of economic growth, full employment, and high living standards. There is also an unease with the welfare state and anxiety about the future burdens it may entail. Repeated revelations of governmental waste and corruption have prompted closer scrutiny of the extent of public expenditures and their objectives, while the threat of tax revolts among voters has strengthened conservative political forces.

From these not entirely consistent perspectives have emerged pressures to cut the growth of public budgets. Objectives have gradually changed from optimizing public services to controlling costs and stabilizing or even eliminating governmental functions. Policy makers have been called upon to carry out the "difficult and unpleasant task of halting the expansion of public expenditures and of reallocating resources within a stagnating and inflation-ridden economy."[1] But their task is not confined to identifying substantial and politically feasible cuts in budgets that have grown in response to social and economic pressures over many years. They are also likely to find that the budget processes through which they have to work are now inappropriate for their purposes. Budget frameworks that had appeared robust and immutable in periods of growth often seem inclined to fall apart when beset with the pressures of constraint. Budgeting for subtraction therefore may mean grappling with and reconstructing deteriorating budget systems.

What happens when institutions are called upon to budget in conditions of scarcity, to subtract rather than to add? For most Western industrialized countries, where the continued availability of public resources has been taken for granted, the experience is a new one. In other, less fortunate countries, where poverty and uncertainty have long been a way of life, their effects on budgetary behavior are only too familiar. Over a decade ago Aaron Wildavsky and I noted the pervasive effects of a long-term lack of redundancy on the strategies and tactics of those charged with public functions.[2] As irrepressible demands continue to press on inadequate resources, the unified budget tends to disappear, fragmenting and splintering into myriad independent accounts and earmarked funds. In the absence of slack resources to cushion the effect of uncertainties, time horizons shrink so that the budget has to be made and remade throughout the year in accordance with the latest predictions for revenues and expenditures. In response to uncertainties and in an effort to conserve resources, central controls are reinforced over the areas that lie within their compass, leading to correspondingly greater effort on the part of spending units to increase their leverage and maintain their autonomy over sources of finance, information, and decisions. Budgeting—defined as the accurate implementation of a comprehensive annual plan for public expenditures—gives way to a desperate and repetitive struggle to maintain cash flow, to the detriment of public accountability, consistent policy making, and unprejudiced information.

In contrast, budgeting in rich countries has until recently been greatly eased by the general expectation of growing public resources. Budgetary conflicts have been mitigated, and the passage of accurate and timely budgets has been ensured through two widely used decision-making techniques, both heavily dependent on assured budget growth. The first of these is incrementalism, the practice of making decisions by relatively small steps at the margin. Budgets are made through additions to the gradually expanding base of previous years' budgets without explicit review of existing programs. Instead of reconsidering the value of all existing programs and all possible alternatives, budgeting is an incremental process "proceeding from a historical base, guided by accepted notions of fair shares, in which decisions are fragmented, made in sequence by specialized bodies, and coordinated through repeated attacks on problems and through multiple feedback mechanisms."[3]

The second means by which budgets have increasingly been made in recent years has been automatic decision making. A growing proportion of budgets in Western industrialized countries is made up of expenditures that are committed in advance and are not subject to decision through the regular channels of the budget process. Frequently these consist of entitlements, sums mandated by law to be paid to those eligible. These payments are often indexed by formula to the cost of living. Therefore the amounts may increase automatically, without anyone's taking any initiative, through the growth of eligible populations and through inflation.

Both incrementalism and automatic decision making facilitate budget making. They provide stable decision rules that cut down the burden of calculation, acknowledge the continuing legitimacy of past claims entrenched in the budget, and avoid pitting demands directly one against another. Incrementalism limits potential conflict by fragmenting power and specializing decisions. Automatic decision making eliminates conflict altogether by resorting to formula in place of deliberation. Both devices help blur and conceal fundamental lack of consensus on public policy and bring interests together through persuasion and accommodation. But both depend on the availability of resources for annual increments and automatic increases. What happens when these resources are no longer forthcoming and resource-intensive budgeting techniques are no longer feasible?

Theoretically, it would seem that budgets might be reduced in the same ways they have grown. Formulas might be adjusted downward, and decrementalism might take the place of incrementalism. Confrontation over basic issues could be avoided by concentrating on the "negative margin" to identify potential reductions.[4] Gradual piecemeal reduction of spending would provide time for adjustments to be made and errors corrected. There would be no need for comprehensive analysis of policies and programs or explicit determination of budgetary priorities.

But subtracting is not the same as adding. Resource-intensive techniques are aligned to budget growth rather than reduction. Although incrementalism may curb growth tendencies somewhat by its small-step-at-a-time approach, its ultimate result is an upward trend in the budget. The dispersal of power it implies increases the number of opportunities for claims to be pressed, with little corresponding counterbalance to make cuts. Similarly, formulas are rigid in design, and their insulation from regular budget processes may make them difficult to adjust. Therefore budget makers who wish to sustain a policy of cutbacks in spending try to devise new budget processes and institutions explicitly designed to curb growth. They seek to establish mechanisms that will force consideration of automatic decisions, set binding ceilings limiting permissible claims, and make authoritative choices that will preempt budget busting. Naturally, these strategies provoke intense resistance from those whose interests are affected. The most sensitive areas, which had been deliberately insulated from annual decision making by automatic formulas, are now opened to fierce contention. While incrementalism protects the base, subtraction, even by decremental means, eats into it, arousing greater conflict as more and more existing commitments are attacked. Previous understandings are disrupted as budget participants seek to pass on cuts and save their own interests at the expense of others. But the resource-intensive methods of conflict resolution are no longer available to cope with the enhanced conflict. Subtraction not only increases conflict but undermines the methods for its resolution.

In the absence of means to keep conflicts at an acceptable level, budget frameworks suffer stress. Even where decision makers are successful in imposing limits on the budget itself, claims may be satisfied through a growing area of overspill: off-budget accounts, loans and loan guarantees, open or disguised deficits, capital accounts, tax expenditures. The unified budget fragments and is no longer a comprehensive representation of government activities. As conflicts rise and uncertainties increase, timetables are disrupted, and budgeting becomes an ad hoc affair in which participants exploit every possibility of leverage to the detriment of consistent or orderly decision making. The stable world of budgeting is shattered, and participants have to adapt to new rules to survive.

Confusion is further confounded because the mechanics of subtraction are by no means straightforward, so that budget makers quickly find themselves entangled in a jungle of competing budget numbers. Everyone knew what an increment was, because it added to a stable base, but a decrement is open to a variety of interpretations depending on the base that is chosen. As Maurice Wright points out, "Different rates of growth or decline can be shown by comparing, for two successive years, plans with plans, plans with outturn, outturn with plans, and outturn with outturn."[5] As the budget process is prolonged, each new set of proposals becomes a base in itself, so that comparisons have to be made not with a single figure but with several. Inflation is an additional complication since the base chosen frequently factors in an allowance for estimated inflation. If, as is usually the case, budget decisions have to be made before definitive expenditure figures for the previous year are available, the base itself may be little more than a guess. The opportunities for obfuscation and manipulation offered by the building of estimate upon estimate and the recalculation of comparison after comparison are legion. Where decision makers once could rely on firm budget figures, they must now base their calculations on estimates that at best seem to evaporate as events unfold and at worst degenerate into mere political numbers.

The question of budget cutting is also a question of budget

capacity. If it is generally agreed that sustained policies of subtraction are called for, what mechanisms may be established to enable them to take place? How can budget makers cope with the increased conflict generated by their attempts to make cuts? What processes of budget making may be devised to counteract resource-intensive decision rules and to replace them as means of conflict resolution? In what ways do pressures to cut the budget transform its frameworks and change the rules of the budget-making game? How can budget capacity be reconstituted to fit the new situation?

Congress now faces all these difficulties of budgeting in an era of limits, but there are additional complications. First, in most countries budget issues may be fought out primarily behind the scenes in the closed worlds of cabinets and bureaucracies, and the executive budget is the final word unless the government is defeated and falls. In the United States the budget drama is played out in the public arena of Congress. Not only must agreement be forged between Congress and the president, but account must also be taken of the dispersal of power and access to decision making that characterize the legislative body and have become more pronounced in recent years.

Second, budget cutting is not the only game in town. While cuts are slated for some areas of the budget, other parts receive additions. Tax cuts and increases are also part of the currency of the budget debate. Because subtraction and addition take place simultaneously, lines of development in the budget process are blurred. Further, while the pressures for subtraction are vocal, they are not the only influence on the budget process—growing uncertainty in economic affairs, difficulties in forecasting short- and long-term economic trends, and demographic changes are only a few of the variables that have had a marked effect on budget making in recent years. It is therefore difficult to isolate the effects of policies of subtraction from other influences on the budget process.

Third, budget processes have not been static. Because the most dramatic developments have taken place in the two years since the Reagan administration took office, it is tempting to ignore previous experience. But pressures for subtraction did not begin with the Reagan administration, and their effects on the budget process had been apparent for several years. To understand why recent demands to cut budget growth have affected the congressional budget process, it is therefore necessary to go much further back and to examine the traditional means by which Congress used to cut the budget and the effects of their erosion and of efforts to find more effective substitutes for them.

The Invisible Hand of Budgetary Accommodation

Although Congress had no formal regular mechanism for setting budget totals or coordinating decisions until the passage of the Congressional Budget and Impoundment Control Act in 1974, it could and did cut budgets. It did so through the ordinary budget process, whose working was underwritten by the understandings and division of labor among the relatively restricted circle of its participants. Their interactions and accommodations constituted the "invisible hand" of the budgetary marketplace, which acted to limit conflicts and also to restrain the rate of budget growth. But by the mid-1960s the traditional institutional means of limiting federal expenditures had begun to weaken, and claims upon the budget multiplied at precisely the time when earlier predictions of ample public resources were being confounded. For a number of reasons the invisible hand no longer operated as an effective means for cutting the budget, and recognition of its demise, as well as more pressing immediate problems, paved the way for reform.

Budget cutting in the traditional budget process, like other budgetary transactions, relied primarily on the specialized roles of the components of the process and the formal and informal rules they understood and accepted. Authorizing committees, ruled by chairmen who owed their positions to seniority, commanded the legislation within their jurisdictions. The president submitted the budget proposal on behalf of the executive branch of government. The House Ways and Means Committee and the Senate Finance Committee dealt with revenue policy. But the keys to the process were the Appropriations committees of each house, which acted as guardians of the public purse.

The Appropriations committees constituted the counter to spending pressures from executive and legislature alike. Fenno's study of selected bureaus between 1947 and 1959 found that the House Appropriations Committee reduced the estimates it received more than 75 percent of the time.[6] Under its guidance, according to Ippolito, Congress reduced almost 90 percent of all regular appropriations bills for fiscal years 1952–1969, as well as most supplemental and deficiency appropriations, below the amounts requested by the president.[7] In general, these two committees accepted a primary commitment to cutting the executive budget.

The methods of the Appropriations committees, as described by Wildavsky, were incremental. Work on the budget was carried out mainly in specialized subcommittees, which rarely impinged on one another's jurisdictions and whose decisions were usually accepted by the whole. Decisions were based on past experience and relied on the validity of previous decisions, so that basic issues did not need to be reopened. Budgets were made in fragments, concentrating on increases or decreases at the margin rather than on the desirability of programs as a whole. There was no attempt at comprehensiveness: problems were dealt with one at a time, by compromise and concession.[8]

The Appropriations committees, along with the tax committees, stood at the apex of the committee structure of Congress, but they did not exercise their power indiscriminately. Caught between the expectations of the executive and members of Congress for increases and those of committee members for economy, the House Appropriations Committee typically reduced presidential spending estimates but granted increases over the previous year's appropriation.[9] Its approach was "a balanced, conservative, incremental response to conflicting expectations."[10] The result was a federal budget that grew incrementally at the margin from year to year but was held in check by the accepted role of the guardians of the public purse.

Budget cutting in Congress, then, depended on the mutual expectations of participants, who assumed stability in relationships and continuity in incumbency through seniority in committee appointments. Budget outcomes derived from decentralized and fragmented decision making held in check by the interactions of the budget system. A well-understood division of roles promoted accommodations and a sense of the limits of acceptable claim pressing and budget cutting. The budget process was a closed world, bounded not only by the assumed prerogatives of the congressional hierarchy but also by "its inherent complexity, the obscurantism of budget documents, the impenetrability of the tax laws, and the failure of affected interests to invest in budget research and data."[11] In other words, federal expenditures, and thus federal government action, were limited by lack of access to budgetary decision making and by the understandings of those who commanded it.

The opening up of the congressional budget process in the late 1960s, in response to demands for greater decentralization of power in Congress and for a greater social role for the federal government, seriously challenged the stability of budget relationships. The growing independence of individual members of Congress and an increase in the resources at their disposal lessened the influence of party leadership. Changes in the seniority rule eroded the power of committee chairmen and liberalized choices. Subcommittees increased in number and power, and their hearings were opened to the public. A gradual change from permanent program authorization to single year or multiyear authorizations for about half the budget gave authorizing committees a greater opportunity to participate in the budget process by setting dollar amounts on authorizations. Simultaneously claims upon the budget were multiplied, and institutional constraints were weakened.

These developments necessarily affected the position of the Appropriations committees and their subcommittees. Members of the Appropriations committees had sometimes tended to favor their own constituencies or to identify with agency or program interests. Now changes in procedures mandated open hearings and self-selection of subcommittee chairmen, who easily became program advocates. Membership was liberalized, and members no longer enjoyed protection in "safe" seats. The Appropriations committees continued to make cuts,[12] but according to Schick they were often illusory:

> Much budget cutting was achieved by fiscal legerdemain— time-honored accounting practices that often veil the true effects of congressional actions. The Appropriations Committees sometimes produced budget "cuts" without taking anything out of the budget by shifting funds backward to the past fiscal year or forward to the next fiscal year, by juggling the estimates for mandatory expenses, or by deferring items for supplemental consideration at a later date. Only by a painstaking, account-by-account examination could one distinguish between real and apparent budget cuts.[13]

The Appropriations committees no longer stood as undisputed guardians of the public purse; to the extent that their guardianship was weakened, the invisible hand ceased to contain incrementalism.

But in any case the influence of the Appropriations committees over the growth of federal expenditures had been lessened by increasing recourse to automatic decision making, whose cumulative effect was to narrow discretion in the annual budget process. During the late 1960s and early 1970s the composition of the federal budget changed as a greater percentage of spending was taken up by entitlements—payments to individuals and others mandated by law and paid according to eligibility. Whereas in 1964 some 25 percent of outlays went to transfer payments to individuals, in 1975 the figure was 40 percent. The growth was due to major increases in social security benefits and the establishment of several new entitlement programs, many of which were indexed to the cost of living. During this period over 90 percent of budget growth was in categories classified as "uncontrollable," that is, programs (including debt interest) that would continue automatically unless Congress made a change in the law.[14]

The enactment of entitlement programs into law meant that they were removed from the arena of budgetary conflict, which stabilized their growth as well as prevented the majority from being cut through the annual appropriations process. Although some, such as Medicaid and supplemental security income, retained the status of appropriations, many fell under the jurisdiction of other committees and were thus excluded from the scrutiny of the Appropriations committees. This increased backdoor spending further weakened the influence of the Appropriations committees over the budget as a whole.[15]

The invisible hand seemed to be disappearing. What was to take its place? One option was to do nothing, to accommodate both the incremental program increases and automatic entitlement increases through either the inflationary dividend in revenues (bracket creep) or tax increases. Although the budget was growing more rapidly, it was still relatively stable in relation to gross national product. Deficits had been an almost inevitable accompaniment of postwar budgets, but their amounts might not appear excessive. Budget growth might be accepted as the price for enhanced individual security and a desired high level of public expenditures. But this solution did not appear universally acceptable. When a tax increase was proposed by the executive, Congress insisted on concomitant cuts in expenditures.[16] And when Congress wished to protect social programs, a president of a different persuasion sought cuts.

A second alternative was to set aggregate limits. No less than five times between 1967 and 1973, Congress adopted a limit on annual expenditures after due consultation and haggling with the president. Since there was no machinery even to coordinate appropriations in Congress, let alone to enforce any limits on them, it is not surprising that just as regularly the limits were exceeded. At the same time, indications began to appear of how such limits might be evaded through the creation of off-budget agencies and increased resort to agency borrowing and loan guarantees.

A third possibility was for Congress to rely on the executive to cut the budget. At one point it did in fact attempt to do so,[17] but the sharpened conflict between legislature and executive of different parties, growing suspicion of abuse of presidential power, and a general reassertion of congressional prerogatives ruled this possibility out too. Thus, if Congress was unwilling to accommodate budget increases without regard to totals, was unable to implement its own self-imposed limit, and wished to prevent the executive from cutting the budget through impoundments, it would have to take a hard look at its own processes. The impoundment dispute of the early 1970s provided the immediate impetus for reform of the budget process, but the origins of the reform movement lay in a more long standing concern about congressional budget capacity.

The New Guardians

The Congressional Budget and Impoundment Control Act of 1974 was an attempt to gain greater congressional control over the federal budget through a measure of integration. Although the act was neutral on its face and was not specifically designed to accomplish budget cuts, the notion of control implied that Congress would have the capacity to subtract as well as add and to abide by its own self-imposed limits. The procedures and institutions of the new process found general acceptance and realigned budget debates toward an awareness of totals. But the new guardians of the act, the Budget committees, lacked power to enforce their decisions, and the steps of the process tended to encourage incrementalism. Although creation of new entitlements was curbed, little was done to modify the effects of automatic decision making. Even so, the increased clarity in budgetary decisions increased conflict in Congress, which in turn brought pressure on the budget process itself, manifest in whipsawing between budget totals and appropriations, a growing area of extra budgetary decision making, and difficulties in maintaining the timetable. When, finally, there were demands for substantial budget cutting, the congressional budget process required further modification.

The Budget Act aimed to improve congressional budgetary capacity by addressing budget totals rather than relying on an invisible hand to coordinate piecemeal dealings over claims. It established a Budget Committee in each house that would propose two budget resolutions—the first to set total and functional targets, the second to confirm and if necessary adjust them. The budget process would fit between the two resolutions, following a timetable designed so that appropriations would follow the framework of the initial targets. Congress would gain its own source of information and analysis in the Congressional Budget Office.

Congress was therefore still free to add to or subtract from the budget as it saw fit. No single source of budget cutting was established; the impetus for cuts could and did come from a variety of sources—the executive, the Budget committees (in either framing or maintaining the budget resolutions), the floor of either house, or in conference. Nor, at least at the beginning of the act's operation, was the issue of budget cutting the most salient. But in one respect a budget-cutting function was crucial to the entire concept of the new congressional budget process: it was essential that appropriations should follow the framework of the budget resolution passed by Congress. True, the first resolution was not binding upon the second, but if it were persistently and flagrantly ignored, the whole process would revert to the position before the act.

The guardian role therefore passed from the Appropriations committees to the Budget committees. The former guardians were now cast as claimants, who had to be watched and controlled lest they "bust the budget."[18] But whereas the Appropriations committees could cut the budget by making detailed, definitive decisions on actual line items, subject only to approval by Congress as a whole, the Budget committees had to operate through the totals of the budget resolutions, by setting the targets of the first concurrent budget resolution at a level that demanded cuts and by keeping committees in line with those targets, both of course requiring the consent of Congress. The actual cutting would have to take place in the executive budget, in authorizations, or in appropriations, which lay beyond the Budget committees' direct jurisdiction. Since the aggregate and functional targets of the first budget resolution were not binding and the Budget committees had no overriding power to enforce them, the Budget committees acted less as guardians than as adversaries. To the extent that they wished to cut the budget, they had to compete on equal terms with other participants. By intention and design the act had made their effectiveness dependent on the normal accommodations of Congress. Provided with a special perspective—the budget as a whole—the new guardians had been granted no commensurate powers. If they wanted to cut the budget, they would have to contend with the accommodations of the congressional budget process, while necessarily participating in those accommodations themselves.

The procedures of the act, born of accommodation and compromise, tended to encourage incrementalism. The presentation of the president's budget to Congress in January each year included a current service budget, or estimate of what services would cost in the coming year if no policy changes were made. The "implicit norm that programs should be held harmless from inflation"[19] easily became the new base for spending requests.[20]

The next stage, the submission of views and estimates of congressional committees to the Budget committees, again introduced an upward bias as spending committees hedged against premature commitments by setting their estimates sufficiently high to accommodate new legislative initiatives likely to pass Congress.[21] The committees were reluctant to endorse cuts in the president's budget and regularly

111

asked for more than the president's estimates. But they were also careful not to overinflate claims so that the Budget committees would be justified in ignoring their estimates altogether and setting their own priorities.[22]

The methods by which the Budget committees produced their reports on the first resolution for submission to Congress also tended to favor increases. The House Budget Committee worked from an initial chairman's mark from which increases or decreases might be made. In practice during the early years of the act, proposals for increases outnumbered those for decreases, although by 1979 the balance was beginning to be redressed.[23] The bias toward increases was further encouraged by the committee's system of line-item review: it was hard for members to vote for reductions when they knew which programs would be affected, and they tended to pass responsibility for making cuts to the House as a whole.[24] Meanwhile the Senate Budget Committee incorporated an upward bias through its use of current policy estimates as its initial mark, ensuring that sufficient funds would be available for programs without specific negotiation with the affected committees.[25]

When the first resolution came to the House or Senate, accommodations to mutual expectations discouraged budget cutting. The targets of the resolution generally met with relatively few amendments, but the Budget committees had tended to avoid exerting downward pressure on budget totals to avert challenges to their own power, rationalizing that changes could be made later in the process.[26]

The real test came at the next stage, when the authorizing and Appropriations committees confronted the limits of the first resolution. The Budget committees attempted to avoid trouble in the first place by setting targets that did not seriously impinge on other committees' plans.[27] When, even so, committees' decisions violated the provisions of the first resolution, the Budget committees were wary about picking fights, since each time it would be necessary for them to put together a new coalition to gain support.[28] Although resolutions generally contained provisions for some program cuts, these were usually described as savings to be realized through efficiencies and improvements. But although savings might be passed on the floor of Congress, they were rarely enacted in the committees.[29] The elasticity of the first resolution caused it to have little effect on the previous practice of deciding funds for each function in turn, thus avoiding open competition among claims.[30]

By the time September 15 came around each year, the process should have been complete, with authorizing legislation for programs and appropriations bills agreed to by Congress. The second concurrent resolution ratified appropriations decisions without much further inquiry. The act provided for reconciliation instructions that would allow Congress to instruct committees to make changes in appropriations enacted during the year so that they would be consistent with the resolution. But to do so would have meant reopening the budget debate, and the procedure was rarely attempted. The second resolution might be modified later in the fiscal year by further resolutions, again providing an opportunity to accommodate incremental increases.[31]

Yet, if the act insisted that budgeting should conform to the normal give-and-take of congressional debate, it by no means made budget cutting impossible. The allocations of the first concurrent resolution consistently made cuts in the president's budget in national defense and international affairs between 1976 and 1980 and in most other functions in certain years.[32] Comparisons between the functional allocations of the first resolution and current policy (or current law) estimates reveal a similar pattern, some functions increasing while others were allowed to lag behind.[33] General impressions were that spending was less than it would have been without the new process.[34] Sundquist saw the Budget committees as

> the fiscal consciences of the two bodies, defending the approved fiscal policy against assault by those who would spend more. . . . The budget committees have not been proven invincible by any means, but they have turned out to be formidable antagonists, their strength derived from their role as guardians of a process that virtually every member of the Congress tacitly recognizes as crucial to the standing of the legislative branch itself.[35]

Ippolito believed that the Budget committees helped prevent new spending initiatives.[36] Schick concluded that most congressional committees accepted the requirements of congressional budgeting and tried to live within the limits of the budget resolutions.[37]

But the jurisdiction of the new guardians, like that of the old, did not extend to the area of automatic decision making. As the proportion of uncontrollable spending expanded to encompass three quarters of the annual budget, this was a serious limitation on the Budget committees' power to gain cuts in the budget. Each year the resolutions assumed levels of spending affected not only by appropriations but by changes in entitlements and other laws. But these legislative changes were not mandated or even listed in the first resolution. They were included in the reports of the Budget committees but were not subject to vote on the floor of Congress; thus conflict on sensitive issues was avoided in the interests of mutual accommodation between Budget and authorizing committees. The result, according to Schick, was that "few of the savings sought by the Budget Committees were enacted into law." More than half the savings assumed in the first resolution were abandoned by the Budget committees when they prepared the second resolution; only a small number of the remaining savings led to legislative action.[38]

The procedures of the Budget Act therefore allowed for budget cuts, but within the context of the normal political accommodations of Congress and with strict regard to previous commitments unless these were explicitly altered by a duly constituted congressional majority. But there were indications that even the relatively weak constraints of the act and the clarity it brought to budget decisions put pressure on the federal budget process. The area of overspill expanded. Outlays of off-budget agencies grew from a little over $7 billion in 1976 to over $14 billion in 1980.[39] Between 1976 and 1980 federal credit programs grew 27 percent a year, and by 1980 loans and loan guarantees reached $462 billion.[40] Tax expenditures, according to Alice Rivlin, became one of the major means of allocating public resources, although their growth is to some extent a function of growing tax liabilities.[41]

The budget process itself came under strain. There were complaints of whipsawing between totals and appropriations—members would vote simultaneously for lower budget totals and higher spending for individual programs.[42] As conflict grew, it became increasingly common for several appropriations to remain unpassed at the beginning of the fiscal year.[43] Accurate estimates of outlays became more difficult to attain. Most attention, however, was focused on the increasing annual deficit, which gradually came to be taken as a major symbol of budgetary incapacity. If Congress was unwilling, in the light of a growing tax revolt, to increase taxes or to live with the deficit, it would once more have to consider more stringent means of cutting the budget.

The Cutting Edge

The Budget Act lacked a cutting edge. The Budget committees were in a weak position to counter the jealously guarded autonomy of the committees that made the actual budgetary decisions. The targets of the first resolution were not binding, and even the totals of the second resolution were likely to change through a supplementary third resolution in the spring of the following year. Most important, given the structure of the budget, the Budget committees could not cut uncontrollable spending, since they had no power to instruct authorizing committees to report legislation to reduce expenditures. Attempts to meet this situation by use of reconciliation related to the second resolution were unsuccessful. It was only when reconciliation was deliberately used with the first resolution that the congressional budget process gained an effective budget-cutting tool, though one that had to be used with discretion.

By 1979 the haphazard victories of the Budget committees no longer seemed an adequate response to pressures on the budget. The Senate Budget Committee therefore attempted to use the reconciliation process to achieve budget cuts. It instructed the Appropriations Committee and six other committees to prepare reconciliation measures to effect savings. Since the House Budget Committee was not prepared to follow suit, the reconciliation procedure was abandoned, and instead Congress passed a declaration that the second resolution totals would not be altered later in the year. In the absence of reconciliation, the committees did not pass the savings requested, and later in the year the totals of the second resolution were exceeded by a large amount.[44]

This experience convinced the Budget committees that if they wished to cut the budget significantly, the time to do so was at the beginning, not the end, of the budget process. The occasion for testing this assumption was immediately at hand: the initial president's budget for fiscal 1981 had called for a deficit, but only two months later it was revised to balance revenues and expenditures, making cuts inevitable. To this end, a key group of House and Senate leaders, together with senior members of the Budget committees, certain committee chairmen, and administration officials, worked together on budget revisions designed to produce a surplus. Advantage was taken of section 301(b)(2) of the act, which allowed the establishment of "any other procedure which is considered appropriate to carry out the purpose of this Act," to transform reconciliation into a more powerful instrument of budgetary control. Tied to the first resolution, a reconciliation bill instructed committees to report legislation to make about $10 billion in deficit reductions. These were duly accomplished, and although several amendments were made on the floor of Congress, the resulting reconciliation bill incorporated over $8 billion in spending reductions and tax increases.

Reconciliation used with the first resolution had the potential to overcome exactly the weaknesses in the Budget Act that militated against budget cutting. First, both the initial resolution instructing committees to change laws to achieve targeted savings and the enactment of an omnibus reconciliation bill duly consolidating the legislative changes demanded a single vote of Congress. Reconciliation integrated budget-cutting measures within a single measure, preventing whipsawing between appropriations and totals and forcing a binding decision on general fiscal policy. Second, the instructions to the committees set compulsory minimum savings to be recommended, although the committees could choose where they wished to make individual cuts. Third, reconciliation directly attacked uncontrollability by mandating legislative changes to fulfill budgetary limits.

To the new administration that took office at the beginning of 1981, reconciliation offered a powerful tool to implement its policy of permanent reduction in the growth of public expenditures. The Reagan administration used the reconciliation process to achieve unprecedented cuts of $53.2 billion in budget authority and $35.2 billion in outlays in the 1982 budget and targeted large cuts for the following two years to culminate, it predicted, in a balanced budget in 1984. It did so in two ways. First, for programs established by authorization and funded through annual appropriations, reconciliation lowered the authorization level, thereby forcing the Appropriations committees to appropriate within that limit. Second, cuts in entitlements, including those that go through the appropriations process, were made by changing eligibility rules and benefit formulas contained in the authorization of various entitlements.[45]

As a budget-cutting measure reconciliation was a stunning success. In the words of David Stockman, director of the Office of Management and Budget, reconciliation addressed "the most difficult problem of budgeting":

> A strong programmatic argument for a specific measure can almost always defeat the general argument about the harm of rapid budget growth. This is because, taken alone, any one measure is not itself significant enough to cause the underlying economic problems that have resulted from the budget policies of the last fifteen years. . . . Reconciliation adds a further dimension to the debate by permitting the argument of overriding national concern for economic revitalization to be weighed against specific program issues.[46]

Reconciliation made possible timely action within a specified period, enabled Congress to ensure that its overall fiscal policy would be carried out by its committees according to a set timetable, enforced aggregate spending totals and broad priorities, and made individual committees accountable to Congress as a whole. In short, reconciliation provided the enforcement mechanism previously lacking in the congressional budget process.[47]

Other observers were more critical. Implementation of the budget process in 1981 had aroused considerable resentment and the accusation that reconciliation, far from fulfilling the Budget Act, had actually short-circuited normal budgetary and legislative processes. Representative Norman Mineta (Democrat, California) charged:

> The haste with which the Administration substitute was thrown together and presented to the House made it impossible for Members to know what they were voting on. Copies of the proposal which was hundreds of pages long were only available to Members just hours before the final vote and after debate had begun on the bill. The legislative document contained handwritten notes scribbled in the margin, dollar amounts of entries pencilled in, others scratched out. In this casual and sloppy manner, Congress was asked to consider the single largest bill ever brought before it, affecting virtually every activity of government.[48]

It was further charged that reconciliation had upset the balance of power within Congress. Although the authorizing committees had been theoretically free to allocate cuts as they saw fit, in practice they had had little option save to follow the guidelines of the OMB.[49] The Appropriations committees, whose discretion had been limited by the lowering of authorizations below appropriations, felt that their role had been undermined altogether and that they were being reduced to ciphers.

There was even greater concern about the balance of power between executive and legislature. The executive, relying on a Republican majority in the Senate and a bipartisan coalition in the House, had played a leading role in steering reconciliation through Congress. To Richard Bolling (Democrat, Missouri), chairman of the House Rules Committee, reconciliation was "the most brutal and blunt instrument used by a president in an attempt to control the congressional process since Nixon used impoundment."[50] Executive direction through reconciliation, according to this view, threatened the prerogatives of Congress and paved the way to dictatorship.

Both critics and advocates, however, were on common ground in understanding that reconciliation had made significant changes in the congressional budget process. Unlike the other procedures under the Budget Act, it was an avowed tool of subtraction, justified for the purpose of budget cutting. Like any other budget mechanism, its use would arouse conflict. It breached previous understandings by examining past decisions. It included in the budget debate areas that had been deliberately excluded from it. It purposely destabilized budgetary

117

accommodations without prospect of future equilibrium as cuts became progressively more difficult. Its procedures ran counter to the normal modes of congressional decision making, substituting integration for fragmentation, decision forcing for bargaining and discussion, and hierarchy for decentralization and autonomy.

Yet, in the last resort, reconciliation depended for its effectiveness on the acquiescence of Congress. Reconciliation could not, of itself, muster majorities or forge a consensus otherwise lacking. Without an underlying political consensus, reconciliation had no means of resolving the conflicts it would arouse which could destroy the fragile framework of the budget process altogether: totals would break apart into individual measures, timetables would be disrupted, committees would reassert their autonomy, and blackmail and deadlock would become the normal order of business.

Despite the potential of reconciliation as a powerful weapon of budget cutting, political prudence precluded its indiscriminate use. The following year budget cutting, whether emanating from the administration or within Congress, was not concentrated exclusively in reconciliation measures. Thus, when the administration required further expenditure reductions at the end of the 1981 budget process, it sought to implement them through across-the-board percentage reductions in appropriations. In 1982 reconciliation was only one deficit-cutting measure among many separately packaged proposals—cuts in appropriations through the first resolution, tax increases, and a separate bill for entitlement cuts under the jurisdiction of the taxing committees. But these measures aroused sharp conflict, and as time went on, the sustained pressures for subtraction appeared to threaten the viability of the budget process itself.

The Budget Process under Stress

The turbulence of federal budgeting in recent years might easily suggest that the congressional budget process was on the verge of collapse. Timetables became meaningless. Fiscal years began and continued without appropriations. Different budget-cutting measures increased the complexity of budgetary procedures and fragmented the budget. Each step of the process crystallized into a fresh focus for conflict and opportunity for leverage. Although measures such as reconciliation were designed to integrate and strengthen the discipline of the budget process, it seemed that they had achieved just the opposite. Under the pressures of subtraction, the budget process appeared to resemble more and more the repetitive and ad hoc decision making of poor countries.

An Incomplete Budget. The most noticeable effect of the budgetary pressures was that the budget debates expanded to fill the legislative calendar; yet at the end of the year there was still no budget. In 1981 a new round of budget cutting initiated by the administration right at the end of the budget process resulted in confrontation, deadlock, and even lapse of budget authority. At the beginning of the fiscal year only one appropriation had been passed, and it was necessary to pass continuing resolutions, renewed every few months, to fund the federal government. The second resolution was a carbon copy of the first—a pro forma measure whose numbers bore little relation to current budget reality. Three appropriations bills never emerged from Congress at all, and the final continuing resolution had to provide full-year funding for the seven departments and various agencies they covered.

The following year the immediate unacceptability of the president's budget heralded an escalation in conflict as Congress struggled to put together a viable budget of its own, yet one acceptable to the president. It took long-drawn-out negotiations in both House and Senate to reach accommodation on the various measures incorporating cuts, and the timetable fell well behind schedule. Action had not been completed on any of the appropriations bills by the beginning of the fiscal year, and a lame-duck session in November also failed to produce a budget. The resort to continuing resolutions meant that different levels of funding were established for different parts of the budget until appropriations could be passed. Agencies would receive allocations at House-passed, Senate-passed, or current operating levels as specifically stipulated in the resolution. Continuing resolutions also increased the complexity of the budget process by carrying over debate on the current year's budget beyond the start of the fiscal year.

Complexity and Fragmentation. A casual observer might have been hard pressed to locate the budget in the second year of the Reagan administration. In 1981 the reconciliation bill incorporating cuts had meshed fairly understandably with the first resolution and the figures produced by authorizing and Appropriations committees. In 1982 it seemed as though there were budget measures all over the place and the budget was being cut through all of them.

Unlike the previous year's cuts, the cuts in 1982 were not concentrated in a single reconciliation measure. In effect the budget was split into several packages, each of which moved on a separate track through Congress. The first package was social security, which, failing agreement early in the process, was shunted off to a special commission, which was to report after the November 1982 congressional elections. A second package consisted of reconciliation instructions concerning entitlements under the jurisdiction of the Finance and Ways and Means committees, to be reported as part of the finance bill. A third included the remaining reconciliation instructions to authorizing committees, and a fourth consisted of the cuts in appropriations levels.

The problem was to keep the packages and the cuts they entailed more or less intact and on track as they passed through Congress. The task was not an easy one, and passage of some packages required acceptance of increases as well as cuts. The Finance Committee, for example, more than accomplished the cuts mandated by the reconciliation instructions but emerged with an extension of unemployment benefits. Certain authorizing committees in the House, such as the Agriculture, Banking, Financing, and Urban Affairs, and Post Office and Civil Service committees, initially resisted reconciliation cuts. To strengthen its position against the president, the Democratic leadership insisted on dividing reconciliation into several bills, so that it required not one but several votes on the floor of the House. The Appropriations committees were uneasy both with the first resolution targets and with the pattern of executive requests and tended to take an independent stance on how much and what should be cut. Although many cuts were accomplished in the passage of the finance and reconciliation bills, the complexity and fragmentation of the budget process increased, as did the number of decisions to be made and hence the opportunities for confrontation, deadlocks, and leverage.

Confrontation, Deadlocks, and Leverage. Just as the steps of the congressional budget process had previously tended to invite incrementalism, the additional steps now provided focuses for conflict. For each consolidated measure it was necessary to gain agreement sufficient for a majority in Congress, to sustain that majority so as to keep the measure intact in the relevant committees or on the floor (and in conference if the committees balked), and finally to ensure that it was not vetoed by the president. Further opportunities for conflict and pressure were provided by the need to pass continuing resolutions and supplementary funding for the previous year's budget and, as the economic situation deteriorated and deficit estimates grew, to legislate increases in the debt ceiling. Each vote constituted an obstacle, to be surmounted by a variety of tactics, which included package splitting, leverage on essential funding measures, avoiding responsibility, negotiating alternatives, and brinksmanship.

Package splitting. Consolidating measures, such as reconciliation, are designed to make budget cutting easier by packaging the cuts together so that voting patterns are blurred. Those who oppose cuts will therefore endeavor to separate them so as to force votes for specific items to be on the record. The Democratic leadership was successful, for example, in splitting open the reconciliation package in the House so that it required several votes, including such sensitive items as cost-of-living allowances for retired civil servants.

Leverage on essential measures. Whenever it is crucial to pass a funding measure, there is an opportunity for leverage. The need to increase the debt ceiling, to pass continuing resolutions during the budget year, and to pass a tax bill gave proponents of increases and opponents of cuts a chance to block a measure and insist on amendments. The trick was to find "veto-proof" measures to gain passage for proposals that would be unable to gain it on their own. This tactic was a variant of the old "Christmas tree" strategy, in which budget measures had been made vehicles for all kinds of amendments. The new situation provided many more opportunities. Toward the end of the 1982 budget process, for example, a measure funding airport development programs through the Airport and Airway Trust Fund was successfully tacked on to the tax bill, and a continuing resolution for the current fiscal year was used as a means of gaining assent to a job creation initiative.

Avoiding responsibility. When one set of participants finds a budget measure repugnant, it may refuse to vote for it at all or may do so behind closed doors. Thus Democrats on the Ways and Means Committee threatened to vote down the cuts incorporated in the tax bill but ended up meeting in closed session and taking the bill directly to conference with the Senate Finance Committee, thus avoiding a vote on the floor of the House.

Negotiating alternatives. Acceptance and rejection of budget measures are only two of many possible responses to budget-cutting initiatives. The art lies in constructing and negotiating packages until one alternative finds acceptance. This may be an exhausting and long-drawn-out process. The first concurrent resolution reported by the House Budget Committee in 1982 faced no fewer than seven alternatives and sixty-eight floor amendments, requiring a highly complex voting procedure (which resulted in defeat for all of them and a need for further negotiations). Virtually every budget measure necessitated a complex balancing of interests to gain compromise and agreement.

Brinksmanship. A difference in party affiliation or a radical difference in views between Congress and the president may easily result in deadlock and a subsequent game of brinksmanship. Deadlocks of this kind occur relatively frequently—over continuing resolutions, spending bills, and supplemental funding. Since the president has no item veto, he may be forced into vetoing items of which he approves or consenting to items he dislikes if Congress packages them together. He also runs the risk of being overruled by a two-thirds vote of Congress. These possibilities are illustrated by the fates of two urgent supplementary funding bills that passed Congress in the summer of 1982. By twice vetoing the first bill, the president succeeded in forcing Congress to delete controversial proposals. But the second, which contained more for social programs and less for defense than the president had requested (although the total was below the president's request), was passed over his veto.

Budgetary Ambiguity. The complexity of the budget process was paralleled by ambiguity about its outcomes. Controversy swirled over the real dimension of the cuts because of the variety of estimating bases. Shifting outlay figures showed continued budget growth even as Congress debated cuts. Changes in terminology blurred budget-cutting actions, and each year the unfinished budget process left reductions in doubt. Lack of space prevents a thorough analysis of the substantive cuts except to point out the major difficulties in assessment.[51]

A primary difficulty lay in determining a base line from which to measure cuts. The general acceptance of a current policy base line—the extrapolation of current spending for the coming year—created two important problems. First, it was necessary to work from an estimate of current year spending, which could not be accurately assessed until near the end of the fiscal year. Second, it was necessary to predict sensitive economic conditions, particularly the rates of inflation and unemployment, whose misestimate would heavily affect revenues and outlays. If initial statements of the base proved inaccurate as the year progressed, Congress would have to either revise the base (which would mean much recalculation) or leave it as it was (giving rise to disputes about the effects of its actions).

The problems of shifting outlay estimates added to the ambiguity. Because Congress actually makes decisions not about outlays but about budget authority, the effects of its actions are not always apparent in the current year, and the actual impact of the cuts is blurred. Moreover, while it was clear that program cuts were being made in certain areas, the progressive upward reestimates of budget outlays seemed to imply that the reductions were having a small effect on the budget as a whole. Although Congress had found in reconciliation a means of affecting uncontrollable expenditures, these continued to account for much budget growth as even more intense efforts were made to cut controllable areas.

In any case, as time went on, emphasis changed from budget cutting to deficit reductions. Tax increases and expenditure cuts were packaged together, to some extent making it more difficult to identify the cuts. Often the cuts themselves were hazy, including such items as management savings, lower interest payments, and accounting changes.

Finally, the fact that the budget remained unfinished at the end of each year was responsible for further uncertainty. Formulas were agreed upon to decide on monthly funding for each appropriate category—last year's spending, last year's spending with an addition, any appropriation that had passed either House or Senate. The absence of regular appropriations also gave rise to confusion regarding permissible apportionment of outlays where the congressional spending level surpassed the administration's request.

Ambiguities about the extent and nature of budget cuts, problems in completing the budget, growing complexity and fragmentation in the budget process, and the increasingly ad hoc methods of budgetary decision making were indications of the strain that policies of subtraction placed on congressional budget frameworks. These frameworks had rested on a shallow consensus, maintained by agreement to exclude the most sensitive issues from annual consideration, to tolerate piecemeal decision making, and to resolve conflicts through accommodation. Sustained policies of subtraction demanded inclusion, integration, and hierarchy in decision making, raising the level of conflict to a point where accepted budget processes seemed in danger of collapse.

Yet in some measure the phenomena discussed in this section reflect the response of Congress not merely to the pressures of subtraction but also to the heightened conflicts they entail. Faced with prolonged struggles over important issues as well as constantly changing estimates for crucial budget totals, Congress chose to make the budget throughout the year rather than curtail debate or accept executive fiat. Confronted with demands to make cuts throughout the budget and to set claim against claim, Congress opted to compartmentalize its choices into packages. In this way decisions might be made more manageable, varying coalitions might be formed, and accommodations might take place over limited areas. Given the acknowledged inadequacy of budget data, Congress sought to supply itself with its own figures through the Congressional Budget Office, to monitor them continuously, and to make adjustments to them when necessary. It was also not averse to blurring the issues when the figures themselves—as was so often the case—were open to debate. The formal structures and procedures of the budget process might suffer from these accommodations, but there were more important issues at stake. These included not only substantive disagreements about what should be cut but also arguments about how the cuts should be made. Implicit in the turmoil of the budget debates was consideration of the future capacity of Congress to make budgetary decisions.

Reestablishing Congressional Capacity

Sustained policies of budgetary subtraction not only are sources of enhanced conflict but also undercut the accepted means by which disagreements and tensions are resolved. Far from strengthening or bringing discipline to established budget processes, long-term pressures on resources are likely to be destructive of budget cycles, cohesion, and clarity. If circumstances dictate continued policies of subtraction, new means for resolving conflicts, which may modify traditional budget principles, need to be found. The potential of any new arrangements to produce budget cuts, however, will be limited by the degree of political consensus on their desirability and by conventions regarding institutional roles.

Efforts to implement policies of subtraction through the congressional budget process in recent years have raised the level of political conflict and brought pressure on budget procedures and institutions. Older means of constraining federal expenditures— through the guardianship role of the Appropriations committees in a relatively closed budget process—are no longer available. Since Congress is unwilling to yield budgetary dominance to the executive branch, it has attempted to deal with the issue of subtraction (among others) by integrating its own budget process through the Budget Act. The weak constraints of the act were accepted by Congress, and the procedures it established were kept more or less intact. But conflicts were resolved only partially within the limitations of the act: spending pressures spilled over into expenditures beyond budget boundaries; previous understandings and commitments entrenched the existing pattern of expenditures; the weaknesses of the act were exploited to maintain the politics of accommodation.

The transfer of reconciliation to the beginning of the annual process was a deliberate effort to find new means of resolving conflict management in favor of subtraction. It attempted to substitute a much stronger measure of integration for piecemeal decision making, hierarchy for autonomy, and inclusion of decisions for exclusion. By cutting across the prevailing modes of conflict resolution in Congress, reconciliation strained formal budget processes, which were no longer facilitated by older patterns of accommodation. But there are also indications that Congress has moved to reestablish its budgetary capacity.

It would be hazardous at this point to predict how Congress will handle budget cutting in the future. Experience has been too short to establish definitive trends. Subtraction is only one of several issues confronting Congress and influencing its processes. Changes in the political balance may transform the situation. If pressures for cutbacks continue, however, it is unlikely that conflict will be reduced and probable that, as the "easy" cuts are accomplished, conflict will rise. How will Congress cope with enhanced conflict, and how will conflict affect its capacity to make timely and appropriate budget decisions? There are a number of possible options, including external limits, executive authority, congressional leadership, and a restructured budget process.

Imposing External Limits. To those who despair of the ability of Congress to control mounting federal expenditures and deficits, the only solution to the problem of congressional capacity to make cuts is to impose external limits on budgetary decision making. Several attempts have been made in recent years to pass constitutional amendments mandating a balanced budget or expenditure limits. One recent proposal (Senate Joint Resolution 58), which incorporated both a limit on revenue increases and a stipulation to balance the budget, failed to gain the necessary two-thirds majority in Congress by a narrow margin in 1982. Further proposals will probably be put forward to place the size of the budget outside the political process and thus enforce budget cutting by an impersonal and neutral formula.

Implementation of a constitutional limit would undoubtedly cause a number of problems, not least of which would be to raise the level of conflict in Congress. Since the proposal provides no mechanism to resolve conflict over budgetary choices, further measures would be needed to alleviate pressure on budget processes.

Reinforcing Executive Authority. In recent years, despite a somewhat inconsistent performance, the executive has been cast in a budget-cutting role. One solution to the problem of cutting the budget might therefore be to increase executive authority over the budget. This development might occur in a number of ways. Congress might be prevented from making additions to the president's budget,

125

although it would still be allowed to make subtractions. This change would probably require a constitutional amendment, would alter the balance between Congress and president in favor of a cabinet system of government, and is not likely to be acceptable in the present political circumstances. A more feasible development of executive authority might occur if the electoral process once more generates a president and a Congress from the same political party. Even so, the diffuseness of U.S. political parties might make presidential dominance doubtful. A third possibility would be to allow the president an item veto, which would permit him to remake the budget after Congress has finished with it, or to expand his power to impound funds. Given the present "resurgence" of Congress, none of these possibilities seems politically feasible. Although a popular or skillful president might be able to gain majorities in Congress for budget-cutting policies through reconciliation, executive predominance in a system of separation of powers is likely to continue to be problematic.

Strengthening Congressional Leadership. If more executive authority over the budget is unacceptable, congressional leadership might provide a focal point for budget cutting inside Congress. To some degree this development is already taking place.[52] The authority of the leadership in both parties has derived from its skill in putting together budget packages acceptable to Congress and steering them through committees. Splitting the budget into politically viable categories allows the leaders of the relevant committees to take the initiative in setting agendas, framing the major budget issues and questions, and suggesting the budgetary trade-offs needed to ensure passage of the packages. Because of the greater information available through the Congressional Budget Office, the leadership may control the essential assumptions on which subsequent budget estimates are built and also monitor the progress of decisions as they move through Congress. And if the leadership can work out acceptable packages and keep them intact, it will limit access to the budget at later stages of the process. The adoption of what amounted to a binding first resolution in 1982 and the agreement by the House to a rule restricting amendments to budget measures strengthened leadership authority in this respect. Further strengthening might occur if the number of steps in the budget process were cut down (for example, by merging authorizations and appropriations) or if political parties became more cohesive entities.

Restructuring the Budget Process. Pressures for subtraction tend to disrupt budget processes because they lay bare controversies otherwise blurred by resource-intensive decision-making techniques. Mechanisms for subtraction tend to intensify conflicts because they integrate and force decisions without providing means for their resolution. Traditional budget frameworks called upon to cope with sustained policies of subtraction may also intensify conflict, and recent strain reflects their inadequacy in the face of the demands, including those for subtraction, now placed on them. Improving congressional budget capacity may therefore require transforming budget frameworks and traditional principles, departure from which constitutes less dysfunction than adaptation.[53] Thus the inability of Congress to complete action on the budget may express the need for a less repetitive, more continuous, and longer-range process than the annual budget. Apparent fragmentation may indicate the suitability of a more differentiated budget process, in which decision making follows agreed upon and manageable budget categories over different time spans. The fast-changing assumptions that yield the bases for budgetary decisions may demand more flexibility in decision making over the budget year, including contingency plans and alternative budgets. In other words, the budget process itself might be restructured to focus and limit conflicts. But the potential of such changes to bring about budget cuts would, like that of the other options discussed here, be limited by institutional and political considerations.

Limitations. All these potential choices in the development of capacity to make budget cuts share a radical redirection in the traditional means by which Congress has coped with conflict. They substitute integration for piecemeal decision making, hierarchy for autonomy, inclusion for exclusion, clarification for blurring of issues, and direct confrontation for avoidance of conflicts. Their implementation would depend on the willingness of Congress to make these changes and to place the value of budget control above the other values it holds. To some extent budget making demands a high degree of cohesion, forced decisions within a strict timetable, and the repeated rationing of claims. Partly for these reasons budget theory places the budget role primarily within the executive, whose abilities to produce clear-cut, consistent, and timely decisions through a bureaucracy are much greater than those of a legislative body. Congress has functions other than the production of a budget: representing different viewpoints, maintaining access to power, flexible negotiating of political compromises. It is involved in constant tensions between the claims of party and individual, leadership and rank and file, which result not in lasting solutions but in shifting balances between centralization and decentralization of power. The resolution of budget conflicts, as well as the framework and rules by which they are decided, will be determined in large measure by the willingness of members of Congress to accept limits on their own autonomy as the price of greater budgetary effectiveness.

A word of warning. Beneath the debates about processes and institutions lie the substantive budget cuts themselves. Budgets are only "the translation of financial resources into human purposes,"[54] reflecting the general consensus of citizens about what public purposes should be. Budgets are therefore difficult to cut not only because of the rigidities or peculiarities of decision processes but because they constitute long-term commitments to individual welfare and security, provision of essential collective services, assurances of stability in an unstable environment, and the granting of special largesse to special groups. Not all areas of the budget are equally susceptible to cuts: in practice budget cutting tends to concentrate on the "controllable" part of the budget and to inflict losses on the politically weaker sections of society. The danger is that the rhetoric of subtraction may cloak the issues of the role of government and redistribution of income in terms of budget control, using pressures to cut the budget as a surrogate for policy determination. Budget cutting may indeed be justifiable to reduce government waste, redistribute public expenditures, restore vitality to the private sector, or adjust to an era of limits. But it should not be overlooked that ultimately the politics of subtraction will be limited by its social and economic consequences.

Notes

1. Bengt-Christer Ysander and Ann Robinson, "The Inflexibility of Contemporary Budgets," *Public Budgeting and Finance*, vol. 2, no. 2 (Autumn 1982), p. 7.

2. Naomi Caiden and Aaron Wildavsky, *Planning and Budgeting in Poor Countries* (New Brunswick, N.J.: Transaction Books, 1980).

3. Aaron Wildavsky, *The Politics of the Budgetary Process*, 2d ed. (Boston: Little, Brown, 1974), p. 62.

4. Daniel Tarschys, "Rational Decremental Budgeting: Elements of an Expenditure Policy for the 80s," *Political Life in Sweden*, no. 12 (February 1982), p. 7.

5. Maurice Wright, "Big Government in Hard Times: The Restraint of Public Expenditures," in Christopher Hood and Maurice Wright, eds., *Big Government in Hard Times* (Oxford: Martin Robertson, 1981), p. 12.

6. Richard F. Fenno, Jr., "The House Appropriations Committee as a Political System," *American Political Science Review* (June 1962), p. 312, quoted in Wildavsky, *Politics of the Budgetary Process*, p. 48.

7. Dennis Ippolito, *Congressional Spending* (Ithaca, N.Y.: Cornell University Press, 1982), pp. 50–51.

8. Wildavsky, *Politics of the Budgetary Process*, pp. 57–62.

9. See Allen Schick, *Congress and Money: Budgeting, Spending, and Taxing* (Washington, D.C.: Urban Institute, 1980), pp. 417–18; and Joel Havemann, *Congress and the Budget* (Bloomington: Indiana University Press, 1978), p. 150.

10. Richard J. Fenno, Jr., *The Power of the Purse: Appropriations Politics in Congress* (Boston: Little, Brown, 1966), p. 411.

11. Schick, *Congress and Money*, p. 21.

12. See Havemann, *Congress and the Budget*, pp. 154–55.

13. Schick, *Congress and Money*, p. 419.

14. Ibid., p. 26.

15. Ibid., p. 427.

16. James L. Sundquist, *The Decline and Resurgence of Congress* (Washington, D.C.: Brookings Institution, 1981), p. 84.

17. Ibid.

18. Schick, *Congress and Money*, p. 442.

19. Ibid., p. 217.

20. Ibid., p. 218.

21. Ibid., p. 203.

22. Ibid., p. 205.

23. Ibid., p. 225.

24. Ibid., pp. 231–32.

25. Ibid., pp. 261–62.

26. Ibid., p. 312.

27. Havemann, *Congress and the Budget*, p. 125.

28. Schick, *Congress and Money*, p. 386.

29. Ibid., p. 318.

30. Ibid., p. 338.

31. Ibid., p. 323.

32. Ibid., pp. 354–55.

33. Ibid., pp. 339–40.

34. Lance T. LeLoup, *The Fiscal Congress: Legislative Control of the Budget* (Westport, Conn.: Greenwood Press, 1980) pp. 149–50.

35. Sundquist, *Decline and Resurgence*, p. 220.

36. Ippolito, *Congressional Spending*, p. 101.

37. Schick, *Congress and Money*, p. 361.

38. Allen Schick, *Reconciliation and the Congressional Budget Process* (Washington, D.C.: American Enterprise Institute, 1981), p. 6.

39. *United States Budget 1983*, p. 9–62.

40. Alice Rivlin, "Statement before the Task Force on Enforcement Credit and Multi-Year Budgeting," U.S. House of Representatives, October 2, 1981, pp. 1–2.

41. Alice Rivlin, "Statement before the Committee on Rules," U.S. House of Representatives, December 9, 1981, p. 5.

42. "Supplemental Views of Hon. David R. Obey and Hon. Richard A. Gephardt," First Concurrent Resolution on the Budget—Fiscal Year 1982, Report of the Committee on the Budget, House of Representatives, April 16, 1981, pp. 327–32.

43. James L. Kirkman, "Congressional Budget Process Reform Ideas: 1981–1982" (Paper presented at the Southern Political Science Association 1982 meeting, Atlanta, Georgia, October 29, 1982), p. 9.

44. Schick, Reconciliation, pp. 6–7; Sundquist, Decline and Resurgence, pp. 227–28.

45. John Ellwood, "Congress Cuts the Budget: The Omnibus Reconciliation Act of 1981," Public Budgeting and Finance (Spring 1982), p. 52.

46. David Stockman, "Statement before the Committee on Governmental Affairs," U.S. Senate, October 6, 1981, pp. 3–4.

47. Senator Peter V. Domenici, "Opening Statement before the Committee on Governmental Affairs," U.S. Senate, October 6, 1981, pp. 9–12.

48. Norman Mineta, "The Budget Process Does Work" (Paper presented at the Committee for a Responsible Federal Government Symposium, "The Congressional Budget Act and Process—How They Can Be Improved," January 12, 1982, Arkadelphia, Arkansas), p. 7.

49. Leon E. Panetta, "Statement before the Committee on Rules, Subcommittee on the Legislative Process," U.S. House of Representatives, September 8, 1981, p. 22.

50. Congressional Quarterly Weekly Report, July 4, 1981, p. 1168.

51. Detailed elaboration of these themes may be found in John Ellwood, ed., Reductions in U.S. Domestic Spending (New Brunswick, N.J.: Transaction Books, 1982).

52. Sundquist, Decline and Resurgence, pp. 387–90.

53. Naomi Caiden, "The Myth of the Annual Budget," Public Administration Review, vol. 42, no. 6 (November/December 1982), pp. 516–23.

54. Wildavsky, Politics of the Budgetary Process, p. 1.

5

Congress and Redistribution

John Ferejohn

Introduction

Legislation almost always entails some redistribution of wealth. But some proposals are justified by their sponsors primarily on the grounds of their intended effects on income distribution. Such proposals are often controversial because they entail the taking of property from some for the benefit of others; their consideration can therefore cause intense political conflict. Since the constitutional biases of the American system, with its multiplicity of decision stages, tend to work against the enactment of controversial laws, the passage of fundamental redistributive legislation occurs infrequently in American politics. Indeed, if one considers only organic acts, many of the most important redistributive programs were enacted in a few congresses of extraordinary partisan imbalance. The New Deal and Great Society congresses passed legislation authorizing social security, medical assistance to the aged, and a variety of programs of public assistance for the poor and the disabled.

Although the inauguration of many of these programs was politically significant, they have grown to many times their original sizes through the actions (or at least the assent) of congresses that were not so atypical. Once previously controversial programs were established, congressional processes often turned to their routine funding and extension in circumstances that might have allowed retrenchment or even dismantling.[1]

The observer of income transfer programs in the United States is struck by two dominant conditions: First, the American system of redistribution is vast and complex. Dozens of programs exist with the purpose of transferring income or services to deserving individuals, and each is administered in some unique fashion in the federal system. Second, despite governmental activity, the effect of redistributive programs on the overall distributions of wealth and

131

income is very limited by comparative standards. The distributions of wealth and income in this country remain highly skewed after decades of governmental involvement and show little sign of evolving in a more egalitarian direction.

In this chapter I argue that the structure of American institutions, particularly congressional institutions, helps account both for the diversity of programs and for their limited aggregate effect. The logic of the explanation is based on the calculus of coalition formation imposed on political actors by the Constitution and by the institutional evolution that has proceeded from it.[2]

It is important, for the purposes of this essay, to make a distinction between the purposes of a program and the means employed to achieve them. A redistributive program or policy has as its primary purpose the alteration of some aspect of the distribution of wealth or income and employs taxing and spending to transfer wealth or income. Programs that use regulatory means to achieve ends of equity are not, in this sense, classed as redistributive even though they may appeal to the same basic values.[3] Redistributive policies are instances of distributive ones. In particular, they are distributive policies that aim at serving values of fairness, equality, or compassion rather than, say, improving highways or limiting flood damage.[4]

Coalition Formation and Policy Making. In spite of their great diversity, redistributive programs in the United States share certain political characteristics. Any program, whether it be redistributive in intent or not, depends on a system of political support (or coalition) both inside Congress and in other critical locations in the federal system if it is to prosper. A number of potential bases of support might be formed to sustain a program; the most common is a coalition of program beneficiaries and service providers (often called an "iron triangle" or subgovernment), but programs may also be based on ideological or partisan systems of support or on coalitions of interest with other programs (that is, logrolling). The maintenance of a public program depends on ensuring that those who could adversely affect the program do not want to and that those whose support is needed provide it at the appropriate times.

Although the supporters of any public policy face the necessity of developing a coalitional base, those who advocate a redistributive program and wish to channel its benefits to a narrow sector of the population face a particularly difficult problem of coalition formation. If they develop a program that efficiently allocates benefits to a relatively small population of needy persons, the program is not likely to be generally popular. Its continued support may depend on the control of Congress by one of the parties. If, however, supporters choose to structure a program so that it has a relatively stable base of support in Congress no matter what the outcomes of elections (that is, if they choose to use program benefits themselves to build and maintain widespread political support), the program will probably not be effective in giving benefits to those who are thought to be most deserving. Either people who are not needy will get a high proportion of benefits, or the "truly needy" will not obtain much help.

In short, the structure of American political institutions militates against efficient redistributive programs with stable political support. This tension between the values that motivate the enactment of redistributive legislation and the necessities of coalition formation can be expected to produce a variety of distinctive political responses within Congress. Three characteristic patterns of redistributive policy making can be discerned.

First, support for a program can be built directly on the distribution of benefits to its clientele. In determining the distribution of benefits, legislators are effectively constructing a base of support for the program. One would expect in this case that there would be a politics of eligibility. Supporters and opponents of a program can affect both the relation of the program to its public purpose and its support in the political process by changing the size and composition of its clientele. And, since much of the problem of program support is centered in Congress, various congressional actors will be involved in these disputes. Insofar as support for a particular program is concentrated in one of the parties, important decision making will take place on the floor (unless the committees can effectively restrain floor activity through the rules) and will tend to involve the leaders or the policy groups of the two parties. For programs that have established sufficiently broad supporting coalitions to obtain bipartisan support, one would expect to observe committee-based decision making; occasionally a full-fledged subgovernment might evolve, whose activities proceed without much reference to partisan tides propagating through the political system.

Second, redistributive programs may be established on a logrolling basis through the exchange of support with proponents of another program. Such arrangements are difficult to organize and are vulnerable to various types of strategic behavior of participants as well as opponents.[5] Because of the potential vulnerability of logrolling agreements, one would expect the ability to arrange them to depend on the capacity of congressional institutions to protect such arrangements. The decline in the power of the standing committees and their chairmen, the decrease in executive markups, and the increase in recorded votes in both chambers may make complicated logrolling agreements more difficult to negotiate and carry out. Conversely, the Speaker's increased capacity to coordinate committee actions[6] and to overcome jurisdictional separations and the evolution of the budget reconciliation process may assist in the formation of cross-jurisdictional logrolling arrangements. While I cannot say which of these tendencies is more powerful, my general point is that the institutional structure of Congress is likely to have an effect on the frequency and stability of logrolling arrangements.

Finally, programs may be based on systems of partisan or ideological support within Congress and its committees. Support for such programs can be expected to respond directly to election returns and to other forces that affect the composition of Congress. To the extent that proponents of redistributive policies are able to gain control of the policy-making committees and to ensure the passage of reported legislation, one would expect relatively effective redistributive legislation to be enacted. Subsequently, when the partisan tides turn, support for such programs would tend to atrophy, and one would expect them to be curtailed or dismantled.

The claim is, then, that effective (or narrowly targeted) redistributive programs are likely to enjoy sporadic support in Congress. They are most likely to be born in periods of partisan imbalance and to be vulnerable when the partisan climate shifts. Programs that spread their benefits more broadly through the population are sometimes able to avoid this instability of support at the price of being relatively ineffective in providing assistance to those in the most need.

Institutions and Policy Making. Thus far this theory does not differ much in its basic structure from the one put forward by Theodore Lowi some twenty years ago.[7] If policy does not mechanistically *cause* politics as it does for Lowi, certain of its features at least constrain the political cleavages that subsequently emerge. There are two senses in which my view departs from his. First, the concrete structure of policies is partly endogenous to the political process. Second, the shape of a policy is influenced by the institutional context within which it is formed. In Lowi's theory, because politics and policy are so tightly connected, there is no need to consider congressional institutions and practices as independent variables that help explain the development of public programs. If a sufficiently long-range view of public policy were taken, one might regard the institutional structure of Congress as either epiphenomenal or endogenous. But in shorter time perspectives the influence of these institutions cannot be ignored.

Institutions structure the strategic opportunities of congressmen. Although the institutional landscape of Congress is diverse and ever changing, a few important features stand out. Most legislation is considered in committees and subcommittees made up predominantly of those most interested in their jurisdictions. The rules of germaneness and of jurisdiction make intercommittee agreements difficult to arrange except in special circumstances. The informal practices of both chambers still discourage members from involving themselves in legislation considered in other committees. Finally, unless a program is enacted as an entitlement, funding is determined in a separate congressional appropriations process.

Congressional committees differ in a number of characteristics that affect their propensity to produce one or another of the coalitional "solutions" outlined above. They differ in the interests of their members, in their access to chamber rules, in the subject matter of their legislation, in their decision-making styles, and in their traditional methods of accommodation. These differences present those concerned with enacting redistributive legislation with diverse strategic opportunities and lead them to behave in different ways in committee. In particular, these committee differences lead to characteristically different coalitions of support for and opposition to redistributive legislation. Thus, to butcher Lowi's epigram: policy plus institutional structure causes politics.

I shall illustrate these principles with cases selected from redistributive policy areas. The examples were chosen to illuminate the theory, not to provide a balanced view of the role of Congress in the formulation and support of redistributive policy.[8] Not only have I chosen a few, possibly unrepresentative, policies, but I have focused more on the political processes associated with program maintenance and support than on the incubation of policy proposals or on enactment of the original legislation. This choice is based on the belief that the issues associated with program support and extension tend to be routine rather than transient and to be dominated by preexisting agreements and alliances rather than by personalities and conjunctional forces.

The Institutional Framework of Congressional Policy Making on Redistributive Issues

The variety and complexity of American welfare programs are partly rooted in the decentralized structure of Congress. Redistributive programs are formed, extended, modified, and funded in diverse institutional milieux within the two chambers. There are important differ-ences in the committee settings in which such proposals are enacted, and these settings have undergone important transformations. To a great extent, the issues associated with programmatic support are worked out in committees: chamber rules and practices make it diffi-cult to overhaul the coalitional basis of a policy completely. Commit-tee recommendations are sometimes modified and reshaped during floor debate, particularly in the Senate; most of these changes do not fundamentally affect the relation of the program to its supporting coalition but make adjustments in the size of the program, eligibility for its benefits, and the degree of congressional supervision. Thus, to understand why a particular program is the way it is, one must examine the congressional institutions that determine who the players in the associated policy process are and their interests, practices, and competencies.

A number of congressional committees have jurisdiction over redistributive programs. The agriculture committees preside over various nutritional programs aimed at supplementing the diets of low-income persons (food stamps, school lunches, school milk). The labor committees pass on aid to education, certain income assistance pro-grams, public jobs, and manpower training. Housing subsidies are referred to the banking committees. But the redistributive programs with the largest expenditures fall within the jurisdiction of the revenue committees.[9]

It is important to emphasize that political logic underlies the linkage of programs with congressional committees. The fact that Medicare was instituted through the social security system and is therefore overseen by the revenue committees of Congress and that the food stamps program is authorized in omnibus Agriculture Department legislation processed by the agriculture committees can only be accounted for by examining the calculus of proponents and opponents of these programs and of other important political actors when the programs were enacted and at later periods of congressional decision.

Committee Differences. The committees of Congress differ from one another in several ways that affect their comparative abilities to consider and report redistributive legislation. For the present dis-cussion, the most important dimensions of variation appear to be these: the composition of the committee, both the partisan, ideo-logical, economic, and geographic interests represented on it and the goals of its members;[10] deference to committee recommendations by the parent chamber during floor consideration of legislation; and the decision-making style and tradition of the committee. The committees that consider redistributive proposals differ greatly in each of these respects, and these differences are reflected in the legislation they produce and the programs they oversee.

Except in the most prestigious and powerful congressional committees, membership is largely determined by self-selection. A member who wants to be on a committee and is willing to wait patiently for an opening has a good chance of getting on it. The parties sometimes temper self-selection by paying attention to other criteria (such as geographic balance), but for the most part committee composition is determined by members' demands.[11]

Fenno has argued that congressmen are attracted to committees for three general reasons: to serve their constituencies, to help formulate important public policies, and to wield influence in Congress.[12] To a great extent the substantive characteristics of committee jurisdictions sort members according to these differing goals. Among committees with important redistributive programs in their jurisdiction, the agriculture committees are dominated by members with a primary interest in serving their rural constituents, the labor committees attract congressmen interested in the formulation of important public policies in a variety of areas, and the revenue committees appeal to people interested either in policy formation or in wielding influence within their chamber.

Committees also differ in the way that their legislation is received by the parent chamber. This difference is reflected in the degree to which legislation is rewritten on the floor. To be sure, there are important interchamber differences: bills are often more heavily amended in the Senate than in the House; the House has been more willing than the Senate to use its rules to restrict amendments. But not all committees are able to make use of the rules in this fashion: the prereform House Committee on Ways and Means was unusually privileged in this respect; it was able to obtain closed rules for much of its legislation. Recent reforms have reduced the House's proclivity to grant closed rules to Ways and Means legislation, although other committees have become more successful in obtaining special rules that limit floor amendments.[13]

Variations in their composition and in access to chamber rules directly affect the decision-making styles of committees. Since members serve on the agriculture committees primarily to further the interests of their constituencies and since the interests of different constituencies can be advanced more or less independently, the committees tend to use legislative alliances or logrolling to enact omnibus bills containing provisions for a variety of loosely related programs.

The committees have traditionally worked through commodity-oriented subcommittees that proceed independently until a general farm bill is put together. Given that the committees are unrepresentative of their parent chambers, this style of decision making is not likely to produce legislation that has an easy time on the floor; as a consequence, Congress has not generally been willing to protect agriculture bills from amendments.

The labor committees are primarily concerned with legislation that is closely related to the major partisan and ideological cleavages in American politics. For most of the past two decades, the House Education and Labor Committee has been strongly polarized between liberal Democrats and conservative Republicans. On the Senate side, the Republican contingent has tended to be a bit less doctrinaire in its orientation to the programs in the Labor and Human Resources Committee's jurisdiction.[14] In any event, since the subject matter of most of their legislation divides their members, these committees could not adopt the logrolling style of the agriculture committees or the accommodating style of the revenue committees. Instead, the committees have been able to report and obtain enactment of major legislation only when the Democratic majority in Congress has been fairly large and the liberal majority on the committees correspondingly lopsided. Both committees have made extensive use of subject-matter subcommittees to assemble legislative proposals, which are heavily rewritten in the full committees. Because the committees are seldom given restricted rules, their legislation is substantially revised on the floor.

Although the composition of the agriculture and labor committees is largely determined by members' preferences, the membership of the revenue committees is shaped by additional considerations. Members have tended to be moderate or conservative (but, in the aggregate, to be fairly representative of the chamber as a whole) and to be more interested in attaining influence within their chambers than in the content of committee legislation. These conditions have made it possible for the committees to adopt accommodating decision-making styles and to report legislation in which many of the important compromises between ideological or partisan factions have already been made. The House Ways and Means Committee developed a reputation for producing broadly acceptable compromises on difficult and delicate legislative proposals and was accordingly rewarded with restricted rules. The reforms of the early 1970s made the committees somewhat more responsive to the liberal majorities in both chambers, but they also reduced the capacity of the Ways and Means and Finance committees to construct and sustain compromises in difficult legislative areas.[15]

Committee Influence on Redistributive Policy. These brief descriptions of committee differences permit the formulation of several hypotheses about the relationship of congressional institutions and practices to the development of supporting coalitions for public policies. The basic idea is simple: committees differ in their capacities and inclinations to develop coalitions. Part of this difference is due to variation in their formal powers and prerogatives and part to differences in their internal makeup: the composition of the agriculture committees or the labor committees seems to constrain their ability to form broad supporting coalitions that reflect the general distribution of opinion in Congress. The proposition is, then, that coalitions based on broad clienteles are more likely to be developed in the atmosphere of the revenue committees. Policies produced by the agriculture committees are likely to be logrolled arrangements, and policies emerging from the labor committees will tend to be based on partisan-ideological coalitions.

I would expect a redistributive program originated by the pre-1974 revenue committees, for example, to have a broad clientele and not to channel most of its benefits to people with low incomes. Such a policy might be generally popular in Congress because it would distribute benefits in many constituencies. But it would not be particularly effective in influencing the distribution of income. Redistributive policy coming from the agriculture committees would be based on the logrolling arrangements practiced by those committees in their traditional jurisdiction. Redistributive proposals from the labor committees or from the post-1974 revenue committees would tend to be based on partisan systems of support because these committees are unable to develop other kinds of supporting coalitions or (when the partisan environment in Congress is favorable) have no need to appeal for broader support to enact their desired legislation.

Congressional Policy-making Processes and Redistribution

This section briefly reviews some major redistributive programs to illustrate the principles enunciated above. I have chosen programs with supporting coalitions that correspond to the ideal types developed in the first section of this paper: broad clientele, logrolling, and ideological-partisan. Although no redistributive program has adopted any of these strategies in its pure form, most large redistributive programs have tended to rely on one characteristic coalition strategy over the others. And, as argued above, this tendency is rooted in the institutional locus within which the policy was developed and extended.

139

Social Security: The Use of a Program to Benefit a Broad Clientele. The history of social security from its authorization in 1935 to the early 1970s offers a relatively pure case of the establishment of a broad supporting coalition for a redistributive policy. Before 1972, when social security benefits were indexed to the price level, and except for a few legislative episodes in which the scope of the social security system was significantly enlarged, the House Ways and Means Committee generally linked increases in benefit payments to expansions in the coverage of the system or to enlargements of the taxable base. Linkage made it possible to achieve a general and immediate increase in benefits along with a deferred increase in taxes that usually affected a relatively small part of the population.

The practice of linking immediate benefits and deferred tax increases was supported by unrealistically conservative assumptions about the likely evolution of the wage level. Each time Congress considered amendments to the Social Security Act, trusted agency people routinely testified that the retirement fund was running an "unanticipated" surplus. The House committee responded by increasing benefits and—in what was generally termed an attempt to maintain the actuarial soundness of the system—broadening the coverage of the system or increasing the tax base so that projected revenues would be adequate to finance projected benefits (under the actuarial assumptions in use). Typically, the committee proposal was considered under a closed rule in the House so that it was not vulnerable to further modification. The legislation was seldom controversial and usually passed by a wide margin.

The Senate usually went somewhat beyond the House proposal in raising the benefit payments and was also more likely to allow certain groups in the population to be excluded from the system if they wished. These tendencies were even stronger on the Senate floor than in the Finance Committee. In other words, the House committee recommended more benefits for constituents than the executive proposed, and the Senate adopted the same general stance relative to the House. Thus both committees evolved strategies that allowed them to grant favors or make exceptions for clientele groups rather than try to restructure the benefit system as a whole.[16] As in much revenue legislation, the House and Senate bills frequently differed substantially, and many of the important decisions were reserved for a closed conference committee.

Until the early 1970s the policy community for social security was a small, closed "subgovernment." A few people in the agency or with close ties to it, together with Wilbur Mills (Democrat, Arkansas), chairman of Ways and Means, and a few other congressional actors, shaped most of the decisions relating to the program and decided whether and when to embark on major expansions. When these moves occurred (as in 1965 with the addition of Medicare), the political process necessarily expanded to include the president and other interested parties. The participation of these external actors was temporary, however, and after the issue of program expansion was settled, they withdrew from the policy-making process.

To a great extent, this pattern of decision making rested on the ability of Mills and the Ways and Means Committee to control the legislation. It was important that expansionary proposals that might undermine congressional support for the program, however attractive they were in the short term, be resisted in markup sessions and in conference until the necessary support was assembled.

Occasionally proposed alterations generated fundamental ideological debate. In her book on the social security system, Martha Derthick describes the intensely partisan conflicts over proposals to expand the system in 1939 and 1950 (which resulted in major expansions in benefits and coverage), 1956 (introduction of disability benefits), and 1965 (enactment of Medicare and Medicaid). The substantial increases in taxes in 1977, though not associated with expansion of the program, also generated significant partisan conflict.

The social security system evolved so as constantly to expand the fraction of the population eligible for its benefits. This growth of beneficiaries was made possible partly by the agency's strategy of linking increases in benefits with expansion in program coverage and partly by establishing an earmarked fund that could not be employed for other purposes. The strategy was maintained by a small community of trusted experts who could be counted on to furnish technical information in support of regular benefit expansions. This strategy allowed congressmen to make noncontroversial decisions that led, over a period of years, to the development of a large and popular program.

The routine pattern of social security decision making appears to have weakened after the 1972 decision to couple benefits with the price level. Once benefits were indexed, Congress no longer had periodic opportunities to adjust benefits upward on the discovery of an "unanticipated" surplus of trust fund revenues. Indeed, because of rapid price inflation since 1972 and because wages (and therefore trust fund revenues) have not kept up with prices, Congress has been repeatedly required to deal with the disagreeable prospect of deficits in the trust fund.

Financing problems have broken down the subgovernment structure that controlled social security policy during most of its history.

The prospect of chronic deficits in the trust funds has led to the involvement of a variety of actors who would not ordinarily have played a policy-making role. But, to a great extent, this intrusion of outside forces has been filtered through the policy community of acknowledged experts. Indeed, although other interests were represented, some of the leading members of President Reagan's commission on social security financing have been major actors in the area for decades.

Social security is a good example of a clientele-based redistributive policy. By rejecting incomes tests and promulgating the idea that benefits are based on contributions, social security has been used to maintain widespread support for an extremely large and expensive program of income transfer. But if the program is effective politically, it is less successful in redistributing income to those most in need, even among the aged. This is an intrinsic feature of clientele-based redistribution. If proponents of redistribution wish to channel assistance effectively to those most in need, they must resort to other techniques of coalition building. In particular, effective redistributive programs can be based either on logrolling arrangements or, if the makeup of Congress permits it, on shared ideological conviction.

The Food Stamps Program: Logrolling as a Basis for Redistributive Policy. Compacts of mutual interest in support of a redistributive program can be formed in a number of ways. The most common methods are found in programs that provide benefits in kind rather than direct cash transfers. Such programs are common in education, social services, and housing. Each has created a constituency of provider groups, separate from the recipients, that are interested in maintaining the program and increasing its funding. These groups often play a major part in the subsequent congressional history of the program by providing a body of articulate and easily mobilized experts who are attentive to congressional actions in the area.

A second sort of alliance found in redistributive programs arises from the use of categorical grants to fund a program. Categorical funding, which is common in health, community services, and urban programs, induces states and localities to act as lobbyists when funding is threatened. This sort of alliance is more fragile than that between the service providers and recipients since the substitution of block grants for categorical grants may easily disrupt its foundation.

The most fragile sort of logrolling relationship is one based only on shared legislative interests. In this case supporters of two programs that have nothing in common agree to support each other's legislative positions for the purpose of enacting both into law.[17] Perhaps the best-known such arrangement is found in the agriculture committees of Congress.[18] Since the early years of the New Deal, these committees have used the Agriculture Department authorization bill to assemble coalitions for commodity programs that separately could not pass. These coalitions have occasionally been quite unstable and have at times collapsed. Such arrangements are vulnerable because they are executed through openly recorded votes; if opponents of a program are clever enough, they can expose coalition members to difficult and embarrassing choices.[19] Thus we should not be surprised that logrolling arrangements are volatile and subject to collapse.

Despite the fragility of legislative alliances, congressional policy making on food stamps (and in nutrition and agriculture generally) has been based on such an arrangement for the past two decades. Although the food stamps program has been relatively successful in maintaining congressional support, its history offers numerous examples of the difficulties of keeping this sort of arrangement together.[20]

If the social security program offers benefits to a very large fraction of the population, blunting its redistributive potential, the food stamps program is sharply redistributive. It is relatively large, with over 20 million participants in 1981, and extends most of its benefits to people living in poverty. One study of poverty programs estimated that 83 percent of food stamps expenditures in 1974 went to the "pretransfer" poor.[21] Like social security, the food stamps program has grown rapidly over the past fifteen years. Part of its growth has been due to economic downturns, since the program has countercyclical features, but part has been due to elimination of the copayment requirement for obtaining stamps, an action that effectively lowered the price of the stamps to recipients.

The political atmosphere within which food stamps legislation has been considered also differs from the environment of social security policy. Although the food stamps program resembles an entitlement program in most respects, it is authorized for a few years at a time, and the authorization contains a maximum expenditure, or cap, that technically limits the obligations of the federal government. Reauthorization of the program often produces ideological debate about its appropriate boundaries, and floor fights are common in both chambers.[22] Food stamps legislation has generally been accorded little deference in either chamber; it is not uncommon for committee compromises to come apart at later stages of the legislative process.

There are several reasons for this. The food stamps program channels its benefits fairly efficiently to the poor, and, as social security executives were fond of saying, "A program for the poor is a poor program."[23] Second, since the program is effectively redistributive, proposed alterations in it touch ideological nerves in Congress. Third, the program is not regarded as part of the basic jurisdiction of the agriculture committees; other committees are also concerned with providing assistance to the poor. But there is a fourth source of vulnerability: food stamps authorizations are usually tacked onto the omnibus agriculture bill, which also contains the various commodity subsidy programs. The arrangement by which these diverse programs are considered has an essential instability at its core. The logrolling arrangement is no one's preferred outcome, and all parties to it can envision a better deal than is embodied in the omnibus bill. Opponents can exploit this instability by offering amendments in the hope that the compromise will unravel.

While each of these reasons helps to explain the controversial floor reception of food stamps legislation, the last one illustrates a basic problem in forming legislative coalitions. The debates over the 1973 Agriculture and Consumer Protection Act are a useful source of material. The agriculture committees of both houses reported legislation extending the cotton, wheat, and feed grains commodity programs and the authorization of the food stamps program for four years. There were two major issues in House debate on the legislation: a proposal pushed by Republicans and northern Democrats to limit support payments to $20,000 per farmer and a provision making strikers ineligible for food stamps. The payment limit was obnoxious to representatives of cotton-producing regions, and they moved to form a legislative alliance that would support a more favorable bill. The antistriker amendment gave cotton interests their opportunity.

Representatives from cotton-producing districts made an agreement with organized labor in which they would work to defeat the amendment barring food stamps to strikers and labor would support an amendment that deleted all cotton from the bill (which would have the effect of removing the support limit). Representative Bob Bergland (Democrat, Minnesota), who had earlier supported the ceiling on support payments, made the first move: he proposed removal of the cotton section from the bill, arguing that he wanted a bill that reauthorized the wheat and feed grains programs and extended the food stamps program without incurring further animosity from cotton interests. Representative Paul Findley (Republican, Illinois) countered by suggesting that the Senate version of the bill was more favorable to cotton interests and would probably be accepted by House conference members if the Bergland amendment were to pass. In spite of strong opposition from Republicans, the Bergland amendment narrowly passed the House, setting the stage for consideration of strikers' benefits.

144

When the food stamps section of the bill was taken up, William Dickinson (Republican, Alabama) moved to deny benefits to strikers and their families. His amendment passed by a division of 213–203, which fell along conservative coalition lines. Speaking for the committee, Thomas Foley (Democrat, Washington) attempted several parliamentary ploys to remove the Dickinson amendment. First he urged defeat of the package of liberalizing amendments to which the Dickinson amendment was attached, but this failed on another close vote, with many southern Democrats (including many from cotton-growing areas) siding with the Republicans. He then offered a substitute amendment that corresponded to the committee bill except that it deleted those sections referring to cotton and food stamps. Dickinson responded by attaching his amendment to the substitute, which, after a ruling from the chair, was allowed to stand. Again the Dickinson amendment passed, this time by a vote of 208–207.

Thus, after two days of intense maneuvering in the committee of the whole, the agreement between labor and cotton had fallen apart: representatives from cotton districts had failed to deliver the votes on the Dickinson amendment that were vital to organized labor. Labor's response was to be expected. Upon consideration of the bill by the whole House, Silvio Conte (Republican, Massachusetts) moved to reconsider the Bergland amendment, which was labor's part of the compromise, and this time it was rejected on a voice vote. At this point the bill was unfavorable to both organized labor and cotton interests. After a number of skirmishes on other sections, the bill was passed and sent to conference, both parties to the original agreement hoping that the labor-cotton alliance could be reassembled there.

The Senate bill did contain a ceiling on subsidy payments, but it was sufficiently porous to be acceptable to cotton interests. Just as important, the bill did not contain a prohibition on food stamps benefits to strikers. With Chairman W. R. Poage (Democrat, Texas) of the House Agriculture Committee speaking for cotton districts, the conference found it easy to accept the Senate position on both these points and compromises on other provisions of the bill. Senate passage of the compromise was essentially a forgone conclusion, and the only question was whether the cotton-labor coalition would hold together in the House.

When Poage brought the conference report to the House, he took advantage of the House rule that only one amendment is in order during consideration of a conference report (normally a motion to recommit) by immediately moving an amendment urging farmers to increase production. If it passed, the conference report would in effect be considered under a closed rule. Although this move angered the Republicans, they did not have the votes to defeat it, and the Poage amendment carried on a party-line vote, southerners showing strong support for the Democratic position. This example illustrates that explicit logrolling coalitions are difficult to maintain and that the rules of consideration can affect their maintenance. Consideration of the conference report under a restricted rule allowed Poage to reassemble a fragile coalition and maintain it even though it was vulnerable to the Dickinson amendment.[24] Because Agriculture Committee bills, unlike Ways and Means bills, usually cannot obtain such rules, the sorts of arrangements that can be made are restricted, and the conference can assume special importance as a locus of coalition formation.[25]

Partisan-Ideological Support Coalitions. Programs built on a broad clientele or on a logrolling arrangement are inevitably shaped by the political accommodations associated with maintaining a coalition. If, as with social security, the clientele is inclusive, the program will evolve in the direction of having a declining fraction of its benefits go to needy individuals. The cost of transferring income to such groups will tend to be quite high since others will receive a substantial portion of the benefits. Programs built on logrolling arrangements are similarly inefficient in transferring income to the poor since the price of such transfers is support for unrelated and possibly costly programs. Thus, although support coalitions based on either principle offer the prospect of insulation from partisan fluctuations in election returns, they lead to legislation that is distant from the program's original purposes. For this reason, supporters of redistributive proposals often find it attractive to construct programs on the basis of support from liberals (mostly Democrats) whose main objective is redistribution.

Because of their ideological appeal, many redistributive proposals achieve their initial successes in a highly partisan and ideological committee context in which liberal Democratic members can report legislation without much concern for the preferences of Republicans on the committee.[26] When the Democrats control Congress, liberal members of the labor committees find it easy to send redistributive proposals to the floor without much concern for the objections of conservatives or moderates, who often constitute a majority of the chamber. As a result, committee legislation is often heavily rewritten and sometimes blocked during floor consideration.

Partisan and ideological committees tend to achieve floor success in congresses characterized by partisan imbalance. Traditional Democratic proposals to aid elementary and secondary schools did not pass until the Eighty-ninth Congress, and the Republicans did not succeed in obtaining a law restricting labor unions until passage of the Taft-Hartley Act in the conservative Eightieth Congress.

The partisan circumstances surrounding the birth of many redistributive programs is often reflected in the programs' characteristics. Large liberal majorities in certain congresses have been able not only to enact redistributive proposals but sometimes to protect them from periodic congressional review by granting permanent authorization or by establishing them as entitlements. Some redistributive programs have been protected from administrative review as well by placing them outside the cabinet departments, as with the Office of Economic Opportunity, or by limiting the authority of the Office of Management and Budget to review their budgets. Congressionally sanctioned insulation of some redistributive programs partially accounts for their rapid growth in less favorable political circumstances. But when the partisan composition of Congress changes, such programs can run into severe difficulties.

Although many redistributive programs are born in such partisan environments and are built on coalitions almost wholly situated in the liberal wing of the Democratic party, some programs successfully broaden their coalitional bases. The best example is, of course, social security. The original act combined a relatively large public assistance program with a fledgling pension plan, which covered only a small part of the working population and deferred payment of retirement benefits for several years after it was signed into law. The expansion of its clientele surely accounts for much of its successful growth in diverse congressional environments over half a century. Conversely, programs that do not expand their coalitional bases are vulnerable to partisan shifts in the composition of Congress or in the presidency.

A good example of this phenomenon was the attitude of the Nixon administration to the War on Poverty. Several major antipoverty initiatives of the 1960s were housed in the Office of Economic Opportunity. Authorizing legislation for the Head Start program, the Job Corps, the Foster Grandparent program, comprehensive health centers, and a number of other programs was routed through the labor committees of Congress and reflected the liberal dominance of those bodies. Its enactment was due not only to strong Democratic majorities in both houses but also to extraordinary support from President Johnson and his staff. These programs had narrowly focused clienteles; indeed, the appeal of the War on Poverty was the belief that poverty in America could be cheaply eradicated by concentrating remedial assistance on needy groups. As a result, some of these programs were vulnerable to a shift in control of the presidency and were poorly protected by succeeding congresses.

After each of his elections to the presidency, Nixon moved to dismantle the Office of Economic Opportunity by executive order, transferring the popular programs to cabinet departments. The programs' proponents in both the House and the Senate contested a number of Nixon's moves but, lacking a broad coalitional base in Congress, were unable to thwart his initiatives. That the OEO existed for several more years is testimony more to the power of inertia and to the characteristic clumsiness of the Nixon administration than to the support the programs enjoyed in Congress. It should be said that the coalitional basis of the War on Poverty was exceptionally weak by any standard. Not only did individual programs have small numbers of beneficiaries, but several were set up in such a way as to invite hostility from state and local officeholders (who, in a categorical grant structure, would otherwise be natural supporters of federal redistributive programs).

The recent assaults on redistributive legislation by the Reagan administration provide additional evidence of the weakness of partisan or ideological coalitions as supports for redistributive programs. Initial attempts by the administration to scale back spending for income support centered on the use of a reconciliation bill to induce legislative committees to reshape program authorizations. President Reagan hoped to focus redistributive program benefits on the "truly needy" who could not be expected to enter the labor force rather than on poor people who might be capable of working. The administration argued for, and obtained, significant restrictions on eligibility in a number of federally funded transfer programs (such as Aid to Families with Dependent Children, food stamps, and school lunches), a reduction in federal payments in programs jointly financed by the states and the federal government (such as Medicaid), replacement of a number of categorical programs with relatively unrestricted block grants in various areas (such as health services), and the outright abolition of some programs (such as CETA public service jobs). In addition, the administration successfully reasserted the OMB's authority to define the poverty level, which allowed it a degree of control over eligibility for a number of entitlement programs.[27]

The use of reconciliation to force congressional committees to rewrite authorizations may have important implications for policy making in redistributive areas. The reconciliation bill was put together without the customary committee hearings and markups, which would have allowed program beneficiaries to express their opinions and to monitor the votes of individual congressmen on the various provisions of the bill. In the House it was considered under a special rule that limited debate and precluded most amendments: House members were faced with an up-or-down vote on the whole package of reconciliation amendments rather than considering them one at a time. In the Senate the reconciliation package was held together by the extraordinary solidarity of the Republicans; members did not defect from the party's position on a variety of amendments to allow increased spending. Only one Senate Republican voted against the reconciliation bill. In other words, the reconciliation bill was essentially an omnibus bill of budget reductions and, like any omnibus bill, was vulnerable to unraveling through well-chosen amendments. That it held together is testimony to the effectiveness of the restrictive rules in the House and special agreements in the Senate under which it was considered.

The effect of reconciliation on redistributive programs was exceedingly uneven. Because of the great diversity of the programs affected, it is difficult to make general assertions, but a few facts stand out. The eligibility restrictions had a substantial effect on expenditures for AFDC and food stamps, two of the most efficient transfer programs in channeling benefits to poor persons. The major federal pension programs (civil service, railroad, and veterans' pensions and social security), which do not primarily benefit the poor, were not cut deeply. By using estimates of the proportion of program expenditures that went to the pretransfer poor, it was possible to construct a graph of the relationship between this characteristic of the program's clientele and the percentage reductions in fiscal 1982 budget authority made in the reconciliation bill (see figure 5–1). It is clear that programs that spent the largest fractions of their budgets on the poor lost most in the reconciliation process.

It seems that programs with narrow clienteles are less able to withstand budgetary assaults of the sort that occur from time to time in American politics than are more broadly based programs. Efficient redistributive programs, because they do not have a broad coalitional base in Congress, are likely to be vulnerable to conservative shifts in electoral majorities.[28]

Conclusions

The argument of this essay is that the way in which a redistributive program is created and its subsequent treatment in Congress depend partly on the institutional setting within which it is developed. Proposals developed in the relatively bipartisan, consensus-seeking

FIGURE 5-1
RELATIONSHIP BETWEEN FISCAL YEAR 1982 BUDGET CUTS AND
PERCENTAGE OF POOR AMONG 1974 RECIPIENTS

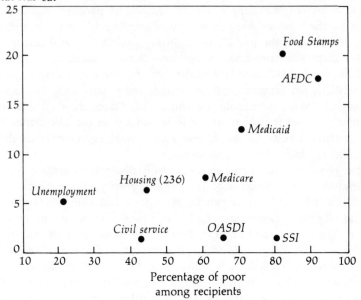

Percentage of poor
among recipients

SOURCES: Congressional Quarterly, *Budgeting for America* (Washington, D.C., 1982); and
Plotnick and Danziger, "Has the War Been Won?"

context of the prereform Ways and Means Committee tend to have
legislative journeys different from those of proposals formulated in
ideological or logrolling environments. This difference is not due to
the power of some committees to get what they want from Congress
independently of the wishes of a majority of members; rather, it
rests on the propensity of committees to produce characteristic kinds
of legislation. The point is simple: redistributive proposals are
endogenously determined within institutional contexts.

Differences in committee development of legislation depend on
the committees' composition, decision-making style, and privileges
and powers in the parent chamber. To a great extent these factors
are interconnected; so it is not likely that one could make clear
empirical separations among them. Moreover, in the long run these
factors themselves are endogenous to the policy-making process.
Nonetheless, purely institutional factors have some independent influence over shorter time spans. Concretely, variations in either the

formal rules of one or both of the chambers (such as the rules associated with the budget process) or in informal conventions (such as allowing much Ways and Means legislation to be considered under closed rules or considering much Senate legislation under informally negotiated unanimous consent agreements) affect the legislative alliances that are formed and therefore the policies produced by Congress.

Furthermore, the way in which a program emerges in Congress has an important effect on its subsequent evolution. Programs that emerge from consensus-building processes characteristic of the revenue committees are not likely to be efficient at achieving redistributive goals. They may be popular and further other valuable, though less ambitious, social purposes. Programs that do not broaden their coalitional bases are likely to display more erratic patterns of development. Yet such programs may be effective in transferring resources to the poorest segments of society.[29]

The distributions of income and wealth in the United States are quite skewed by comparative standards. Some observers have argued that the considerable inequality they evince implies that the American political system is somehow incapable of redistributing resources. In my view, this conclusion is clearly wrong: a great amount of income is transferred among individuals, but the transfers do not always redistribute income between income classes. This does not mean that there are no winners or losers from redistribution. Transfer programs put resources in the hands of the aged and the disabled. But the largest transfer programs are not means tested, and the tax system is not particularly progressive in its overall effects. On balance the overall distributions of income and wealth are not much affected by the mechanisms of redistribution employed in American politics.

The structure of the political system in general and of Congress in particular helps to account for this condition. Because of the constitutional separation of the constituencies of elected officeholders and because of the absence of disciplined parties, coalitions have to be built separately in support of particular policies. These supporting coalitions must be formed in the context of a political institution that divides its workload among committees and subcommittees of specialists. Coalition building is not assisted by the existence of unified political parties organized on class lines: both major parties appeal for support to all important social categories. In this setting the three general methods that could be used to develop supporting coalitions in Congress—building a broad clientele through program benefits, logrolling, and appealing to shared partisan or ideological values—do not offer much possibility of creating stable political support for effective redistributive programs. For short periods, when partisan conditions in Congress are favorable, efficient redistributive programs may evolve; but their ability to endure or grow is inversely related to their effectiveness.

Congress has not transformed the distribution of income or wealth in this country. But it has helped to ameliorate a variety of harms that would otherwise occur in a society with a very uneven distribution of wealth. The price that the constitutional system imposes for such improvements is reflected in the trade-off between the effectiveness of a transfer program in getting benefits to its intended targets and the support for the program within Congress.

Notes

1. Evidence of the congressional propensity to enlarge redistributive programs is found in the rapid and steady growth in federal expenditures on social insurance programs (social security, other federal retirement schemes, and unemployment insurance) and income maintenance programs (Aid to Families with Dependent Children, Supplemental Security Income, food stamps, and other forms of public assistance). Collectively, these programs expanded from 2 percent to 37 percent of the federal budget between 1945 and 1980. In the decade from 1970 to 1980, after the increase in social legislation during the Great Society, the expansion was from 27 percent to 37 percent of the budget. These figures are from John L. Palmer and Isabel V. Sawhill, eds., *The Reagan Experiment* (Washington, D.C.: Urban Institute, 1982). Income security programs have not merely kept up with inflation in the last decade; they have grown very substantially in relation to the rest of the public sector.

Many of the increases in expenditures on redistributive programs are due to more or less autonomous processes. Economic and demographic forces directly affect the demand for expenditures in entitlement and categorical grant programs independently of short-term congressional actions. But Congress has, in effect, assented to systems of finance for these programs that insulate expenditures from the ebb and flow of congressional sentiment. It could withdraw that assent if the basic support for a program were to recede sufficiently.

It is important to note that not all redistributive programs have fared equally well. Some have grown rapidly, and others have withered or disappeared. Programs aimed at providing assistance to the poorest segment of the population have generally not grown as rapidly as programs that transfer income to broader classes of recipients. The number of recipients in some programs has actually declined over the past few years because of tightened eligibility requirements.

2. It is well known in the theory of collective choice that legislative outcomes are inherently unstable in the sense that there is always a coalition that could be formed to defeat any particular proposal. But such

coalitions are difficult to locate and assemble, especially in large legislatures, and so, in real world settings, a variety of institutions have evolved to carry out this task. It is important to realize that these institutions cannot be expected to construct coalitions in a neutral or unbiased fashion. Rather, they will generally tend to build certain characteristic types of coalitions and to ignore other logically possible alternatives. In Congress the primary institution of coalition formation is the committee, although the party leadership and the administration sometimes play a role.

3. Particularly good examples of such regulatory programs are found in the civil rights legislation of the 1960s and in certain programs of the War on Poverty, which sought an eventual redistribution of income by rectifying the distribution of political and legal power in local settings.

4. This notion of redistribution differs somewhat from that offered by Lowi in his seminal article on policy formation. While he classifies programs as redistributive on the basis of their aims, he also asserts that their "categories of impact are much broader [than for regulatory programs], approaching social classes." Lowi seems to be arguing that programs with redistributive purposes tend to have categories of impact that correspond with classical notions of social class. He writes that the categories are the "haves and have-nots, bigness and smallness, bourgeoisie and proletariat. The aim involved is not the use of property but property itself, not equal treatment but equal possession." Theodore J. Lowi, "Distribution, Regulation, Redistribution: The Functions of Government," in Randall Ripley, ed., *Public Policies and Their Politics* (New York: W. W. Norton, 1967), p. 28. In the present framework, there is no necessary connection between the intent of a program and the size or identity of its clientele. Congress can decide to redistribute income to broad categories of its citizens or to narrow ones; it can use as a test of eligibility income or wealth or some other criterion, such as the existence of a disability, age, or the presence of dependents. In other words, the shape of a program is not determined by its classification as redistributive; rather, it is worked out within the political process.

5. The supporters of each of the programs in a logrolling agreement can be expected to try to reduce benefits (or restrict eligibility for benefits) for supporters of the others, though not to the point of making the overall agreement unattractive to their partners. Further, opponents of a program can be expected to try to disrupt the coalition by confronting logrollers with difficult votes in the House or Senate.

6. Because of his increased control over assignments to the Rules Committee and to his capacity to make joint and multiple referrals.

7. But for Lowi redistributive policies divide the classes and cause their organized representatives (organized business and labor) to confront each other in a zero-sum conflict; in turn, this conflict structures the political disputes within the institutional contexts where they occur. Lowi's main example of redistributive policy making is one in which the principal disputes were between the "peak" associations, were resolved within the

executive branch, and were subsequently ratified in Congress. He concludes that the typical locus of decision in redistributive policy making will be between the executive and the peak associations. In my view, rather too much is drawn from a case that occurred during the height of the New Deal when Franklin Roosevelt was at the peak of his popularity and the Democrats had solid control of Congress.

8. Most of the case material is drawn from prereform congresses. Recent changes in the rules or in the composition of committees would be expected to affect the substance of enacted legislation if not the logic of the process.

9. Congress dispenses funds in two general ways: it can enact laws that authorize expenditures for some purpose and then determine the amount to be spent each year through the appropriations process; or it can authorize automatic expenditures on the receipt of a valid claim by some individual (or institution) who can demonstrate entitlement to such funds. Entitlement programs obligate the federal government to appropriate public funds upon application by those eligible and are not subject to the normal appropriations process of Congress.

Although an entitlement program confers a legal right to benefits on eligible individuals, there may still be room for administrative and political discretion. In particular, eligibility for the program and its benefit structure may be determined in a variety of ways. For some programs these issues are addressed by the states or localities; for others executive officials are given the discretion; and sometimes Congress reserves these issues for itself. In all cases, even if other officials have a say in resolving the issues, Congress may decide to override their decisions. Furthermore, entitlement programs differ in the nature of their authorization: some, like social security, have a permanent or open-ended authorization with no ceiling on expenditures; others, such as the food stamps program, are authorized for short periods of time and for limited dollar amounts.

10. Richard Fenno, *Congressmen in Committees* (Boston: Little, Brown, 1973).

11. Kenneth Shepsle, *The Giant Jigsaw Puzzle: Democratic Committee Assignments in the Modern House* (Chicago: University of Chicago Press, 1978).

12. Fenno, *Congressmen in Committees.*

13. See Bruce Oppenheimer, "Policy Implications of Rules Committee Reforms," in Leroy N. Rieselbach, ed., *Legislative Reform: The Policy Impact* (Lexington, Mass.: Lexington Books, 1978).

14. Polarization has increased since the Republicans took control of the Senate in 1981.

15. The withdrawal of the closed rule had a particularly striking legislative consequence during the consideration of President Ford's energy tax bill in 1975. That bill came up under what was termed an "orderly open rule" in the House and attracted over 200 amendments. The bill was completely gutted during floor consideration, partly because Chairman Al

Ullman (Democrat, Oregon) could not even count on committee members to defend the bill against amendments. See Catherine Rudder, "The Policy Impact of Reform of the Committee on Ways and Means," in Rieselbach, *Legislative Reform*.

16. Martha Derthick, *Policymaking for Social Security* (Washington, D.C.: Brookings Institution, 1979).

17. It is well known in the formal theory of legislatures that this sort of logrolling arrangement will generally be vulnerable to amendment. This proposition has been independently established by several authors; the earliest proof was given by Jay Kadane in "On Division of the Question," *Public Choice*, vol. 13 (1972), pp. 47–54.

18. David Mayhew has argued that the traditional Democratic coalition of urban and rural interests was built on a logrolling arrangement organized within the Democratic party. See David R. Mayhew, *Party Loyalty among Congressmen* (Cambridge, Mass.: Harvard University Press, 1966). It seems clear that such arrangements now have to be negotiated separately, issue by issue, and cannot be left to the party leadership.

19. Gordon Tullock makes a useful distinction between "implicit" logrolls, which are based on an omnibus bill composed of a group of independent proposals, and "explicit" logrolls, which are based on coordinated voting strategies on independent bills. See Tullock, "A Simple Algebraic Theory of Logrolling," *American Economic Review*, vol. 60 (1970), pp. 419–26. Of course, unless the legislature considers an omnibus bill under a closed rule, the bill can be disassembled into its components, forcing proponents to engage in explicit arrangements. The capacity of a legislature to make stable logrolling arrangements depends crucially on the availability of rules restricting amendments.

20. I chose to discuss the 1973 bill because the course of its congressional consideration provided particularly striking illustration for the theme of this chapter. But the reader should be assured that the same sorts of issues have arisen each time that Congress has had to reauthorize the program.

21. Sheldon Danziger and Robert Plotnick, "Has the War on Income Poverty Been Won?" (in preparation).

22. I borrow the notion of "boundary" from Derthick's study of social security policy making. Many of the disputes during the reauthorization process have centered on who should be eligible for benefits. Some of these arguments have been motivated by concern over the increasing expenditures for the program during the economic downturn after 1974, but the more divisive issues centered on eligibility of strikers and students for food stamps and on copayment and work requirements. It seems that the stakes here had less to do with costs than with more general arguments about the relative powers of various social groups and the appropriate role of the government in alleviating poverty.

23. Derthick, *Policymaking*, p. 217.

24. This situation is a particularly clear example of cyclical majorities in a legislature. A majority of the House was in favor of the unamended bill

over the bill with both the anticotton and the antilabor provisions, but the antilabor amendment would pass against the unamended bill, and the anticotton amendment would, in turn, pass against a bill with the antilabor provision. There is no position in this case that could be said to represent the "sense of the House." Rather, the outcome of the legislative process will be a function of the particular rules of the chamber under which such cyclical situations occur. In this case, if a closed rule is available, depending on the preferences of the committee leaders, essentially any of the four outcomes could be sustained as that of the legislative process. While clear examples of cyclical majorities are rarely observed during legislative consideration, there are good theoretical reasons for believing that they are rather common in real legislative settings. Chamber rules often mask these phenomena, however, and produce the erroneous impression that there is some outcome that represents the will of the majority.

25. The viability of the 1973 cotton-labor alliance rested on the assumption that the Senate bill would be acceptable to the alliance partners in the House. When in 1981 this assumption failed because of the shift in partisan control of the Senate, the politics of food stamps authorization was bound to change substantially. While congressional consideration was still based on an alliance between the commodity programs and supporters of food stamps, the alliance had to be formed and sustained in the House without the prospect that the Senate would reassemble the pieces of a failed package. The alliance that formed during House consideration of the 1981 legislation centered on dairy price supports and on the overall funding of the food stamps program. After a long and bitter conference, Congress extended the food stamps authorization for only one year in 1981 (while extending the authorization for the commodity programs for four years) and finally included the controversial provision barring strikers from receiving program benefits; the dairymen also had to settle for 73 percent of parity (rather than the 80 percent payments contained in the 1977 authorization).

26. Because membership in most committees is, in the long run, essentially self-selected, programmatically oriented liberal Democrats and conservative Republicans tend to dominate those committees most concerned with social welfare programs. Only where the leadership has systematically intervened to counter self-selection (as in the appropriations and revenue committees) have such tendencies been moderated.

27. In 1969 the Bureau of the Budget adopted a standard data series on poverty for use in determining the poverty line. The OMB's poverty line in 1981 was $8,450 for a family of four and was calculated without regard to the receipt of in-kind payments (such as Medicaid or food stamps). Liberals feared that the Reagan administration intended to alter the basis by counting such benefits as income. When administration supporters included a provision in the House's Gramm-Latta substitute to the reconciliation bill authorizing the administration to define poverty, liberals suspected that this language was intended to provide a basis for including

in-kind transfers. A partisan struggle ensued in which the OMB asserted that it already had the right to define the poverty level (which it had exercised since 1969) and that it did not intend to alter the basis of the calculation. It would simply continue to make inflation adjustments using Census Bureau income data. The Democrats were unsuccessful in removing the provision, but the legislative history will probably circumscribe the administration's authority in the area to some extent.

28. There is also evidence that, more or less independently of the effect of the characteristics of its clientele, the mechanisms of a program's administration affect its vulnerability to budget cuts. Although the data available for such comparisons are scarce, it appears fairly certain that categorical grant-in-aid programs suffered particularly large cuts in the fiscal 1982 budget in relation to entitlement programs. The administration's success in consolidating many such programs into a small number of relatively unrestricted block grants was based on its ability to break down the natural alliance between state and local officeholders and program recipients by offering the states and localities an increase in discretion in return for a budget reduction. The administration's success in this area was spotty: categorical grant programs with strong congressional support were kept separate from the block grants.

29. The effectiveness of programs based on partisan-ideological support in transferring income or services to the poor is based on the fact that they employ means tests. While liberals and conservatives differ over the application of such a criterion for determining eligibility, the existence of such a test implies that recipients at some benefit levels will face a high marginal tax rate on any income-generating activity they engage in. To the extent that punitive tax rates keep recipients out of the economic mainstream, programs with partisan-ideological support may have pernicious effects on their beneficiaries.

6

The Cry-and-Sigh Syndrome: Congress and Trade Policy

Robert Pastor

"The U.S. Congress is not the center of the world," complained Michel Jobert, the French minister of trade, after a tense meeting with trade ministers from eighty-eight nations in November 1982.[1] The meeting was held in Geneva under the auspices of the thirty-five-year-old General Agreement on Tariffs and Trade (GATT), which serves as the forum for negotiating the reduction of trade barriers and adjudicating trade disputes. The U.S. trade representative, William Brock, requested the meeting—the first GATT ministerial in nine years—to stem protectionism abroad and at home. Jobert's expression of annoyance and bewilderment that Congress had become a modern "middle kingdom" came in response to Brock's warning that Congress would begin to protect the U.S. market if our trading partners would not open theirs.

If Congress had indeed become so powerful in trade policy, few would rejoice at such a development. The conventional view of Congress is that its members are so entangled with special interests and so preoccupied with reelection that the institution's vision is necessarily limited, short term, and narrow.[2] In domestic policy Congress's limitations are viewed as bothersome and sometimes scandalous; in foreign policy, where the nation's very security is at stake, the failure of Congress to take a broad and long view puts the nation at risk.

Sitting at the intersection between domestic and foreign policy, waiting for Congress and an accident to happen, is foreign trade policy. Congress has the primary constitutional responsibility for formulating trade policy; yet the choice that trade policy poses—between protecting U.S. jobs and firms against cheap imports and resisting such pressures to defend an abstract general interest in an open international trading system—is one that Congress does not seem well suited to make. If Congress chooses to defend the domestic rather than the international interest, the consequence for the United States is neither as final as war nor as transient as a scandal, but it could be as serious as economic depression. Our nation's present and future prosperity is linked increasingly to an open international trading system.

Those who believe that trade policy is dominated by special-interest groups and that Congress serves its constituents better than it serves the national interest are likely to see a gloomy future for the international trading system. Some economists who have analyzed long-term economic trends, rather than congressional behavior, have reached equally pessimistic conclusions.[3] Editorials and articles in the *New York Times* and the *Washington Post* have warned repeatedly of the threat of "a revival of every-man-for-himself protectionism."[4]

Predictions of the imminent collapse of the international trading system due to congressional irresponsibility are hardly new. In 1955 Speaker of the House Sam Rayburn warned that if the House of Representatives did not accept a closed rule to debate the trade bill, the result could be another Smoot-Hawley, the 1930 act that raised U.S. tariffs to their highest rates in the twentieth century. In 1961 the economist Jacob Viner warned: "In Congress . . . the tide is running in a protectionist direction." A decade later Harald Malmgren and C. Fred Bergsten, two distinguished economists and trade experts, warned about approaching "trade wars" and a genuine "crisis" in the international trading system. Malmgren wrote that "we are seeing a resurgence of mercantilism, whereby governments meet domestic economic demands with conscious policies of manipulation, passing the costs of these policies as much as possible on to other countries."[5] After each of these predictions, Congress surprised itself and the country by passing liberal trade laws, which lowered barriers rather than raised them. The cry of protectionism often precedes a sigh of relief that the open trading system has survived. If everyone is predicting gloom and doom, how are we to explain the cry-and-sigh syndrome?

Even if this cry-and-sigh syndrome applied to past trade policies, will it persist? During the last fifteen years there have been significant changes in the U.S. and the world economy and in the agenda of international trade issues. During this period Congress has altered its mode of doing business. What are the implications of these changes for U.S. trade policy in the 1980s? Can Congress cope with the new complexities of interdependence? Is Congress biased toward mortgaging the long-term interests of the United States for the short-term interests of specific industries or labor unions? These questions are addressed in this chapter.

U.S. Trade Policy

Trade policy has been defined as "the sum total of actions by the state intended to affect the extent, composition, and direction of its imports and exports of goods and services."[6] From 1789 until the completion of the Kennedy Round of multilateral trade negotiations in 1967, the most important trade issue for American legislators, administrators, and negotiators was the tariff: whether and how to raise, lower, or eliminate tariffs on a particular product or group of products. Today trade policy has become almost as complicated as the economy. It still includes the promotion, restriction, and regulation of imports and exports, but as tariffs were lowered to an inconsequential level and world trade grew and became a significant engine of economic growth, trade became intertwined with virtually all economic policies.

Today any government policy that affects the price or the market for a product or a service, conferring either an advantage on a nation's exports or a disadvantage on its imports, is a legitimate issue for international trade. This means, for example, that agricultural price supports, health and safety standards, and a city's procurement policies have become trade issues. Thus the definition above, which was accurate in 1968, needs revision; today trade policies include those state actions that affect trade unintentionally as well as those intended to affect it. Moreover, trade is a tool for development, and therefore a key element in the north-south dialogue, and a strategic weapon, and therefore an important item in east-west relations.

To understand trade policy and Congress's role in making it, one also needs to distinguish among policies and between policies and "signals." To paraphrase an Orwellian quip, all policies may be equal, but some are clearly more equal than others. Some of the confusion about U.S. trade policy and whether it is liberal or protectionist—open or closing—is based on a failure to distinguish between a major trade law and the introduction of a trade bill, between a decision by the International Trade Commission (ITC) and a petition filed there, between an executive order by the president and a comment made by an under secretary of commerce in the course of negotiating with a Japanese delegation.

Trade policy is made in three arenas: in Congress, by law; in the executive branch, by administrative decision, executive order, or agreement; and internationally, by GATT decision or negotiated agreement. Congress plays a key role in all three arenas but obviously plays the most decisive role in the first. The cries of protectionism are often provoked by congressional bills, resolutions, speeches, or hearings, but these are often intended more as signals to the executive branch, foreign governments, or local constituents than as policy; they are not commitments. In 1969 Congress defined a "national commitment" as an act that involves "affirmative action taken by the executive and legislative branches."[7] These acts, which include laws and treaties (and, implicitly, those executive orders and agreements and administrative decisions that are not vetoed by Congress) are discrete policy actions. "Policy" should be considered the sum of these various actions, capped by presidential or cabinet statements that ought to imbue them with a sense of coherence and direction. Therefore, trade laws and agreements are the most important items of trade policy; congressional resolutions, bills, speeches, and hearings are more useful in explaining the process and the politics than the policy.

The Legacy of Smoot-Hawley

Since the passage of the Reciprocal Trade Agreements Act in 1934, U.S. trade policy and the process by which it is made have passed through three periods: (1) bilateral negotiations to reduce tariffs, 1934–1945; (2) multilateral trade negotiations in GATT to reduce tariffs, 1945–1967; and (3) multilateral negotiations to harmonize, reduce, or eliminate nontariff barriers, from 1967 to the present. To understand the evolution of both the policy and the process, however, one needs to begin with the Smoot-Hawley Tariff Act of 1930, which raised U.S. tariffs to their highest rates in the twentieth century, 52.8 percent ad valorem, and, when combined with the world depression, had a devastating effect on world trade.[8]

The Smoot-Hawley Tariff Act of 1930 is to commerce what the Munich agreement of 1938 is to peace. Hailed at the time, both decisions soon betrayed their promises, and they remain indelibly imprinted on the consciousness of the world as historical errors of such magnitude that every generation of leaders has pledged to avoid repeating them. "No more Munichs"—meaning that appeasing an aggressor cannot bring peace—remains today a powerful slogan, even though it was used and discredited as a justification for U.S. involvement in Vietnam. "No more Smoot-Hawleys" certainly does not generate the same emotions, but it remains a gripping symbol among those concerned with U.S. trade policy. Each time protectionist pressures seem irresistible, someone is there to remind others of the consequences of the Smoot-Hawley tariff.

Although Smoot-Hawley constituted the end of an era of high tariff policies and unquestioned congressional obeisance to interest

161

group pressure, the act continues to shape popular perceptions of U.S. trade policy and how it is made.[9] The final bill included specific tariff schedules for more than 20,000 products, almost all of them increases. The Senate passed 1,253 amendments to the House bill, 1,112 on the Senate floor. "I might suggest that we have taxed everything in this bill except gall," Senator Caraway of Arkansas told his colleagues. "Yes," Senator Glass replied, "and a tax on that would bring in a considerable revenue."[10]

Before the final vote in June 1930, the *New York Times* reported that fifty-nine countries had sent formal protests, and 1,028 economists sent President Hoover a telegram urging him to veto it. Hoover ridiculed the cable and signed the bill into law. Within months Canada, France, Mexico, Italy, Spain, Cuba, Australia, and New Zealand raised tariffs. By the end of 1931 twenty-six countries had enacted quantitative restrictions and exchange controls, and by 1932 the United Kingdom abandoned free trade and established the Ottawa system of imperial tariff preferences. Scholars have since concluded that "the world depression and the Hawley-Smoot tariff are inextricably bound up one with the other, the latter being not only the first manifestation of but a principal cause of the deepening and aggravating of the former."[11] From 1929 to 1933 U.S. exports fell from $5.2 billion to $1.7 billion; imports fell from $4.4 billion to $1.5 billion. World trade (the average of exports and imports) fell from $34 billion to $12 billion.

How did Smoot-Hawley happen? The consensus at the time was, and the conventional wisdom remains, that the policy resulted from the political pressure of interest groups whose influence derived more from their contributions to congressional campaigns than from economic need.[12] The public interest was sacrificed to the sum of narrow private interests. Although this explanation is reasonably accurate in explaining the Smoot-Hawley trade policy, it does not help to explain why Congress passed the Collier bill, which reduced many tariffs, two years later or the Reciprocal Trade Agreements Act in 1934.

Although President Hoover started the process on April 16, 1929, by requesting "limited changes in the tariff," Congress dominated the issue. Then, as now, the bill was reported by the House Ways and Means Committee and then went to the House floor, the Senate Finance Committee, the full Senate, a conference committee to iron out the differences, and finally the president for his signature. Each step of the way Congress raised the tariff on individual products —20,000 by the time the bill emerged from conference. The operating procedure was to grant a little protection to almost every business that requested it. Congress did not restrain itself, nor did the president try to curb its excesses. The result, said Senator Robert La Follette of Wisconsin, was the "worst tariff bill in the nation's history."[13]

Bilateralism and Reciprocity, 1934–1945

On June 12, 1934, President Franklin D. Roosevelt signed the Reciprocal Trade Agreements Act, which delegated authority to him for three years to negotiate bilateral, reciprocal trade agreements, which could reduce tariffs by as much as 50 percent of the 1934 rate. The process by which the 1934 trade law was enacted was as different from that of Smoot-Hawley as the policy was. In 1930 the president initiated the process, but Congress took it away from him. In 1934 presidential leadership was decisive from the initial draft to the signing ceremony, but Roosevelt consulted with congressional leaders every step of the way, and the final act reflected congressional concerns almost as much as the president's perspective.

In 1934 the House Ways and Means and the Senate Finance committees did not even debate tariffs on individual products, whereas in 1930 they did little else. Interest groups were hardly evident in 1934, and they would never again exert the kind of influence that they had in 1930. The key debate was between Congress and the president, and although they differed on prerogative and other matters, they found common ground in devising mechanisms to insulate the trade negotiating process from interest groups, though not by ignoring or suppressing them. In 1934, at the request of Congress, the president established an Executive Committee on Reciprocity, which would listen to the concerns of individual interests and groups and convey them to the trade negotiators. This principle of giving industries a say and perhaps also relief from tariff concessions became known as the escape clause and was accepted as an essential element in trade policy by both branches.

The trade act of 1934 was a watershed. For the first time the argument for protection became an argument of exception rather than one of principle. For nearly 150 years, since the birth of the Republic, U.S. trade policy had consisted mainly of tariffs, which went up and down but mostly up, and had been made primarily by Congress. Committees were important, but so too was debate in the two houses. Smoot-Hawley was the last and worst gasp of this policy and process. After 1934 tariffs went in only one direction—down—and Congress shifted its attention from individual tariffs to general trade policy: how much and what kind of authority to delegate to the president, for how long to delegate it, and how to ensure that firms with legitimate grievances would be heard without biasing the entire trade policy.

Although it appeared that the president came to dominate both the policy and the process after 1934, the reality was different. Both president and Congress recognized that the trade issue had changed and new procedures were needed. Before 1934 trade policy was viewed, in Hoover's words, as "solely a domestic question in protection of our own people."[14] Smoot-Hawley taught Congress and the president that trade policy was not like distributing water projects to different states; it was more like foreign policy, in which Congress and the president could legitimately argue about the general outlines, but the details—the specific tariff schedules—had to be left to the negotiators. Moreover, if the pulling and hauling between the branches was to be constructive rather than self-defeating, the two branches would have to strike a tacit understanding: the executive would implement the law in a manner responsive to congressional concerns, and Congress would permit the executive sufficient discretion to negotiate effective agreements.

Congress retained its influence on trade policy by accepting rules that encouraged self-restraint on specific points and by focusing on general issues. Anticipating congressional concerns, the president modified his proposal before sending it to the Hill. Roosevelt and his secretary of state would have liked to begin multilateral negotiations in the 1930s, but they recognized that Congress preferred to start more modestly and therefore recommended bilateral agreements. Similarly, the president requested authority to negotiate reductions item by item, though he clearly preferred to negotiate "linear reductions" across the board. Congress also made a number of changes in the bill, such as requiring the executive to take into account the concerns of injured interests through the Executive Committee on Reciprocity. Although the president had requested permanent negotiating authority, Congress preserved its power by giving him only three years.

The Reciprocal Trade Agreements Act was extended by Congress routinely for three years (by joint resolution) in 1937 and 1940 and for two years in 1943. Between 1934 and 1940 the State Department negotiated twenty-two reciprocal trade agreements; by 1945 the number had risen to twenty-eight. Tariffs fell from an average of 59.1 percent in 1932 to 28.2 percent in 1945; to put it another way, the tariff rates on 64 percent of all dutiable imports were reduced by 44 percent.

Multilateralism and Tariff Reduction, 1945–1967

Almost all the original negotiating authority mandated in the 1934 act "has been used up," President Roosevelt told Congress in 1945; so too had bilateralism. The president requested new authority for three years to reduce tariffs by 50 percent of the 1945 rate. Although Congress was in a resurgent mood, strong leadership by the president and Speaker Sam Rayburn stemmed any deviation from the free trade policy adopted in 1934. Rayburn and Ways and Means Chairman R. L. Doughton led the fight in the House to defeat twelve amendments that would have circumscribed the president's authority to negotiate a reduction of trade barriers, and the trade bill passed 239–153 on May 26, 1945. In the Senate President Truman's leadership led to defeat of the Finance Committee bill; instead, the Senate passed the House bill, 54–21.[15] In November 1946 the United States invited twenty-two countries to the first round of multilateral trade negotiations in Geneva. Within a year the GATT reduced tariffs on more than 45,000 items that accounted for more than one-half of world trade.

Between 1945 and 1962 Congress kept the president on a short leash, giving meager grants of new negotiating authority—the maximum permitted tariff reductions were 20 percent in 1958—for short periods. Still, the State Department participated in five rounds of international trade negotiations. Each renewal proved more difficult because of the success of the previous round. As U.S. tariffs came down, there was less insulation from the chilling winds of international competition, and those industries that either could not adjust or had a high labor-capital ratio, such as textiles, began to request relief. Congress persistently asked the executive to obtain international agreement to the escape clause that permitted relief to injured industries—first through bilateral agreements and then by inserting it in GATT (Article XIX). In addition, Congress formalized and mandated the escape clause in law and gave itself a legislative veto to ensure that the executive would implement the provision.

Since the end of the war, the United States had permitted its allies to take advantage of lower tariffs without requiring them to lower their own barriers. With the establishment of the European Economic Community in 1958 and the recovery of Japan, Congress began hearings, and members introduced resolutions aimed at getting these countries to reduce their trade barriers or, if they proved unresponsive, raising our own. In an article in Foreign Affairs in July 1961, Jacob Viner warned that "in Congress . . . the tide is running in a protectionist direction."[16]

165

Trade negotiating authority was due to expire in 1962, and President Kennedy decided to press for comprehensive legislation that would grant authority to negotiate tariff reductions by 50 percent, phased in over a five-year period and negotiated on an across-the-board, linear method rather than product by product. Congress voted a bill that granted the president sufficient authority to eliminate tariffs as a significant barrier to trade, but in hearings and in committee reports it sent a clear message that the executive would have to negotiate harder with the Europeans.

Concerned that the State Department was more interested in maintaining good relations with our allies than in pursuing U.S. trading interests, Congress removed the responsibility for negotiations from State and created a special trade representative in the White House. Because Congress believed that the executive was ignoring the escape clause, in 1958 it provided for an override of the president's decision by two-thirds vote; in 1962 it revised the law again, permitting an override by majority vote, and it added adjustment assistance provisions. In 1962 Congress also insisted on giving its representatives the status of observers in the U.S. trade delegation. Some have described these actions as protectionist, but Congress used these devices to ensure that the executive would remain responsive to the intent of the law, to petitioning industries, and to Congress itself. It was Congress's way of remaining engaged and making the process work.

On June 30, 1967, the expiration date for U.S. negotiating authority, the United States joined with forty-five other nations in signing the General Agreement of 1967 concluding the Kennedy Round. The tariff cuts were wide and deep. The average cut for all industrial products was about 35 percent, bringing the average duty for the industrialized countries down to about 9 percent. Harald Malmgren wrote that the Kennedy Round constituted "the most successful trade negotiations in history,"[17] and congressional participation contributed to its success. Representative Thomas B. Curtis, a member of the Ways and Means Committee and of the trade delegation, called the new relationship "experimental but successful."[18] After this experience Congress increased the number of congressional representatives in future negotiations, and their influence and involvement increased as well.

Although there was still room to negotiate tariff reductions, particularly because some products had very high tariffs, the conclusion of the sixth round of multilateral trade negotiations—the Kennedy Round—was the end of the second period in U.S. trade policy and the modern liberal world trading system. From 1946 to 1967 the average duties levied on imports to the United States declined gradually but consistently from about 25 percent to about 11 percent. U.S. exports tripled from about $10 billion to about $31 billion, and world trade expanded from about $55 billion to about $235 billion. Future negotiations would give greater emphasis to nontariff barriers.

Multilateralism and Nontariff Barriers since 1967

Three significant changes since 1967 reopened for many professional economists the question whether the United States would maintain a liberal trading policy and impelled many political scientists to ask whether Congress could act constructively in making U.S. trade policy. These changes transformed the agenda of trade policy, the structure of the international political economy, and the way Congress makes policy. I will examine each of these changes, then review U.S. trade policy during the last fifteen years in an effort to assess their likely effect on future policy.

A New Agenda. The success of the Kennedy Round created a new and different set of trade problems for the international community. As one writer graphically put it: "The lowering of tariffs has, in effect, been like draining a swamp. The lower water level has revealed all the snags and stumps of nontariff barriers that still have to be cleared away."[19]

Robert E. Baldwin defines nontariff barriers broadly as "any measure (public or private) that causes internationally traded goods and services, or resources devoted to the production of these goods and services, to be allocated in such a way as to reduce potential real world income."[20] Nontariff barriers include not only measures (such as quotas, export subsidies, and border tax adjustments) whose purpose is to affect the volume and composition of trade directly, but also those regulatory policies—safety, health, or pollution standards, regional development subsidies, and discriminatory procurement—whose purpose and orientation is predominantly domestic (to set standards or assist an industry or region) but that nonetheless have an effect abroad. Like tariffs, nontariff barriers can be used for short-term advantage by a particular government, but only at the risk of retaliation.

Nontariff barriers are the ultimate issue of economic interdependence: not only have they pressed trade issues to the center of foreign economic policy, but they have also broadened the concept of trade policy to the point that it has become virtually identical with all national policies that affect prices and markets. If government

167

intervention in the economy were declining, the removal of nontariff barriers would be easier. But while tariff barriers have been declining, every nation has increased its involvement in the regulation and control of its economy.

The next, and most difficult, stage of international trading negotiations will aim at reducing the advantage that national policies give to domestic goods and services; if this stage were carried to its logical conclusion, nations would negotiate the harmonization of their economic policies. Of course, this would be the end point of policies that have barely been broached. In 1967 the executive decided to start down the road without the authorization of Congress and was blocked. When Congress learned through its observers that U.S. negotiators in Geneva were bargaining on two nontariff-barrier issues—an antidumping code and a revision of the customs valuation system (from the American selling price system)—it sent a signal, through Senate Concurrent Resolution 100, urging the president to instruct his negotiators to bargain only on provisions authorized in the Trade Expansion Act of 1962. The warning was ignored, and when the president sought Congress's agreement on the two codes, it was denied. This incident served somewhat the same purpose for the executive on future negotiations on nontariff barriers as Smoot-Hawley did for Congress on tariffs. During the debate on the Trade Act of 1974, the executive was determined to devise a procedure for ratifying agreements on nontariff barriers that would be acceptable to Congress and would avoid a repetition of the mistake of 1967.

International Political Economy. The Kennedy Round of tariff reductions was implemented in the early 1970s, removing one of the last layers of insulation from cold trade winds. At about the same time, the first energy shock sent a chill throughout the world. To pay for more expensive petroleum imports, the non-oil-exporting countries had to expand their exports dramatically. U.S. dependence on trade, which was quite small—about 4.2 percent of GNP in 1970—doubled during the decade.[21] As trade theory would have it, the decline in the barriers between countries encouraged greater convergence of factor prices within each country: differences in real wages among the industrialized countries narrowed, as did the ratio of capital to labor. There were three important implications for the international political economy of the decline in trade barriers and the convergence of factor prices among the industrialized countries.

First, small changes in costs could henceforth cause large and rapid shifts in trade, with severe unemployment consequences for the losers. Similarly, national policies that affected the costs of production (or the exchange rate for the national currency) could—however unintentionally—rapidly promote exports.

Second, trade in manufactures among industrialized countries became highly differentiated. Using subsidiaries in each country to market specialized products, multinational corporations have proved well suited to this new trade and have accounted for an increased proportion of world trade. Both trade and foreign investment have increased at faster rates than domestic production. The trade and foreign investment issues are now closely related, as illustrated by the local content bills, which are aimed at encouraging successful automobile exporters to invest in the United States.

Finally, for virtually all the industrialized countries, the share of the gross national product devoted to manufacturing, agriculture, and mining declined while the share attributed to services increased. The United States has led this shift, with 65 to 70 percent of its economy now accounted for by services, and it has also led the way in the export of services. One-third of U.S. exports today are services; receipts from services and investment increased fivefold during the last decade to about $100 billion. The exchange of services has increased among all countries, however; it now accounts for about one-quarter of all trade and has been increasing at double the rate of merchandise trade. In 1981 William Brock, the U.S. trade representative, described the "services" issue as "the number one negotiating priority" for the United States because of its importance to the U.S. economy and also because "we don't have any rules governing trade in services in the international marketplace."[22]

Two trends have reshaped the international economy, but there has been a lag in adjusting obligations and responsibilities to reflect these changes, creating tensions in the international trading system. The first is the shift from U.S. predominance in the international economy to a situation in which there are now other poles of international economic power. In 1958 the United States accounted for more than half of total world capital; by 1975 its share had slipped to slightly less than one-third while the Japanese share had increased from 4 percent to 15 percent and West Germany's from 6 percent to 11 percent. The international trading system has still not fully adjusted to this change.

The second international shift is the rapid rise of economic power of the newly industrialized countries, including Brazil, Mexico, the OPEC countries, South Korea, Hong Kong, Taiwan, and Singapore. Between 1970 and 1980 the share of manufacturing imports purchased by the countries of the Organization for Economic Cooperation and Development from the developing countries doubled, from

5 percent to 11 percent. The newly industrialized countries sustained extraordinary rates of export-led growth in the 1970s, some by accumulating dangerously top-heavy debt profiles. The debt burden has become a major impediment to their further growth and also to their feasible graduation in the short term to greater obligations and responsibilities in the international trading system.

One school of thought argues that the liberal international trading system cannot survive a shift from U.S. hegemony to a world of greater pluralism. According to this view, the international economy is adjusting to the structural change in power and moving toward either regional economic blocs or greater protectionism and perhaps closure.[23] This process began in 1971 when the United States abandoned the gold standard. Predictions of the imminent collapse of the international trading system grew in number and forcefulness in the 1970s. Robert Gilpin wrote that the world was moving away from "an interdependent world economy" and "in a mercantilistic direction."[24]

Congressional Changes. Three developments in Congress in the 1970s strengthened particular interest at the expense of the general interest: the dispersion of power in Congress; the increasing abilities of individual congressmen and senators to obtain a platform and press their policies; and greater access by the public to the legislative process.

Starting in the streets of the South with the civil rights movement and culminating in antiwar marches on Washington, the political changes that swept the United States in the 1960s gradually worked their ways into the halls of Congress, changing laws and congressional procedures. In 1970 Congress was largely run by committee chairmen, most of whom were southern and conservative; the seniority system reigned. By 1980 power had flowed downward and outward, to subcommittees and to individual congressmen and senators. In Roger Davidson's words, Congress is now run by "subcommittee government."[25]

This change was accompanied by dramatic enhancement of congressional capabilities—enlargement of staff, legislative support mechanisms, and external resources—in a way that accentuated and reinforced the shift in power. Until the 1946 Legislative Reorganization Act, neither the House Foreign Affairs Committee nor the Senate Foreign Relations Committee had a single professional staff member; the State Department wrote their reports. In the 1950s and 1960s the numbers of personal and committee staff increased; in the 1970s subcommittee staff almost doubled.

Regardless of staff size, the environment on Capitol Hill hardly permits long-term original research. Staff members can digest outside research and package it for legislators. Fortunately, external research capabilities increased even more rapidly than congressional staff. Two of the four central legislative support systems—the Office of Technology Assessment and the Congressional Budget Office—were established in the 1970s. By the end of the decade each had a budget of about $12 million; the OTA had a professional staff of 130 and the CBO of 218 (see table 6–1). During the decade, the budget of the Congressional Research Service grew sixfold, and its staff increased by 169 percent. The General Accounting Office tripled its budget and increased its staff by 15 percent. Since the budget of the International Trade Commission is not reviewed by the OMB, it is more responsive to Congress and can be said to work as much for Congress as for the executive. The ITC staff grew by 65 percent during the decade.

Congress also taps into universities and two major sources of policy-related information: public interest and private lobbying groups. Congress also expanded its access to the informational resources of the executive branch by means of reporting requirements, broadened freedom of information, and extension of the congressional and committee veto.

The decentralization of power and the enhancement of the policy-making capabilities of individual legislators have enabled Congress to formulate alternatives to executive branch proposals and to question the executive's policies. The third set of changes—opening access to Congress—began with the Legislative Reorganization Act of 1970, which permitted committees to allow the televising, broadcasting, and photographing of committee hearings. Subsequent decisions opened markup sessions to public and private lobbyists and to journalists.

The overall effect of these changes has been, in Norman Ornstein's words, to produce "less consistent and more erratic policy outcomes."[26] Others have suggested that legislators are now, more than ever, connected to the short-term whims of their constituents. They use their new powers and capabilities to seek media visibility rather than private influence over policy, credit taking rather than advice giving, and posturing rather than policy making. Davidson shows that Congress holds more meetings but accomplishes less.[27]

The implications of these congressional changes for trade policy are as ominous as one would expect from the shifting structure of the international political economy. The decentralization and individualization of Congress have coincided with a shift in the trade

TABLE 6–1

PERMANENT STAFF AND APPROPRIATED BUDGET IN THE CONGRESSIONAL
SUPPORT AGENCIES WITH PERCENT CHANGE, 1970–1980
(budget in thousands of dollars)

Fiscal Year	Congressional Research Service		General Accounting Office		Office of Technology Assessment		Congressional Budget Office		International Trade Commission	
1970										
Staff	323	—	4,569	—	—	—	—	—	265	—
Budget	4,683	—	68,641	—	—	—	—	—		
1971										
Staff	363	12	4,692	3	—	—	—	—	280	6
Budget	5,653	21	79,991	17	—	—	—	—		
1972										
Staff	438	21	4,768	2	—	—	—	—	285	2
Budget	7,166	27	89,208	12	—	—	—	—		
1973										
Staff	528	21	4,852	2	—	—	—	—	322	13
Budget	9,155	28	98,065	10	—	—	—	—		
1974										
Staff	618	17	5,080	5	—	—	—	—	389	21
Budget	11,662	27	109,450	12	—	—	—	—		
1975										
Staff	703	14	5,230	3	56[a]	—	—	—	408	5
Budget	13,722	18	124,989	14	4,000	—	—	—		
1976										
Staff	778	11	4,894[b]	−6	93	66	193[c]	—	426	4
Budget	17,170	25	141,541	13	6,500	63	5,927	—		
1977										
Staff	809	4	5,144	5	125	34	208	8	395	−7
Budget	20,300	18	150,580	6	6,624	2	8,931	51		
1978										
Staff	813	0.5	5,144	0	130	4	208	0	395	0
Budget	22,991	13	175,980	17	8,204	24	9,935	11		
1979										
Staff	856	8	5,274	3	130	0	218	5	395	0
Budget	26,584	16	185,756	6	10,215	25	11,386	15		

TABLE 6–1 (continued)

Fiscal Year	Congres- sional Research Service		General Accounting Office		Office of Technology Assessment		Congres- sional Budget Office		Inter- national Trade Com- mission	
1980										
Staff	868	1	5,275	0	130	0	218	0	438	11
Budget	28,690	8	209,067	13	11,284	10	12,299	8		
Change over	169		15						65	
entire period	513		205							

NOTE: Figures on appropriations do not necessarily include supplemental appropriations. Figures on size of staff are not necessarily actual staff but may be appropriated staff. All figures are relatively accurate and compare with other studies. Compare John F. Bibby et al., *Vital Statistics on Congress, 1980* (Washington, D.C.: American Enterprise Institute, 1980).

a. 1975 was the first full year of appropriated funds for the OTA.

b. The transportation audit responsibility of the GAO was moved to the GSA during this fiscal year.

c. January 1 through September 30. The CBO began operating on appropriated funds on January 1, 1975; before this it operated on the Senate Contingency Fund.

SOURCES: U.S. Congress, Senate, Committee on Appropriations, *Legislative Branch Appropriations*, various fiscal years. The figures of staff for the International Trade Commission are authorized positions (ITC Staff, Budget Preparation, October 1982).

agenda toward nontariff barriers, which, in effect, relate to all domestic policies. Foreign policy used to be debated only in the foreign affairs committees and trade policy in the Ways and Means and Finance committees. No longer. Nowadays it is more difficult to locate a congressional committee that does not involve itself in trade policy than to identify those that do.

The House Banking, Finance, and Urban Affairs Committee has jurisdiction over the international development banks, over trade, investment, and monetary policy, and over the Export-Import Bank. The Senate Banking, Housing, and Urban Affairs Committee has jurisdiction over U.S. export policy, the Export-Import Bank, the International Economic Emergencies Act, the Trading with the Enemy Act, and foreign investment in the United States, and it shares legislation on international monetary matters with the Senate Foreign Relations and Finance committees. The House Government Operations Committee has oversight of international trade issues; the

House Agriculture Committee has jurisdiction over legislation on international commodity agreements, export controls, and foreign agriculture trade; the House Merchant Marine and Fisheries Committee has jurisdiction over the law of the sea; and in 1982 the House Energy and Commerce Committee reviewed local content legislation to the evident displeasure of the Ways and Means Committee.

The House has a steel caucus, a textile caucus, an auto task force, an export task force, a mushroom caucus, and a North American trade caucus. The Senate duplicates several of the House caucuses and also has a coal caucus, a copper caucus, and an export caucus.

Everyone seems to have got into the act. The Senate Judiciary Committee has considered legislation to require other countries to adopt antitrust laws similar to those of the United States to be eligible to sue American corporations abroad for antitrust-related reasons.[28] This attempt to insist on reciprocity in antitrust is typical of the way that committees with no experience in trade policy are being drawn into issues of nontariff barriers. Canadian discrimination against U.S. truckers impelled the Senate Commerce, Science, and Transportation Committee to threaten Canadian truckers unless Canada accepted precise reciprocity; concern about other governments' procurement policies brought in the Senate Armed Services Committee and the commerce committees of both houses; and Senator Jesse Helms, chairman of the Senate Agriculture, Nutrition, and Forestry Committee, played an active role on the U.S. delegation to the GATT ministerial meeting in November 1982.[29] Bill Bradley, a first-term senator, persuaded forty-five of his colleagues to cosign a letter sent September 10, 1982, to Prime Minister Suzuki of Japan expressing Congress's deep concern about Japan's exchange rate policies and nontariff barriers and implying that Congress might take action if Japan did not change its policies.

As a result of the changes in Congress, cases such as trade policy made by the "domestic" Judiciary Committee and negotiating by a "dear colleagues" letter might be a harbinger of future trends. Power is more widely distributed in Congress today, but this does not necessarily mean that Congress will become more protectionist. To understand the implications of these changes for U.S. trade policy in the 1980s, it is essential to review their effect on trade policy in the 1970s.

Trade Policy in the 1970s

In 1971, after two years as the senior economist on the National Security Council, C. Fred Bergsten wrote: "U.S. trade policy has been moving steadily away from the liberal trade approach which had characterized it since 1934."[30] Bergsten was referring, in part, to a modest trade bill submitted by the Nixon administration in 1969 to extend negotiating authority for four years. After a long and difficult debate, Congress transformed the bill into what Frank Fowlkes of the *National Journal* described as "the most protectionist trade act since the depression of the 1930s."[31] In December 1970, however, Congress adjourned before passing it.

Congress used this trade bill as a signal to the executive branch, the Japanese, and the Tariff Commission. (The commission got the message first and began processing petitions more quickly and with more evenhandedness; that is, it did not deny every petition.[32] Japan also reduced some of its nontariff barriers and subsequently agreed to limit its textile exports.) A 1971 report entitled "The United States in a Changing World Economy," written by Peter Peterson, described the need for the United States and the world to adjust to the decline in the U.S. share of wealth and income and for Japanese and European responsibilities to increase commensurately with their new economic power.

On September 28, 1971, Representative James A. Burke and Senator Vance Hartke introduced the trade and investment bill, which was drafted and supported by the AFL-CIO and targeted multinational corporations and free trade as the cause of unemployment. The bill signaled the desertion of the labor movement from free trade and was to many the most persuasive sign that the trading system was in peril.

On April 10, 1973, President Richard Nixon, already under fire because of Watergate, sent the most complex trade bill in U.S. history to Congress, requesting "unprecedented negotiating authority" for five years to conduct multilateral trade negotiations to harmonize, reduce, or eliminate all tariffs and nontariff barriers and to give special preference in the U.S. market to the exports of the developing countries. Twenty months later, after long debate, despite the prophets of doom and neomercantilism and despite the fall of a president, the Trade Act of 1974 passed intact and liberal. Edwin L. Dale, Jr., of the *New York Times* admitted that, to his own astonishment, "the protectionist forces essentially lost the battle."[33]

The bill was a compromise between congressional and presidential views of the best policy and process to ensure the continued liberalization of the international trading system. Congress argued successfully for more automatic and generous adjustment assistance, more flexible and equitable criteria for import relief, and more participation and power in the negotiating process for itself and the general public. The executive insisted on maximum flexibility to negotiate and administer the law but reached compromises on both. On the key issue of how to obtain congressional approval of future agreements on nontariff barriers, both branches forged an innovative compromise that gave Congress the power to accept the agreement affirmatively but clear deadlines for it to act.

On the path to passage of the Trade Act, the executive negotiated voluntary export restraint agreements on steel and textiles, just as President Kennedy had done before the passage of the Trade Expansion Act of 1962 (and Eisenhower had done in 1955 on textiles). The agreements, however, were not static cartels but placed limits on the growth of imports each year.

One reason why protectionist pressures became so powerful in the late 1960s was the success of the Trade Expansion Act of 1962, which gave the administration freedom to maneuver away from petitioning industries. Between 1962 and 1969 there were fifteen petitions for adjustment assistance, and all were rejected by the Tariff Commission; there was not a single affirmative vote in the twelve escape clause cases brought before the commission during this period. When the administration testified in 1974 before the Senate Finance Committee and asked for even greater presidential discretion, Senator Abraham Ribicoff responded angrily: "What is the use of seeking liberalization of this clause if you have been so reluctant to apply even a stricter clause?"[34]

By tightening the clause, Congress wanted to ensure that injured industries would have a fair opportunity to obtain relief. It is incorrect to equate this with protectionism. Evaluating the work of the Tariff Commission—renamed the International Trade Commission by the Trade Act—a year after passage of the law, Senator Russell Long said:

> I am pleased to observe that you Commissioners have in
> your determinations since the passage of the Trade Act of
> 1974 observed both the letter and spirit of the Trade Act as
> it emerged from the Congress. Sometimes the Commission
> has found that domestic industries were not being hurt and
> in other cases it was found that injury was taking place.
> Each case has been judged on its own merits.[35]

The Trade Act of 1974, like its predecessors, succeeded in channeling the pressure for industry-specific remedies into general principles, which would allow an adjudicatory body, the International Trade Commission, to determine the legitimacy of the complaint. The ultimate decision on relief rested with the president.

When Jimmy Carter came into office in 1977, he found a number of trade complaints—on nonrubber footwear and on color television sets—awaiting his decision. He rejected the ITC recommendations for stringent tariff quotas and instead ordered negotiations for orderly market arrangements with Taiwan and Korea on shoes and with Japan on color television sets to limit the rate of growth of imports from these countries. In addition, Carter instructed department heads to develop a comprehensive program to enhance the efficiency of these industries.[36]

Pressures for protecting the declining steel industry were deflected by an ingenious mechanism called a trigger-price system devised by a task force headed by the under secretary of the Treasury, Anthony Solomon. The trigger price was the world's most efficient cost of production; if the price of steel imports fell below that, the government was immediately required to investigate whether foreign steel producers were dumping.

At a conference at the American Enterprise Institute in 1977, Robert Baldwin, an eminent trade economist, declared that "the [Carter] Administration is facing protectionist pressures from particular industries and labor groups that are stronger than at any time since the early 1930s."[37] He accepted with dismay the theory that détente and its declining power had reduced U.S. interest in trade liberalization. While acknowledging that the Trade Act of 1974 was a forceful reaffirmation of the U.S. interest in freer trade and therefore inconsistent with the theory, Baldwin chose to keep the theory and dismiss the act as "something of an aberration."[38] But, as before, this cry of protectionism underestimated the strength of the forces for freer trade that were already moving toward another international negotiation to open the trading system further.

On May 8, 1977, at the international economic summit in London, President Carter joined with the leaders of the United Kingdom, France, Japan, West Germany, Canada, and Italy to pledge "a new impetus to the Tokyo Round of Multilateral Trade Negotiations." Before undertaking negotiations, Robert Strauss, President Carter's special trade representative, sought to solidify his relationship with the congressional leadership, particularly with Russell Long, chairman of the Senate Finance Committee, and the premier congressional maker of trade policy. Strauss consulted congressmen often but could never obtain much of a commitment. Describing the process in 1978, Strauss said: "It is something like this: They say, Bob, you go out there and do what you think is best, and we will support you unless you make a bad mistake!"[39]

Pressure for protection of steel and textiles continued but was resisted. On November 10, 1978, President Carter pocket-vetoed an amendment that would have excluded textiles from negotiations on tariff reductions. At about the same time the Europeans expressed reluctance to negotiate new agreements on reducing nontariff barriers unless the Carter administration sent an unequivocal signal that it would not back out of such agreements, as it had in 1967. The sign that was requested was an extension of the waiver on countervailing duties, which was due to expire on January 3, 1979. Carter asked Congress to extend the waiver, but it adjourned before completing action. The textile interests then succeeded in tying this issue to Carter's veto of the textile amendment. To continue negotiations, Strauss had to persuade Congress to extend the waiver, but he first had to satisfy U.S. textile producers. He did this by March, and the negotiations moved forward to completion.[40]

On April 12, 1979, after substantial agreement on reducing tariffs and unprecedented agreement on nontariff barriers, trade negotiators representing forty-one countries that accounted for 90 percent of world trade completed the seventh round of multilateral trade negotiations. The United States agreed to cut its tariffs on industrial goods by an average of 31 percent—from 8.2 percent to 5.7 percent—over an eight-year period beginning in 1980. On import-sensitive products, such as textiles and steel, tariff reductions would be deferred until 1982 but would be almost 40 percent. In addition, sectoral arrangements were negotiated on steel, civil aircraft, and agricultural trade; and five new nontariff codes of conduct were negotiated to bring the practices of governments more in harmony on subsidies and countervailing duties, government procurement, products' standards, import licensing, and customs valuation.

Strauss had taken care to consult congressional leaders throughout the negotiations, but it was Congress that devised the novel procedures that ensured successful ratification of the agreement. The Trade Act of 1974, which authorized the Tokyo Round negotiations, precluded legislative amendment of the final agreement and required that Congress accept or reject it within sixty days. The full implications of this unique procedure for the legislative process were not fully understood in 1974 when it was written. Four years later, as the trade agreement was almost completed, the Senate Finance Committee staff devised a procedure that increased the probability of passage of the trade bill in exchange for greater congressional involvement.

By denying Congress the opportunity to amend the executive bill, the Trade Act of 1974 had forced a double role reversal on both branches. The original intent of the Founding Fathers was that Congress would write laws and the president would approve or veto them. Over time the executive's role in this process increased, and after Franklin D. Roosevelt's presidency the roles were almost completely reversed—the president drafting most of the laws and Congress amending, accepting, or rejecting them. As devised by the Senate Finance Committee staff and accepted by that committee, by Ways and Means, and finally by Robert Strauss in July 1978, the two committees would draft legislation in closed "nonmarkup sessions" with executive officials present and the trade agreements as the text. Then a "nonconference" would meet—again in closed session—to reconcile the differences between the two committee bills. The executive would take the congressional bill on advice and then submit a revised version. According to I. M. Destler, the nonmarkups "were essentially a technocratic, staff-managed enterprise, particularly on the Senate side."[41] In other words, Congress drafted a bill, the executive then had the responsibility of final revision and amendment, and then Congress had to accept the bill or veto it.

Trust and mutual responsiveness between the two branches of government have been essential ingredients in keeping U.S. trade policy constructive and liberal since 1934. If the executive fails to negotiate in a way that reflects congressional concerns, one might expect Congress to reduce the executive's negotiating authority and discretion, as it has done on foreign aid.[42] The Trade Agreements Act of 1979 reflected the refinement of an informal and trusting relationship between the branches on trade policy into a formal procedure.

The White House formally submitted the legislation on June 19, 1979. Two days later the House Ways and Means Committee approved it 35–0. Representative Barber B. Conable, Jr., the ranking minority member, said: "The potential opinion-setters who were likely to lead the alarm against the bill have been defanged. The bill has fallen into a benign environment of disinterest."[43] The House passed the bill 395–7 on July 11 and sent it to the Senate, where the Finance Committee approved it unanimously the next day. But the committee decided to delay sending it to the floor until the administration submitted a proposal for reorganizing the executive branch's structure for making trade policy. On July 19 Strauss officially announced the president's intention to do just that, and four days later the Senate passed the trade bill by a vote of 90–4. On July 26, 1979, President Carter signed the Trade Agreements Act of 1979 (P.L. 96-39), calling it "perhaps the most important piece of trade legislation in the history of the United States."[44] The 173-page law had spent a mere five weeks on Capitol Hill; barely eighteen months before, Baldwin had warned that protectionist pressures were the strongest ever.

True to his word, President Carter sent a trade reorganization plan to Congress on September 25. The movement for trade reorganization had been building since 1977, when Senators Roth and Ribicoff introduced a bill to consolidate all the trade functions of the executive branch into one mighty department modeled after MITI, the Japanese trade ministry. The executive branch naturally opposed the idea, as it has virtually all congressionally sponsored reorganization proposals, but the bill picked up support for three reasons. Some senators liked the idea of strengthening Strauss, who had proved much more responsive to their concerns at the expense of the State, Commerce, and Treasury departments. Others wanted to take away Treasury's authority on countervailing duties and dumping because they felt that Treasury was lax in implementing those provisions. Others felt that better coordination on the part of the executive branch was essential to implementing the new codes. These were all legitimate reasons, but President Carter's proposal did not really respond to them. Instead, it called for renaming the special trade representative as the United States trade representative and strengthening it with "international trade policy development, coordination, and negotiating functions" taken from the State Department and elsewhere. The Commerce Department gained Treasury's authority on countervailing duties and dumping and the State Department's commercial attachés.[45] Congress did not reject this partial reorganization, but there were few who were very satisfied with it.

The Tokyo Round was hardly over and not yet implemented when predictions of "the gradual deterioration and ultimate economic collapse of the [international trading] system" could be heard once again.[46] As in previous cycles, the most recent warnings began during a recession. In addition, the United States was burdened in 1981–1982 with an overvalued currency due to high interest rates, the highest unemployment in four decades, and a more open international trading system. Once again, as in the past, the ailing industries were steel and textiles, and this time automobiles were added to the list. Japan, with a $16 billion trade surplus with the United States in 1981 and about $18 billion in 1982, was again seen as the villain.

The Reagan administration, like its predecessor, started off with "conflicting signals" about what its trade policy would be.[47] Like all presidents since Franklin Roosevelt, Reagan publicly took an unequivocal position for freer trade and made decisions—for example, terminating four years of import quotas on shoes—reflecting that commitment. But at the same time his administration was under severe pressure to reduce automobile and steel imports.

Both the House and the Senate had pressed President Carter to negotiate curbs on Japanese automobiles in 1980, but Carter resisted, preferring other methods to assist the automobile industry. By 1981 Reagan could no longer deflect the pressures. U.S. automobile sales plummeted to their lowest level in two decades and declined further in early 1982. The Japanese, who sold 639,000 cars in the United States in 1971, doubled their market share to 12 percent by 1978 and almost doubled it again to 22 percent in 1981. Congress threatened legislation to curb imports, and using that leverage, the administration negotiated a voluntary export restraint agreement in April 1981.[48]

The agreement with Japan neither solved the problems of the automobile industry nor mollified them. Paying the price of high labor costs and poor management decisions, the industry laid off 250,000 workers, and more than double that number were laid off in related industries. The United Auto Workers (UAW) devised a general formula to suit its specific problem, and the idea gained broad support in Congress, even among advocates of free trade. Introduced in December 1981 by Representative Richard Ottinger, the Fair Practices in Automotive Products Act—sometimes referred to as the local content bill—would have required that cars sold in the United States include a large percentage of parts and labor from North America. The more cars a country sold in the United States, the higher the required percentage of local content. By 1985, according to the bill, 90 percent of the parts of Japanese cars would have to be produced in the United States.

U.S. Trade Representative William Brock called the bill "the worst threat to the international trading system and our own prosperity to be put before the Congress in a decade." Hobart Rowen of the *Washington Post* cited studies from the Congressional Budget Office to argue that the bill is "the wrong way to save auto jobs." The CBO study calculated that if other nations were to retaliate, by 1990 there would be a net gain of only 70,000 jobs in the automobile industry and a loss of 220,000 other jobs. A study by the Congressional Research Service estimated that the bill would cause a drop in automobile imports of 810,000 per year by 1985.[49] Support for the bill came from those who believed it would create jobs in the United States, from those who saw it as a way of opening other markets to U.S. goods, and from those who wanted to encourage more Japanese investment in the United States. Ottinger pointed out that thirty-one nations, including Japan, have domestic content requirements for their automobiles. "This bill is a shot across the bow to alert the Administration and foreign countries that there is some concern about the decline of the American auto industry," said Ottinger. "The United States has been a sucker in this trade business and has generously given away free access."[50] With over 200 cosponsors, the bill passed the House of Representatives in the last days of the Ninety-seventh Congress but went no further.

Both Trade Representative Brock and the Japanese responded to the congressional signal. At the GATT ministerial meeting in November 1982, Brock pressed the other members to negotiate the issue of local performance requirements, but only the Japanese took the issue seriously. Brock's deputy, Michael Smith, warned: "We may have been crying wolf once, but we're not crying wolf any longer. Should the [local content] bill become legislation, you'll suddenly see this place [GATT] start hopping with a lot of proposals to get performance requirements back on the agenda." The Japanese also responded to congressional concern by accelerating their automobile investments in the United States. On February 14, 1983, Toyota and General Motors announced an agreement for joint manufacture of a subcompact car in the United States.[51]

The steel industry took a different tack, using provisions of the trade law to seek relief, precisely because it offered less administrative discretion. Also ailing badly from the recession and poor management, the industry in mid-1982 was using less than 50 percent of its operating capacity; 30 percent of its work force (over 100,000 workers) were unemployed. The industry filed a formal petition in January 1982 claiming that nine foreign governments were unfairly subsidizing their steel exports. In August 1982 the Commerce Department found that the governments were subsidizing their steel companies, and on October 15, 1982, the ITC ruled that the industry had suffered "material injury" as a result of the subsidies. As a remedy it prescribed countervailing duties of up to 26 percent. Rather than accept the tariffs, the producers—mainly Europeans— negotiated a three-year agreement to limit their steel exports to the United States.[52]

Much of what Congress does is a reaction to what the executive does or does not do, but the major thrust of congressional concern on trade policy since the Trade Agreements Act of 1979 has not been to close U.S. markets to imports but to open foreign markets to U.S. exports. An example that illustrates both the source of congressional concern and the purpose of its response is the "reciprocity" bill, which aimed to open other countries' markets to an extent that is "substantially equivalent" to the openness of the U.S. market. The bill, whose chief sponsor was Senator John C. Danforth, chairman of the Subcommittee on International Trade, included procedures for retaliation if the foreign governments did not respond. Congress had already given the president sufficient authority to retaliate in the Trade Act of 1974; but the president showed little inclination to use it in twenty-eight cases, and even when the administration petitioned GATT for redress, the cases were delayed indefinitely. Congressional frustration with this lack of responsiveness led to the reciprocity bills.

The arguments against the reciprocity bills are that they are protectionist and that demanding precise reciprocity product by product would be counterproductive. Danforth protested that reciprocity should not be equated with protectionism: "In trade policy, reciprocity means that the U.S. ought to enjoy and actively seek the same degree of commercial opportunity that we routinely accord others." Senator Heinz was more candid in saying that he saw the legislation as "leverage to achieve our open market objectives."[53] Walter Mondale was taken to task by columnist James Reston of the *New York Times* for "striking a more strident and protectionist theme." Actually, in the interview and speech on which Reston's article was based, Mondale said: "Now, I'm not a protectionist, but I'm not a sucker. And I believe our country and its leaders and its negotiators simply must get tougher in negotiations and say something like this: 'From now on, it's going to be fair. If you want to close your markets, then we're going to take steps to make certain our markets are not going to be available to you.' "[54]

There are few leaders in the United States today who do not recognize the importance of freer trade for U.S. prosperity. Although some legislators are willing to risk the free trading system to protect a firm or industry, the major debate on trade in Congress has come to pivot on the tactics necessary to preserve U.S. interests in a freer trading system. In that arena the debate is increasingly between what Raymond Ahearn has called the "economic purists," who believe that threats of retaliation are not helpful to negotiations and could be harmful, and the "political realists," who believe that we are more likely to open up the markets of other nations in negotiations if they believe that the alternative is that we will close our own.[55]

Congress and Trade Policy in the 1980s

Despite significant changes in the trade policy agenda, in the structure of the international political economy, and in the way Congress makes policy, trade policy has remained quite liberal. The politics of U.S. trade policy continues to follow the same pattern that it has followed for the last fifty years—the cry of protectionism, followed by an audible sigh of free trade.

Despite dramatic success in reducing world trade barriers and in expanding world trade, the United States seems to be always on the verge of "another Smoot-Hawley." In the 1960s and before, people feared protectionism; in the 1970s it was called neomercantilism; now it is called the new protectionism.

The debate is sometimes confusing because the warnings of doom appear to be analyses of trade policy based on decisions, but they are really arguments in a continuing debate and signals in a subtle process of national and international negotiation. On the eve of important international negotiations, a cry comes from Congress that the United States is tired of being taken to the cleaners by the Europeans or the Japanese. As Senator Russell Long put it in hearings in 1973: "I am tired of the United States being the 'least favored nation' in a world which is full of discrimination. We can no longer expose our markets while the rest of the world hides behind variable levels, export subsidies, import equalization fees, border taxes, cartels."[56] The message from Long then or from Mondale today is not for protectionism but for reciprocity; the message signals to foreign nations the need for adjustments and gives added leverage to the executive in its negotiations. Mistaking a signal for a policy, economists and others rush to defend free trade and protest politically motivated distortions. Their warnings have proved inaccurate but successful.

While observers remain preoccupied with the question of why Congress always seems the source of protectionist pressures, *the far more interesting and important question is why such pressures have been successfully and consistently resisted during the last fifty years.* There are four reasons. First, and most important, since 1934 the principle of free trade, not the principle of protection, has been the reigning ideology of trade policy in the country and in the world. There is perhaps no other position that would obtain as much support among economists, and there are few, if any, competing approaches that could claim support from experts. A politician would find himself on shaky grounds if he contested such a consensus: none has since Herbert Hoover. The second and third reasons—presidential leadership and congressional restraint—both derive from a shared belief in free trade.

Second, presidential leadership replaced Hoover's passivity. The president is the protector of national rather than specific interests, and free trade and defense are among the most important national interests he defends. On behalf of the national interest and free trade, the president can command a majority in Congress despite the pressures of specific interests or economic stagnation. The executive branch remains the most awesome lobbyist on Capitol Hill. In the Ninety-seventh Congress the executive easily diluted or deleted the three principal threats to freer trade that emerged from Congress:

the "buy American" provision of the jobs and defense bills were deleted; the Danforth reciprocity resolution was diluted to reaffirm the U.S. commitment to the principles of GATT; and the local content legislation first was defanged with a clause that required it to conform to GATT rules and then failed to pass the Senate. One trade bill that came close to passage in the Ninety-seventh Congress was the administration's Caribbean Basin Initiative to reduce—not raise—trade barriers for products exported from that region to the United States. The two trade bills that passed—the Export Trading Company Act and an omnibus law to reduce duties on a number of commodities—will increase trade, not reduce it.

Third, Congress has accepted—indeed welcomed—self-discipline in the final stage of passing trade policy. On major trade bills the House has generally accepted a closed rule on amendments. Many other devices are available to make a congressional point without making it a policy. During the last fifty years the Ways and Means Committee and the Finance Committee have alternated as the more protectionist and restrictive, but they have never adopted that stance concurrently. The purpose, of course, is to press others to be more open, not for Congress to be more protectionist. Because the ideology of free trade is shared, the committee system has been used more to send signals to the executive than to shape policy.

The staff and members have become much more aware and sophisticated over the years; no one seriously questions the importance of trade for the U.S. economy. The legislative support agencies are an additional bulwark for national interests in freer trade. As Robert Russell, the minority staff director of the Senate Banking Committee, said, half seriously and half in jest, "It's hard to get a good protectionist study out of" the Congressional Budget Office, the Congressional Research Service, or any other source of expertise.[57] Studies from these institutions poked holes through the original reciprocity bill and the local content bill; there is little doubt that they would quickly point out the flaws in any protectionist trade bill initiated by Congress.

The decentralization of power in Congress has made it more difficult to pass legislation. As Norman Ornstein put it, Congress is today *"less* able to act."[58] It is easier to introduce new initiatives than to pass them. This works to the advantage of the nation in trade policy, where "domestic" committees and individual legislators are more interested in sending signals than in making policy. The slow congressional process gives U.S. negotiators time to convert congressional leverage into U.S. advantage.

Since Smoot-Hawley, interest groups have organized at the

sector level and have lined up on both sides of the issue, canceling out their influence in all but two kinds of cases. First, when specific interest groups, such as the dairy or footwear industry, have a genuine complaint, they force Congress to address the source of their grievance at a general level, for example, by liberalizing the law on adjustment assistance or by tightening the law on unfair trade practices. Second, between major trade laws Congress and the executive have sought to insulate themselves from the political pressures of injured industries by delegating authority over such decisions to an autonomous agency, the International Trade Commission.

Robert Hormats, who served in senior economic positions in the last four administrations, found a great deal of continuity in the way Congress and the executive make trade policy. "Some [in Congress] want to protect industries," he said. "But the general attitude on the Hill is to strengthen the hand of the executive and to force the executive to get tougher in negotiations."[59]

There is a fourth reason why no major trade bill in the last fifty years has been protectionist: trust and responsiveness on trade policy between Congress and the president. The executive has negotiated hardest on those issues of greatest concern to Congress, and Congress has therefore provided sufficient discretion and negotiating authority to enable the executive to negotiate successfully.

Before concluding that this pattern will characterize the role of Congress in future trade policy, one needs to confront two hard questions about the policy and the process. First, how important is the new protectionism? Is there a danger that the proliferation of export restraint agreements will erode the international trading system to the point of collapse? Second, will the cry-and-sigh syndrome that has characterized U.S. trade policy in the past persist in the future? Will Congress continue to stop at the edge of protectionism, or could it take the United States over the brink?

A 1982 International Monetary Fund study of international trade developments found "the rise in protectionist pressures . . . worrisome," and a statement by the influential British–North American Committee noted ominously "a daunting constellation of circumstances, both long and short term, that challenge" the world trading system.[60] To assess the significance of new restraints on trade, one needs to place them in the broader context of the international trading system and also examine whether they prevent trade or just limit its rate of growth. In an excellent analysis of the current "regime" of international trade, Charles Lipson concludes that it is characterized by "neither openness nor autarchy—[it is] a regime of profound discontinuities."[61] Lipson found that the central norms of liberalizing world trade, reciprocity, multilateralism, and the right to safeguard against import surges are "still intact." But he also found that the norm of nondiscrimination has been "violated with increasing frequency" and that dispute settlement by GATT has not retained its effectiveness or credibility. He found that trade liberalization has continued relentlessly in the most advanced sectors and that these sectors not only contribute most to the growth of the international economy but also account for an increasing proportion of world trade. Those sectors at the rear of international trade—steel, textiles, shoes, automobiles—have succumbed to agreements that restrain trade.

These declining industries reflect national, not just special, interests in their effect on employment, industrial production, and the entire economy. National security questions are raised by the possible phase-out of such industries, but they are also raised by the protection of declining industries from import competition.

An examination of the restraint agreements and of changes in the industries in the last two decades, however, suggests that the agreements have permitted rather than precluded adjustment. Despite two decades of agreements restraining textile exports, the industry has undergone dramatic changes, both within the United States and internationally. The value of textile imports into the United States from 1970 to 1980 increased by 270 percent, from about $1.9 billion to $7.2 billion. U.S. production increased by 1 percent annually and became more efficient, leading to annual reductions in employment of about 2 percent. In a pessimistic analysis of world trade in the 1980s, the British–North American Committee found some grounds for optimism in the "promising" example of adaptation in the textile industry—"Considered doomed fifteen years ago, [the U.S. textile industry] now exports more than it imports."[62]

From 1974 to 1980, despite a number of restraint arrangements, U.S. steel production declined from 132 million tons to 102 million tons, and employment in the steel industry dropped by 18 percent. In other industries restraint arrangements generally limit the rate of growth of imports, thus providing opportunities for adjustment but not for complete protection.

To assess the state of the international trading system, one should examine not only the industries at the rear but also those on the frontier. In the 1970s U.S. exports of services increased by 260 percent, and high-technology exports constituted an increasing share of U.S. exports. International trade has grown almost twice as fast as world production in the last two decades; both stagnated in 1982 not because of protectionism but because of global recession.[63]

187

In brief, the increasing proliferation of agreements to restrain trade is not halting world trade or precluding necessary adjustment.

Restraint agreements are negotiated by the executive branch, not by Congress. Since Smoot-Hawley Congress has passed seventeen laws to reduce trade barriers. It would be as mistaken, however, to conclude that because the restrictive agreements are made by the executive it is more protectionist than Congress as to conclude that Congress is more protectionist because it introduces more protectionist legislation. Both branches are continually prodding each other, and it is impossible to explain U.S. trade policy by focusing on only one branch. Trade policy is the product of the interaction of the two branches.

The international trading system is not in danger of collapse; all nations have a large stake in preventing that. Of course, one could argue in a similar vein that nuclear war is unlikely since all nations have a stake in preventing it. Assuming rough parity in strategic weaponry, that is true, but the key difference is that few defense experts believe that a limited nuclear exchange is possible without rapid escalation where recent history is replete with trade skirmishes that were contained well short of trade war. It is easier to apply the brakes and contain a trade dispute because people expect nations to strike deals on economic issues but not to retreat when their dignity or sovereignty is at issue.

Even though an across-the-board trade war is unlikely, the future is likely to see an increase in trade disputes. Congress will continue to pressure the system. In explaining his support for local content legislation, Senator Ernest Hollings viewed it as "signaling the Japanese on the need for reduced barriers and trade reciprocity. But, much more, I want to signal the President on the need to compete for economic survival."[64] If the U.S. trade representative remains sensitive to such concerns, as the last several have been, the pressure will shift to our trading partners. The issue becomes whether our partners will be sufficiently responsive. It is safe to say that without any pressure Europe and Japan have no real incentive to open their markets since that would jeopardize politically sensitive declining industries and agriculture. Because Europe and Japan have much more to lose than the United States from closed markets, congressional threats may spur them to take politically costly steps.

There are problems that might inhibit international responsiveness and might transform the cry-and-sigh syndrome into a gloom-and-doom scenario. First, it is difficult to lower trade barriers when national economies are stagnant or depressed. Moreover, given the high degree of economic interdependence, even small changes in the exchange rate or in a national policy can have devastating consequences for other countries. In these circumstances, it is understandable why other nations may be reluctant to reduce trade barriers any further or might even want to freeze trade.

Second, several of the most difficult trade problems of concern to the United States—exchange rate problems, local content, services, safeguards, national support for high technology—have only recently been placed on the agenda of international trade; others, such as agriculture, have been so intractable that they have been kept off the agenda until recently. It will take time to define the problems in a way that will permit nations to start negotiating their resolution. For these reasons the future of trade policy may be more precarious than the past; Congress may feel the need to push harder and faster than the system can respond.

Recommendations

Congress and the United States will have to be more patient and not expect instant or complete satisfaction. Moreover, Congress should be responsive to complaints about U.S. trade policies from the Europeans and the Japanese. Special braking devices should also be developed to keep Congress from pushing U.S. trade policy over the brink. The executive needs to communicate regularly with the relevant congressional leaders about the actions it is taking in response to legitimate congressional concerns about the trade practices of other countries.

What one nation considers legitimate—say agricultural price supports or local content requirements—another nation may see as an unfair trade practice. The United States is likely to view Japanese trade concessions as trivial while the Japanese may view them as significant and burdensome. The only way to prevent diverging perceptions from triggering a trade war is for the GATT to play a more active role in national debates as a conveyor of impartial information on government trade practices. The GATT also needs to strengthen its dispute settlement procedures by setting firm deadlines on cases and enforcing its decisions. Nations, especially the United States, should turn more to the GATT to settle disputes, considering retaliation only after the GATT sanctions it.

Congress and the United States need to view trade problems from a broader perspective of U.S. firms failing to adapt to domestic and international competition. Paula Stern, a member of the International Trade Commission, has proposed that when the ITC examines a firm's complaint, it also undertakes a comprehensive analysis—

beyond the international dimension—of the firm's problem and suggest a comprehensive program for revitalization.[65] This proposal is pregnant with implications for current U.S. policies on everything from environmental protection to job safety; it clearly deserves further study.

Increasing attention should be directed at trade restraints to ensure that they permit the growth of imports, that they are related to revitalization programs, and that they are not permanent. Tensions are built into the international trade system. Although these brakes will not avoid the tensions, they could help to keep policy from going over the edge.

In brief, Congress can cope with the increasing complexity of trade issues; indeed, it remains on the cutting edge of U.S. policy, forcing the executive to address the new issues and forcing other governments to adjust their trade policies to the realities of an increasingly pluralistic world economy. The changes in Congress have reinforced its institutional instincts. With enhanced capabilities, legislators can now stay familiar with the rapidly changing issues. Fifteen years ago, when there was one-third the staff, it would have been impossible for congressional staff to draft a bill of 173 pages, as it did in 1978.

Despite the traditional view of Congress as a parochial, con-stituent-bound body, Congress has played a constructive role in breaking down trade barriers and in harmonizing the policies that separate nations. And it will continue to play that role. "Danger invites rescue," Justice Cardozo once wrote, and that is an apt characterization of how the United States makes trade policy. The cry of protectionism, which one hears when Congress turns to trade policy, invites the forces of freer trade to wrestle once again with new and more difficult barriers. When the match is completed and the trade barriers have been surmounted, we will hear once again a sigh of relief. Until the next match.

Notes

1. Cited by Clyde H. Farnsworth, "Fragile Consensus on Trade Reached in Eighty-eight-Nation Talks," *New York Times*, November 29, 1982.

2. For a good survey of this perspective, see David R. Mayhew, *Congress: The Electoral Connection* (New Haven, Conn.: Yale University Press, 1974).

3. C. Michael Aho and Thomas O. Bayard, "The 1980s: Twilight of the Open Trading System?" *The World Economy* (October 1982); and J. Tumlir, "International Economic Order: Can the Trend Be Reversed?" *The World Economy* (March 1982).

4. For a sample, see the following editorials and articles: "One Planet, One Recession," *New York Times*, October 18, 1982; "Playing Games with Protectionism," *New York Times*, November 8, 1982; Hedrick Smith, "In Congress, a Rising Tide of Protectionism," *New York Times*, December 14, 1982; and Stuart Auerbach, "Cry for Trade Protectionism in U.S. at Fever Pitch," *Washington Post*, December 12, 1982. See also, Christopher Madison, "The Protectionist Congress—Is This the Year That the Trade Barriers Go Up?" *National Journal*, January 1, 1983, pp. 18–21.

5. The incident involving Sam Rayburn and the quotations from Jacob Viner, C. Fred Bergsten, and Harald Malmgren are cited in Robert Pastor, *Congress and the Politics of U.S. Foreign Economic Policy* (Berkeley: University of California Press, 1980, paperback edition, 1982), pp. 103, 105, 198 (hereafter cited as Pastor, *Congress*).

6. Benjamin J. Cohen, ed., *American Foreign Economic Policy: Essays and Comments* (New York: Harper and Row, 1968), p. 20.

7. U.S. Congress, Senate, *National Commitments*, Senate Report 91-129, 91st Congress, 1st sessions, April 16, 1969, p. 5.

8. This historical survey borrows heavily from Pastor, *Congress*, chaps. 3–6.

9. Although E. E. Schattschneider's chronicle of the passage of Smoot-Hawley remains a classic text on trade policy, he predicted that the process that led to that act was so entrenched that the United States could not expect any other kind of policy. He was proved wrong even before he completed his book. E. E. Schattschneider, *Politics, Pressures, and the Tariff: A Study of Free Enterprise in Pressure Politics, As Shown in the 1929–30 Revision of the Tariff* (New York: Prentice-Hall, 1935).

10. Cited in "Senate Completes Revision of Tariff after Weary Fight of Six Months, Eighteen Days," *New York Times*, March 23, 1930.

11. Joseph M. Jones, *Tariff Retaliation: Repercussions of the Hawley-Smoot Bill* (Philadelphia: University of Pennsylvania Press, 1934), p. 2.

12. Contemporary critics of the bill called it the Grundy tariff after the senator who brazenly stated that the people who gave money to congressional campaigns had a right to expect compensation in higher tariffs. *New York Times*, March 25, 1930.

13. Cited in the *New York Times*, March 25, 1930.

14. William Staff Meyers and Walter H. Newton, *The Hoover Administration: A Documented Narrative* (New York: Charles Scribner's Sons, 1936), pp. 493–95.

15. Pastor, *Congress*, pp. 93–96.

16. For a description of the negotiations within the executive branch, between Congress and the executive, and between the United States and the other GATT members in the Kennedy Round of trade negotiations (1961–1967) and its aftermath (1967–1971), see Pastor, *Congress*, chap. 4.

17. Harald B. Malmgren, *International Economic Peacekeeping in Phase II* (New York: Quadrangle Books, 1972), p. 16.

18. Thomas B. Curtis and John Robert Vastine, Jr., *The Kennedy Round and the Future of American Trade* (New York: Praeger, 1971).

19. B. A. Jones, *New York Times*, July 10, 1968, quoted in Robert E. Baldwin, *Non-Tariff Distortions of International Trade* (Washington, D.C.: Brookings Institution, 1970), p. 2.

20. Baldwin, *Non-Tariff Distortions*, pp. 2–5.

21. In the postwar period foreign trade has become increasingly important to most countries, although this was not true for the United States until the 1970s. From 1970–1980 U.S. real GNP grew at an average annual rate of 3.2 percent while U.S. real exports of goods and services grew at the rate of 8.6 percent. By 1980 the export share of the U.S. GNP rose from 4.2 percent to 8.2 percent. U.S. payments for about the same quantity of petroleum imports rose from $8.1 billion in 1973 to over $78 billion in 1980. *Twenty-fifth Annual Report of the President of the United States on the Trade Agreements Program, 1980–1981*, p. 20.

22. U.S. Senate, Subcommittee on International Finance and Monetary Policy of the Committee on Banking, Housing, and Urban Affairs, *Foreign Barriers to U.S. Trade: Service Exports*, pt. 1, 97th Congress, 1st session, November 9, 1981. For statistics and statement by Brock, see pp. 2, 4, 7.

23. "Economic regionalism has already become seriously entrenched," in Douglas Evans, *The Politics of Trade: The Evolution of the Superbloc* (London: Macmillan, 1974), p. viii. See also David Calleo and Benjamin Rowland, *America and the World Political Economy* (Bloomington: Indiana University Press, 1973); Ernest Preeg, *Economic Blocs and U.S. Foreign Policy* (Washington, D.C.: National Planning Association, 1974); and Theodore Geiger, "Toward a World of Trade Blocs?" in National Planning Association, *U.S. Foreign Economic Policy for the 1970s: A New Approach to New Realities*, a policy report by an NPA Advisory Committee (Washington, D.C.: NPA, 1971), pp. 67–78. Steven D. Krasner focuses on the question of "closure" in "State Power and the Structure of International Trade," *World Politics*, vol. 27, no. 3 (April 1976), pp. 317–47.

24. Robert Gilpin, *U.S. Power and the Multinational Corporation: The Political Economy of Direct Foreign Investment* (New York: Basic Books, 1975), pp. 261, 268.

25. Roger H. Davidson, "Subcommittee Government: New Channels for Policy Making," in Thomas E. Mann and Norman J. Ornstein, eds., *The New Congress* (Washington, D.C.: American Enterprise Institute, 1981), p. 99.

26. Norman J. Ornstein, "The House and the Senate in a New Congress," in Mann and Ornstein, *The New Congress*, p. 366.

27. Davidson, "Subcommittee Government," p. 116.

28. Interview with Burton Wides, counsel, Senate Judiciary Committee, October 15, 1982.

29. Interview with Ted Kassinger, professional staff member, Subcommittee on International Trade, Senate Finance Committee, October 7, 1982;

and interview with Dr. Robert Russell, minority staff director of the Senate Banking Committee, October 7, 1982.

30. C. Fred Bergsten, "Crisis in U.S. Trade Policy," *Foreign Affairs*, vol. 49 (July 1971), p. 619.

31. Frank V. Fowlkes, "White House May Lose Gamble: Protectionist Bill Is Emerging," *National Journal*, November 21, 1970, p. 2555.

32. In the 1960s virtually every petition for relief or adjustment assistance was either interminably delayed or denied. Petitions were taken more seriously in the early 1970s, but the real change occurred with the Trade Act of 1974. Within a year fourteen industry investigations under the escape clause were completed, as compared with only one such investigation in the preceding twenty months. Injury was found in only two cases, and in only one of these—specialty steel imports—did the president recommend restrictive quotas. Congressional hearings reveal considerable satisfaction by Congress at the rapid response by the Tariff Commission. Although only one of fourteen petitions was granted relief, Congress viewed this as serious and fair. See Pastor, *Congress*, pp. 171–76.

33. *New York Times*, May 23, 1976.

34. U.S. Senate, Committee on Finance, *Hearings on Trade Reform Act of 1973*, H.R. 10710, pt. 1, March 1974, p. 233.

35. U.S. Senate, Committee on Finance, *Hearing: Authorization of Appropriations for the U.S. International Trade Commission*, 94th Congress, 2d session, March 5, 1976, p. 2.

36. *Public Papers of the Presidents of the United States, Jimmy Carter, 1977*, vol. 1, pp. 551–54. For a good analysis of trade policy during the Carter administration, see I. M. Destler, *Making Foreign Economic Policy* (Washington, D.C.: Brookings Institution, 1980), pp. 197–210.

37. Robert E. Baldwin, "Protectionist Pressures in the United States," in Ryan C. Amacher et al., eds., *Challenges to a Liberal International Economic Order* (Washington, D.C.: American Enterprise Institute, 1979), p. 223.

38. Ibid., p. 234.

39. Quoted in I. M. Destler, "Trade Consensus, SALT Stalemate: Congress and Foreign Policy in the 1970s," in Mann and Ornstein, *The New Congress*, p. 335.

40. For a summary of negotiations and results of the Tokyo Round of trade negotiations, see Congressional Quarterly, *Congress and the Nation*, vol. 5, 1977–1980, pp. 270–74. See also I. M. Destler and Thomas R. Graham, "United States Congress and the Tokyo Round," *The World Economy*, vol. 3 (June 1980), pp. 53, 70.

41. Destler, "Trade Consensus," pp. 334–40.

42. For an analysis of congressional policy making on foreign aid, see Pastor, *Congress*, chap. 10, "Congressional Foreign Policy by Amendment, Two Cases: Investment Disputes and Human Rights."

43. Congressional Quarterly, *Congress and the Nation*, vol. 5, p. 272.

44. Cited in U.S. House of Representatives, Committee on Foreign Affairs, *Congress and Foreign Policy, 1979*, p. 127.

45. Destler, *Making Foreign Economic Policy*, p. 209; and Stephen D. Cohen, *The Making of United States International Economic Policy*, 2d ed. (New York: Praeger, 1982), chap. 8.

46. Aho and Bayard, "The 1980s"; and John C. Boland, "Protectionism Rears Its Ugly Head," *Barron's*, September 27, 1982.

47. Clyde Farnsworth, "U.S. White Paper Stresses Free Trade," *New York Times*, July 8, 1981.

48. Gordon T. Lee, "Detroit's Advocates in Congress Want to Stamp Cars with 'Made in America,'" *National Journal*, July 10, 1982. This agreement was extended for another year in February 1983.

49. For Brock's remarks and reference to the CRS study, see ibid., p. 1221. Hobart Rowen, "The Wrong Way to Save Auto Jobs," *Washington Post*, September 2, 1982.

50. For Ottinger's statement, see Lee, "Detroit's Advocates," p. 1221.

51. For Smith's statement, see Clyde H. Farnsworth, "What U.S. Achieved at Trade Conference," *New York Times*, November 30, 1982; see also John Holush, "G.M. and Toyota to Produce Cars in Joint Venture at Plant on Coast," *New York Times*, February 15, 1983.

52. For comparison of import penetration in steel industries, see S. J. Anjaria, Z. Igbal, N. Kirmani, and L. L. Perez, *Developments in International Trade Policy* (Washington, D.C.: International Monetary Fund, 1982), Occasional Paper 16, table 17, p. 88 (hereafter cited as IMF Report). For a description of the agreements on restraining steel exports to the United States, see Federal Reserve Bank of Chicago, *International Letter*, October 22, 1982. See also Clyde Farnsworth, "U.S. Rules against Imports of Steel from Europe," *New York Times*, October 16, 1982; and Christopher Madison, "U.S. Finding of Steel Subsidies May Be First Shot in Trade War with Europe," *National Journal*, June 19, 1982.

53. "Administration Tries to Avert Congress' Protectionist Spree," *Congressional Quarterly Weekly Report*, March 27, 1982, pp. 703–4.

54. James Reston, "Mondale's Tough Line," *New York Times*, October 13, 1982; and Martin Shram, "Big Fritz: Tough Talk and a Flag," *Washington Post*, October 7, 1982.

55. Raymond Ahearn, "Political Determinants of U.S. Trade Policy," *Orbis* (Summer 1982), pp. 418–19.

56. Cited in Pastor, *Congress*, p. 167.

57. Interview with Russell.

58. Ornstein, "House and Senate," p. 367.

59. Interview with Robert Hormats, former assistant secretary of state for economic and business affairs, October 10, 1982.

60. IMF Report, pp. 2, 3; "A Policy Statement by the British–North American Committee," in Sidney Golt, *Trade Issues in the Mid 1980s* (Washington, D.C.: National Planning Association, 1982), p. ix.

61. Charles Lipson, "The Transformation of Trade: The Sources and Effects of Regime Change," *International Organization*, special edition on

international regimes, ed. Stephen D. Krasner, vol. 36, no. 2 (Spring 1982), p. 446.

62. For an analysis of several of the export restraint agreements, see IMF Report, pp. 19–23; and Twenty-fifth Annual Report of the President of the United States on the Trade Agreements Program, 1980–1981, pp. 49–80. "A Policy Statement by the British–North American Committee," p. x.

63. See a summary of research of C. Fred Bergsten in Robert D. Hershey, Jr., "A Perilous Time for World Trade," *New York Times*, August 1, 1982.

64. Quoted in *Washington Post*, Outlook section, December 19, 1982.

65. Paula Stern, U.S. international trade commissioner, "Trade Policy in Perspective," unpublished speech, September 23, 1982. I am grateful to George Eads for pointing out some of the implications of the idea.

7

Tax Policy: Structure and Choice

Catherine E. Rudder

The requirements for making responsible tax policy seem to run counter to open, decentralized legislative procedures, especially when organizing forces, such as strong political parties, that can facilitate cohesion are lacking. As James Madison warned in *Federalist* No. 10, "The apportionment of taxes . . . is an act which seems to require the most exact impartiality; yet, there is perhaps no legislative act in which greater opportunity and temptation are given to a predominant party, to trample on the rules of justice."[1] John Manley found in his study of the House Ways and Means Committee that members repeatedly emphasized the complexity and importance of tax policy and recognized that a unique and controlled process is necessary to protect public interests.[2]

Given the significant national implications and widespread effects of tax policy, the main problem facing Congress in the area of tax policy is how to structure the process so that the resulting legislation is responsible, that is, is equitable and efficient, raises sufficient revenues, and is coordinated with other components of fiscal policy.[3] This chapter compares congressional formulation of tax legislation before and after the reforms of the 1970s and analyzes how the changes have affected the capacity of Congress to produce responsible legislation.

The Mills Era: Restricted Access

From 1958 through 1974 Wilbur Mills (Democrat, Arkansas) chaired the House Committee on Ways and Means. During his long rule as chairman, Mills was recognized as a leader who could move Congress to produce responsible tax legislation.

I am indebted to Joyce Murdoch, John Gist, William Johnstone, and Thomas Mann for their helpful comments on this chapter. Patricia Spellman assisted by typing the manuscript.

The Ways and Means Committee under Mills was congenial and small (twenty-five rather than the present thirty-five members) and was tightly run and controlled by the chairman, whose political and tax expertise was rarely challenged successfully. Mills could put together a coalition in support of a tax measure and hold that coalition together throughout the legislative process. The combination of Mills's political skill and the tools at his disposal produced a remarkable record of legislative success.[4]

One method of control within the committee was the careful recruitment of its Republican and Democratic members. Those selected to serve on Ways and Means tended to be from safe districts, and they could resist political pressure for unpopular decisions more effectively than the average representative. Moreover, each member was chosen with consideration of the composition of the entire committee and of the legislation it would produce. Ways and Means members tended to be party regulars with relatively high scores on party unity. They were reliable legislators, team players who helped build consensus and worked within the agenda and substantive boundaries set by the chairman.[5] Democratic aspirants had to support the oil depletion allowance and, at one time, health insurance for the aged to receive active consideration for a committee slot. To ensure that they were fair to all regions when assigning other House Democrats to committees, the Ways and Means Democrats tended to be geographically representative of the nation. The role of Ways and Means as the committee on committees helped it obtain passage of tax legislation in the House. Its composition also facilitated coordination of the tax policy goals sought by committee Democrats with those of their party's leadership.

Just as the House tightly restricted access to the committee, committee members severely limited access to their deliberations. Most Ways and Means bills were drafted, amended, and passed in executive sessions. Therefore, no member had to take public responsibility for particular provisions. Because there was no public record of deliberations or of their positions, committee members were free to take responsible positions on issues without openly rejecting the demands of lobbyists or openly taking unpopular positions that could be used against them by challengers. It should be noted that members were also free to take irresponsible positions, with little or no accountability, so that closed sessions did not inevitably produce responsible legislation.

A third element of the tight control of tax matters was Mills's ability to set the tax agenda. All tax matters had to go through the Committee on Ways and Means; most tax legislation originated there.

Because of the closed rule under which most tax legislation was considered, members had no opportunity to amend specific provisions on the floor of the House. The only way to change the tax code was through Ways and Means. And in Ways and Means a tax proposal was considered only when Mills wanted to consider it. There was no externally required periodic review of the tax code, nor were there any subcommittees to pursue their own legislative objectives independently of the chairman's.

The agenda was further restricted and tax policy making simplified by regarding the main purpose of tax legislation as raising revenue "equitably."[6] Other aspects of fiscal policy, such as stabilization, were only occasionally considered—for example, the 1964 tax cut and the creation, suspension, and enlargement of the investment tax credit. Furthermore, nontax objectives—provisions to achieve substantive rather than fiscal policy goals—were not typically pursued through the tax code. Although there was a gradual growth in special tax provisions, they were generally justified on the grounds of equity within the prevailing context of the tax system or were isolated tax breaks for certain people or industries.[7] Usually the tax code was restricted to tax matters and was subject to little change over time.

A fourth method of restricting access to tax policy making was control of tax expertise and information. House members who wanted to challenge the work of the committee did not have tax experts to explain proposals and suggest alternatives. The staff of the Joint Committee on Taxation (formerly the Joint Committee on Internal Revenue Taxation), which serves both the Ways and Means Committee and the Senate Finance Committee, was not available to noncommittee members and was answerable primarily to senior committee members, especially Mills. Individual members, on or off the tax committee, did not typically have staff aides to assist on the legislation. Because all tax matters in the House were referred exclusively to the Committee on Ways and Means, Mills—a master of the tax code—controlled the flow of information about tax proposals, their implications, and alternatives.[8]

How Mills Built a Majority Coalition. Mills could not have maintained this tightly controlled system if he had remained totally unresponsive to the wishes of the House.[9] Even in this system of lack of participation or decision making by congressmen outside the committee, some decisions had to be made. As Manley contends, the House could have voted down closed rules and committee bills if it had been dissatisfied with the committee's product or its autonomy.

Instead, Mills enjoyed remarkable success, at least until the 1970s, when, it could be argued, his system of power was dismantled because he was no longer sufficiently responsive.

Mills used several techniques that deflected pressure from his tightly constrained system and allowed him to build majorities. First, he was responsive to demands from those outside his committee. He was generally responsive to presidential requests, although Ways and Means always put its own stamp on tax legislation.

Moreover, he was selectively responsive to interest groups and other outside pressures. When there was sufficient pressure, his committee would respond, as it did with the 1969 Tax Reform Act, which grew out of public outrage that some wealthy persons were paying no federal income taxes. Third, to obtain Ways and Means Committee members' support on committee bills, Mills allowed them to submit special-interest bills. Fourth, his style of legislating within the committee was slow and deliberative and offered all members an opportunity to participate, although not all chose to do so. The final product was based on a painstaking consensus-building process. Finally, the legislation could command support in the House because the committee tended to be representative of the House, and the coalition held together on the floor because under the closed rule the logrolled product could not be dismantled.

Mills produced coherent, well-crafted, and politically palatable legislation because he took care to do so and because he forged instruments that enabled him to do so. A less able chairman might not have been nearly so successful, although it should be noted that Ways and Means floor success preceded Mills's chairmanship. The procedures by themselves did not guarantee a good legislative product and never produced a "pure" one devoid of special privileges, which steamed through the built-in safety valves of members' bills and selective responsiveness. Moreover, the resulting legislation was produced at the expense of individual members' accountability and of meaningful participation by members of the House who were not on the committee. Presumably, because of the composition of the committee, the product was representative of centers of power within the Democratic party both nationally and in the House and, to a lesser degree, accommodated Republican interests. The tax policy process in the House was not very democratic, but it was skillfully controlled.

Other Sources of Responsibility. In developing legislation, Mills had considerable help from Treasury tax staff and the staff of the Joint Committee on Taxation, both of which participated in closed markups of tax legislation and were concerned about the effects of legislation on the equity, efficiency, and integrity of the tax code. Treasury officials, in particular, were concerned about protecting federal revenues and constituted a key center of control and responsibility for tax policy in Congress.[10]

Like closed markups, however, participation of Joint Committee on Taxation or Treasury staff did not necessarily produce responsible legislation. The 1969 Tax Reform Act, landmark legislation that increased the equity of the tax code and eliminated some tax breaks, could not have become law without the help of the Treasury tax staff. Treasury developed the legislation, worked closely with the Ways and Means chief of staff, Lawrence Woodworth, and provided the expertise and convincing arguments in markup sessions.[11] Yet the 1971 Revenue Act, which to some degree reversed the direction of the 1969 tax act and increased neither the equity nor the efficiency of the code, was also developed with the participation of Treasury and joint committee staff in secret sessions during Mills's chairmanship. But committee members who relied on Treasury to provide discipline, as it had in the past, were instead given a green light to include a number of special-interest provisions, such as those for domestic international sales corporations, which deferred tax payments of certain companies engaged in exports. With that signal from Treasury, Ways and Means was blind to the stop sign being waved by the staff of the Joint Committee on Taxation.

Senate Finance Committee. Whereas Ways and Means served fairly consistently, until recent years, as a center of responsibility, the Senate Finance Committee did not. During the Mills era, the Senate committee was much less restrained on tax matters than Ways and Means and saw itself as a court of appeals for those who felt their interests had been damaged or neglected in the House. It was susceptible to special-interest appeals, a susceptibility that continued in the postreform period but was controlled during the Mills era.

The Senate had almost as many instruments of control over tax policy as the House, but they were used substantially less. The Joint Committee on Taxation and Treasury tax staff, closed meetings, and a deft and able committee chairman did not suffice to provide the tools with which to legislate responsibly.

Part of the difference between the Senate and the House can be explained by the different roles of the two bodies and their tax committees. The House's role was to exercise responsibility, the Senate's to be responsive. Even the chairman of the Senate Finance Committee valued responsiveness more than responsibility. In part, the Senate's behavior was symbolic in that it sometimes added provisions to House-passed bills with the tacit understanding that some of them would be moderated or excised in closed conference committee meetings. Senators were thus provided with an excuse for disappointed constituents and lobbyists: Mills said no.

Provisions were added by the Senate not only because of senators' self-image as a court of appeals but also because recruitment to the Finance Committee, its work, and Senate rules were different from the situation in the House. Party unity was less important in recruitment of Senate committee members, and senators serving on the Finance Committee did not typically express concern about the integrity of the tax code until Senator Robert Dole (Republican, Kansas) forced them to do so in 1982.

The behavior of the Finance Committee was affected by the fact that it normally considered major tax legislation that had already passed the House. As a result, less time was spent on tax legislation in Finance than in Ways and Means. There also tended to be less tax expertise among senators than among representatives, although this distinction has faded in recent years. Lack of knowledge led some Finance Committee members to take lobbyists' arguments at face value. It also enhanced the power of Dole's predecessor, Senator Russell Long (Democrat, Louisiana), who headed the committee during much of the Mills era and until 1981, when the Republicans took control of the Senate. One of Long's many famous remarks was, "If the members insist on knowing what's in this bill, we'll never get it passed!"[12] Although Long could have constrained the generous impulses of the Finance Committee and the Senate, he tended to share them, especially when dealing with the oil industry.

Finally, in the Senate as in the House, there were no external controls to force consideration of the effect of special provisions on the overall tax code or to evaluate their efficiency or equity. Not subject to annual or multiannual reviews, as many authorizations and appropriations are, tax policy was changed primarily on the initiative of Ways and Means, and provisions were added or altered unsystematically. The lack of decision making that characterized the House was equally applicable to the Senate.

Congressional Reforms: The Weakening of Ways and Means as a Control Committee

The tax process no longer resembles the stable and predictable process or produces the stable tax policy of the Mills era. The political inclinations of members have not changed, but the harnesses that kept their individualism reined in have been loosened, if not entirely removed. Specifically, the congressional reforms of the 1970s have led to a loss of internal leadership, heightened individualism, increased responsiveness to organized interests, and erosion of the autonomy of

Ways and Means. To the detriment of the House, the Senate, and the nation, Ways and Means no longer functions as a control committee.[13]

Other sources should be consulted for a full recounting of the reforms and changes in Congress.[14] What makes a conclusive assessment of the effects of the reforms so difficult is that a great many changes were going on at the same time. The most important ones affecting the tax policy process were these:

• secret ballot selection of committee chairmen instead of complete reliance on the seniority system
• modification of the closed rule under which Ways and Means bills could be considered on the House floor without amendment
• open committee proceedings, including House-Senate conferences, except when a majority of a committee agrees by roll call vote to close a meeting
• enlargement of the Ways and Means Committee by one-third
• transfer of House Democratic committee assignments from Ways and Means to the Democratic Steering and Policy Committee
• routine assignment of new members and members from unsafe districts to the Ways and Means Committee
• creation of Ways and Means subcommittees

The Positive Side of Reform: Increased Potential for Deliberation. Several of the reforms have strengthened the potential for high-quality deliberation on tax matters and the capacity of the tax committees to handle their enormous workload.

Not only are all revenue matters handled by the tax committees, but 40 percent of all direct spending is also under their jurisdiction. Without subcommittees to oversee social security, trade, health, welfare, and unemployment compensation policy, Ways and Means could not function as well as it has in recent years. Appropriate oversight of the executive branch could not take place without this division of labor. A comparison of the workload of Ways and Means in the Ninety-third Congress (1973–1974) with that in the Ninety-fifth Congress (1977–1978) demonstrates this point, although the workload has since declined as part of a general decline in congressional activity. As table 7–1 shows, the percentage of bills referred to Ways and Means, the number of days spent in hearings and markups, and the number of bills reported to the House were considerably higher in the Ninety-fifth than in the Ninety-third Congress. The existence of subcommittees probably contributed to the increased workload.

The Subcommittee on Select Revenue Measures could weed out questionable requests for small revisions in the tax code and could constrain Ways and Means members if it chose to do so. When Daniel Rostenkowski (Democrat, Illinois) became chairman of that

TABLE 7–1
WORKLOAD OF THE HOUSE COMMITTEE ON WAYS AND MEANS, 1973–1982

	93d Congress (1973–1974)	95th Congress (1977–1978)	97th Congress (1981–1982)
Bills assigned to Ways and Means	3,370	3,922	2,414
Percentage of total House bills	16	22	26
Hearings (days)	102	325	165
Markups (days)	176	332	100
Bills reported to House	45	144	37
Bills passed by House	39	121	33
Bills reported to Senate	34	57	19
Bills passed by Senate	39	69	20
Bills enacted into law	34	49	21

SOURCE: Legislative Record of the House Committee on Ways and Means, 93d, 95th, and 97th congresses.

subcommittee, some of this potential was realized. It became more common, for example, to identify beneficiaries of special-interest provisions.[15]

Other reforms have the potential for improving the quality of deliberation on tax matters. Additional staff and technical information have given rank-and-file members the opportunity to develop tax expertise in a way that would have been much more difficult a decade ago. Some observers have argued, however, that increased staff for members has undermined the role of Treasury and the Joint Committee on Taxation in making tax policy.

The Cost of Reform. Although the reforms were in accord with democratic precepts, the verdict on their effect on the capacity of Congress to do its job has been distinctly negative. Congress is now a place of "buzzing confusion" and "organizational chaos."[16] It is more open and accessible but also more fragmented. Its accessibility is useful only to those who master its complexity. In this "new Congress" it is much "harder for followers to follow and leaders to lead."[17]

The reforms had a devastating effect on Ways and Means. As its autonomy was diminished, the committee was weakened. Without its function of assigning members to committees and the virtually automatic closed rule, Ways and Means had few resources for imposing its will on the House. The committee was opened up, not only by opening its meetings to the press and public but also by enlarging its membership and altering its composition. It now has a larger proportion of members from unsafe districts, who are more responsive to constituency-based interest groups than to the chairman or the ranking minority member. Since many members feel electorally insecure, the absence of committee constraints has had an adverse effect on the entire membership, not only on those who have experienced close elections. With the power of the chairman significantly curtailed, the inclination of members to pursue their own goals rather than those of the committee or their party has been encouraged.

The chairman no longer has the tools to control Ways and Means, which, because of its diverse composition and size, would be difficult to contain even without the other reforms. In trying to develop legislation, the chairman now has little to offer members as inducements to cooperate. In the light of open meetings and roll call votes, members often find it more beneficial to support provisions pushed by interest groups rather than the chairman's position, particularly since Washington lobbyists have learned how to exploit the new environment in Congress.[18] Moreover, the chairman no longer has the luxury of using members' bills to induce cooperation; members have often pushed through their own legislation without the chairman's nod.

The once prevalent understanding of Ways and Means members that they were selected to be "reliable" lawmakers, that is, team players, watchdogs of the federal Treasury, and protectors of their party's interests and the committee's power, has given way to an attitude of each for himself. Without self-discipline or effective leadership, it is difficult for the committee to develop legislation that is not riddled with special-interest provisions and other items that entail revenue losses. When no one has to take responsibility for the final product and no one is attending to the committee's reputation, the result is the disorder of recent years.

Various scholars and observers have questioned the effects of congressional reform on tax legislation. Stanley S. Surrey has concluded that "the consideration of tax legislation by the Congress has completely disintegrated. The picture has been one of almost utter chaos without responsible control residing anywhere."[19] A primary culprit, according to Surrey, is congressional reform, especially the enlargement of the House Committee on Ways and Means and the proliferation of its subcommittees and staff. Thomas J. Reese blames open sessions and other reforms for decreasing the influence of professional centers of expertise, such as the tax staffs of the Treasury Department and the Joint Committee on Taxation, and for increasing the influence of lobbyists on tax policy.[20] Reese goes so far as to suggest that closed conference committees might be more conducive to achieving the tax reform goals that he and others who originally supported congressional democratization advocate.[21]

The 1981 and 1982 Tax Bills:
Case Studies in Legislative Disarray

These assessments seem to be confirmed by the Economic Recovery Tax Act of 1981. Congressional tradition, if not the Constitution, was violated when that bill originated in the Senate, but more important was the absence of any careful review of its provisions or deliberation in the Ways and Means Committee.[22]

Characterized as "an unprecedented bidding war" between House Democrats and the Republican administration to attract floor votes for their two versions of the act, the tax policy process was turned into an auction.[23] Each time the Ways and Means Committee incorporated a new tax privilege into its bill, the administration followed suit. By the time the bill was reported out of the committee, Ways and Means Democrats were bragging that at least thirteen provisions in their bill had been added to the administration's proposal.[24] These costly provisions included elimination of federal estate taxes for all but 0.3 percent of estates, savings incentives worth $5 billion in 1983 alone, reduced taxes for Americans working abroad (the first $95,000 of income earned overseas would be exempt from federal taxes by 1986), a prohibition against Internal Revenue Service regulations to tax fringe benefits, substantially reduced taxes on the oil industry, and authorization of tax-exempt bonds to finance mass transit and volunteer fire departments.[25] Perhaps the most criticized provision allowed companies to sell their unused tax credits to more profitable companies. Businesses buying the benefits could reduce their own tax liability—an ingenious back-door method for the federal government to subsidize both profitable and unprofitable companies and to do so without having to enact legislation through the authorization and appropriations processes.

The administration's original proposal had only two basic elements: a 30 percent across-the-board tax cut (including a reduction from 70 percent to 50 percent of the top rate of taxation on unearned income) and a substantial liberalization of depreciation rules for business (so substantial that some businesses have negative tax rates for purchasing depreciable assets because benefits from the new rules were combined with those from the existing investment tax credit). These two highly stimulative proposals, known respectively as the Kemp-Roth tax cut and the Capital Cost Recovery Act, had been incubating in Congress for several years.[26] Each proposal was very generous to high-income individuals and to business. Each had faced an uphill battle in Congress, especially since the Revenue Act of 1978 had taken some strides in the same direction by cutting taxes to encourage investment.[27]

The Reagan administration's original bill was moderate in comparison with the final version. Called "the Republican substitute," the final administration bill entailed a five-year revenue loss of $732 billion, only $26 billion more than the staggering $706 billion loss that would have resulted from enactment of the final Ways and Means bill. Even the business-supported Tax Foundation called the changes in corporate taxes "astounding" and said they "would have been inconceivable only a few years ago."[28]

It was in reference to the 1981 tax policy process that David Stockman, director of the Office of Management and Budget, remarked that the hogs were feeding at the trough.[29] The process was out of control. The primary interest of participants was in winning, that is, writing a bill that could attract a majority of votes in Congress. Absent were careful deliberation, a sense of limits, an ability to say no to claimants, and an overriding concern for the quality of the bill and for the integrity of the tax code. Even though individual provisions might be justified on various grounds, the process and the total product were irresponsible. Once the spigot was opened, there seemed to be no way to shut it off.

When Ways and Means approved a provision to allow distressed industries to claim $3.3 billion of unused investment tax credits, committee member W. Henson Moore (Republican, Louisiana) remarked, "You guys have come a long way toward being Republicans on taxes, but this goes too . . . far."[30] Although that particular provision was subsequently dropped, Moore's warning was applicable to the entire chaotic process that produced the revenue-draining bill Congress passed in 1981. Within months after the bill's enactment, the Reagan administration was discussing the need for "revenue enhancers," its euphemism for tax increases, and Paul Volcker, chairman of the Federal Reserve Board, was warning that the federal government would have to consider raising taxes if large deficits and their economic consequences were to be avoided.[31]

By early 1982 it was clear that the unprecedented tax cuts of the previous year would necessitate unprecedented tax increases to reduce the soaring deficit. Several factors, in addition to the 1981 tax cut legislation, led the Congressional Budget Office and others to estimate that the fiscal 1982 deficit would approach $180 billion. The recession simultaneously lowered tax collections and raised federal spending for programs such as unemployment compensation. Meanwhile, persistently high interest rates increased spending to service the national debt and pushed deficit estimates still higher.

The deficit projections had a sobering effect on Congress and led to the Tax Equity and Fiscal Responsibility Act of 1982. Given

CATHERINE E. RUDDER

the performance of Congress in 1981, this was a surprising corrective to the tax cut bill. The act will raise an estimated $99 billion over three years in additional revenues. The shape of the legislation enacted can largely be attributed to the leadership of Senator Dole, chairman of the Senate Finance Committee, and his effective use of closed caucuses of Republican committee members and to a strict germaneness rule limiting amendments in the Senate.[32] Dole produced a consensus among Finance Committee Republicans even though six were up for reelection and were vulnerable to heavy pressure from interest groups. His feat was accomplished in part by excluding the press, the public, and even committee Democrats in constructing the tax package. He maintained complete control of the process, as the House declined to produce its own bill and decided to go directly to conference with the Senate.

Rather than risk blame in an election year for enacting a tax increase, House Democrats completely abdicated the House's traditional lead in tax matters. Not only did House conferees fail to take their own bill to conference, they "had not studied the issues or reached a consensus before the conference began."[33] At the same time, however, not having a House bill strengthened the hand of House Ways and Means Chairman Rostenkowski; he and the other House conferees consequently had considerable leeway to negotiate with Senate conferees. On behalf of the House conferees, he acceded to the Senate's position on provisions that some senators had hoped would be softened or eliminated, as is usual in tax conferences. The Senate conferees were thus forced to accept the potent Senate version of a number of provisions.

With a few exceptions the 1982 bill, as well as the process that produced it, was a model of restraint. Provisions that had been unsuccessfully proposed by Treasury for years to increase tax compliance were included in this bill. Withholding on interest and dividends, which had been blocked for years by the skillful lobbying of financial institutions, was included. (The provision was replaced one year later, however, before it was put into effect.) The bulk of the revenue raised in the bill came from increasing compliance, accelerating corporate tax payments, and adjusting some of the provisions in the 1981 bill affecting business. The minimum tax, which is meant to ensure that wealthy individuals pay some income tax, was tripled. Yet the individual tax cuts of 1981 were maintained, an achievement that averted a presidential veto.[34]

The tax bills of 1981 and 1982 give credence to the assessment that the congressional reforms failed. The decentralization and democratization of Congress, and of the House in particular, seem to have left the legislative branch in a state of semianarchy and capable of acting responsibly on taxes only by circumvention of normal procedures, such as reverting to secret sessions, and only in response to a severe economic crisis.

It is true that 1981 and 1982 were somewhat unusual in that the Republicans controlled the Senate and White House while the Democrats had a nominal majority in the House (which evaporated when southern Democrats voted with House Republicans). This divided government can account to some degree for the tax outcomes of 1981 and 1982. The difficulties experienced in 1981 and the extraordinary means necessary to enact the 1982 tax increase suggest, however, that the tax process is malfunctioning. Have the democratic reforms failed in the tax area, where enormous pressures bear upon members even when the process is tightly controlled?

The erosion of the tax policy process in Congress has been spurred by three related developments: ad hoc decision making, bypassing of normal legislative channels, and increased use of the tax system for nontax purposes.

Ad Hoc Decision Making

Members of Congress want to be helpful, Stanley Surrey once pointed out in explaining why special tax privileges get enacted.[35] That posture has grown as members increasingly see themselves as ombudsmen. In addition, because many members are worried about the next election and cannot rely on a stable base of electoral support, they are less able to take a long-range view and less willing to disappoint claimants on the federal treasury. Congressional reforms have stripped away the protections that permitted responsible tax policy making. The problem is exacerbated by the fact that another control mechanism, the political party system, is also in disarray, even though during the first year of Ronald Reagan's presidency the Republicans were temporarily unified on tax issues.

When parties are fragmented, there is little basis on which to form governing coalitions. The lack of a philosophical-political-historical context makes members susceptible to taking arguments for tax provisions at face value, without considering them in any larger context. In such an environment, lobbyists can be successful if they gain access to members, demonstrate a connection with members' political interests, and show that the proposal is virtually identical with a provision already in the tax code, will remove an impediment to free enterprise, or will encourage a desired activity, such as replanting trees.

The repeal in 1980 of a 1976 tax reform, the carry-over basis provisions, is a good example of the ad hoc decision making increasingly characteristic of the tax policy process. Before 1976, heirs could avoid paying taxes on the amount an asset has appreciated between the time it was purchased and the death of the buyer. If the owner had sold the asset before he died, he would have had to pay a capital gains tax on the amount by which its value had increased between the purchase date and the selling date. Congress agreed in 1976 to eliminate the discrepancy between the tax treatment of assets sold before death and those held until death. Under the new law the original basis of appreciated assets would carry over to heirs.

For example, an investor bought stock worth $1,000 in 1950, he died in 1970 when the stock was valued at $10,000, and his heir sold the stock in 1980 for $20,000. Under the old provision the heir would owe a capital gains tax on a gain of $10,000, the amount the stock had appreciated since the original investor's death. Under the new provision the heir would pay capital gains on an appreciation of $19,000, the amount the stock had increased in value since it was originally purchased in 1950.

To ease the burden of this change, Congress increased the size of estates that would be exempt from taxation. Thus estate taxes were lowered in exchange for raising the capital gains tax on inherited property to that paid on other property. The effective date of the carry-over basis provision in the bill was to be 1978, to allow for estate tax planning.

Opponents subsequently postponed the effective date until 1981 and then killed the provision outright in a Senate rider attached to a windfall profits tax bill. The second half of the 1976 compromise, the expanded estate tax provision, remained in the tax code even though the original justification for it had been abandoned.

Those who worked to repeal the 1976 rule counted on the fact that few members knew or cared that estate taxes had been lowered in exchange for the carry-over basis provision. They also pointed out the disparities in the treatment of estates during the transition period —disparities created primarily by postponements sought by the opponents themselves—and the impossibility of calculating the original value of assets purchased years earlier.[36]

Although these arguments alone did not bring about repeal of the 1976 provision, without them the heavy lobbying for repeal could not have been nearly so effective. Members were susceptible to these arguments because the arguments seemed reasonable when taken at face value and out of context. Larger issues faded under the weight of arguments that seemed perfectly legitimate. If either political party had supported the 1976 provision because of some overall philosophy about taxes and if members of that party had been able to count on support from a stable coalition of party voters in their districts, the outcome of the repeal effort (17 to 0 for repeal in the Senate Finance Committee) might not have been nearly so one-sided. Furthermore, if either party had had a general tax policy, voters could have held members responsible for tax legislation on the basis of party affiliation— without having to follow every action of their representative or having to understand the ramifications of complex provisions, such as carry-over basis.[37]

Bypassing Legislative Procedures

The absence of a tax philosophy offers a fertile opportunity for manipulation of the tax code. What passes for deliberation and reasonable argument resembles on closer inspection discordant, random policy making. This haphazard process is furthered by the increasing tendency to bypass the committee stage altogether. The Ways and Means Committee has lost considerable control over its subject matter as amendments affecting the tax code have been added on the floor, and the Senate has added tax provisions to House-passed bills with increasing impunity. Much more frequently than in the past, Ways and Means is bypassed altogether in significant tax matters. Repeal of the carry-over basis, for example, circumvented the Committee on Ways and Means, although the House did have a separate vote on it and overwhelmingly instructed its conferees to support repeal.

One way House members can alter provisions or interpretations of the code without going through the Ways and Means Committee is to offer floor amendments to appropriations bills. Under House rules legislation is not supposed to be included in appropriations, but when amendments are written in the form of limitations, they often are not ruled out of order. The House amended the fiscal 1981 Treasury-Postal appropriations bill, for example, to prohibit the IRS from using funds to study withholding taxes on interest or dividend income, to implement certain vesting rules under the Employment Retirement Income Security Act of 1974, to charge penalties for underpayment of taxes due to erroneous written advice given to the taxpayer by IRS, or to evaluate the tax-exempt status of private schools.[38] All these amendments fell within the substantive jurisdiction of the Ways and Means Committee, but none had received committee scrutiny. No hearings or committee markups were held, and thus no adequate legislative history was developed to shape and justify these restrictions. The deliberative function of the legislature was truncated to the detriment of coherent, carefully considered tax policy.

In floor debate on the vesting amendment, high-ranking Appropriations member Tom Steed (Democrat, Oklahoma) complained, "I think that of all the amendments I have seen, the most undesirable one to be made part of an appropriations bill would be this one, because it is a technical and complex legislative matter that only legislative committees can hope to cope with properly. . . . There is no emergency. . . . The amendment may be a fine thing, but this is not the place to solve it."[39] Nevertheless, despite assurances that Ways and Means was looking into the vesting problem and would act, the amendment passed overwhelmingly, 310 to 86.

Perhaps the most pernicious of the legislative amendments passed that day was the one prohibiting IRS from issuing regulations to establish procedures for revoking the tax-exempt status of private schools that discriminate racially. The amendment, which passed overwhelmingly (308–85) in the absence of constraining influences and committee review, was an end-run tactic that violated orderly legislative process, interfered with administrative rule making, and left affected parties in limbo with a public policy of nondiscrimination but no regulations to ensure compliance.

Substantive considerations regarding the civil rights laws aside, many members who voted for the amendment seemed unconcerned about circumventing normal procedures. The institutionally responsible position of opposing the amendment could have meant loss of campaign support in the next election. Moreover, the amendment provided the only opportunity for voting in favor of private schools. It is infrequent that a member is willing or able to defend a position by saying, "I voted to preserve the legislative process."

Just as the House often bypasses Ways and Means, the Senate—no longer willing to take a back seat on tax policy—has successfully bypassed the House, sometimes with the consent of the House, as in the 1982 tax bill. House-passed bills are used as vehicles for unrelated amendments. Although this practice is not new, it was rarely successful in the Mills era without Mills's consent. These additions, because they are part of a House-passed bill, go directly to conference without any prior consideration by the House or its tax committee. Given the Senate's past proclivity to accept "helpful" amendments, the consequences of this procedure for the tax code are unfortunate. The process has become so manipulable that in some ways it resembles an open caucus that can be taken over by virtually any group. With the proliferation of specialized interest groups and the increasing effectiveness of business lobbying, organized interests are at a great advantage in this environment.

Tax Solutions for Nontax Problems

Another trend that can be exploited by well-organized interests is the use of the tax code to solve substantive policy problems. President Carter proposed to solve the problem of inflation through a tax incentive policy that would lower the taxes of workers who accepted wage increases below the rate of inflation. Many of Carter's proposals concerning the nation's energy problems depended on the tax system. Businesses were to be rewarded with a tax credit for hiring certain hard-to-employ workers.

Although Carter was probably the first president to propose such extensive use of the tax code for nontax purposes, many such provisions preceded him, and many others were enacted after he left office.[40] These tax expenditures, which include credits, deductions, exemptions, exclusions, and deferrals, are the functional equivalent of direct spending programs but have certain strategic advantages over them. Because tax expenditures are counted as revenue losses rather than outlays, Congress can stay within expenditure limits and still distribute benefits to claimants. A second, related advantage of tax expenditures is that they are not regularly reviewed through the authorization and appropriations process, although they are reported annually. A third advantage is that tax expenditures such as the child care credit or individual retirement accounts are not viewed as spending by the public. Indeed, certain groups argue that using taxes to encourage and reward desired behavior is not the same as spending, that the tax expenditure concept itself is "an exercise in fiscal impressionism," and that many of the tax expenditures simply make taxes more fair.[41] Is the deduction for medical expenses, for example, an unfair subsidy for sick taxpayers, or does it simply adjust for their ability to pay? Finally, tax expenditures are seen by some people as more efficient than direct spending programs in that they are administered through the tax system automatically rather than through a costly bureaucracy.

It is clear why proponents would use tax expenditures to advance their goals, but there are costs. In addition to altering the equity and efficiency of the code and increasing its complexity, tax expenditures constitute a tremendous and growing drain on the federal treasury. Between 1975 and 1980 the revenue losses from tax expenditures rose faster—14 percent a year—than direct outlays, which increased 11 percent annually during that period. From fiscal 1974 to fiscal 1980, tax expenditures grew by 162 percent while outlays rose by 111 percent. In fiscal 1982 total tax expenditures exceeded $260 billion.[42]

Although some tax expenditures help low-income families—for example, the earned income tax credit, which is not available to low-income individuals—the benefits of most tax expenditures go to middle- and upper-income people.[43] The effects of these tax breaks are mitigated to some degree by the minimum tax, which was instituted to ensure that all individuals—even those who can fully exploit the tax system—pay some taxes.

Whatever the merits of individual tax expenditures, their cumulative effect on the tax code and on congressional process is enormous. With recourse to tax solutions for nontax problems, the effective jurisdiction of the tax committees is virtually unlimited. The tax policy process is already exploitable because of the Ways and Means Committee's no longer serving as a control committee, the circumvention of normal legislative processes, and ad hoc decision making. The pressure to use the tax code for non-fiscal-policy purposes has proved irresistible to many members of Congress.

The Budget Act: A New Source of Responsibility

A sense of limits, the ability to consider legislation on its merits and within some philosophical or historical context, rational and predictable procedures—these are the elements lacking in the tax policy process described thus far. The addition of subcommittees, new attention to oversight, increased staff, and wider availability of tax information have increased the possibility that the process could be deliberative, but by themselves these elements have been insufficient to produce responsible policy making.

Rules and procedures are no substitute for political will. If members have no desire to preserve the integrity of the tax code, it is unlikely that procedural changes would measurably improve the situation. Members who are concerned about the code, however, should be able to protect it and certainly should not be prevented from doing so.

It is here that rules and procedures matter since they structure the situation in a particular way. "Organization is bias," as E. E. Schattschneider said.[44] The bias needed in the tax area is one of responsibility, defined here as a concern for raising appropriate levels of revenue fairly, efficiently, simply, and in a manner consistent with other elements of fiscal policy.

To do that, the legislative process must be structured to permit careful consideration of the implications and long-run consequences of proposals. Deliberation of this sort is not facilitated by the current tax policy process.

Senate Finance Committee Chairman Dole was able to produce legislation that meshed with fiscal policy and improved the integrity and equity of the tax code. He did so, however, only under extraordinary pressure stemming from the economy and with the aid of a new source of responsibility, the congressional budget process, which was established in 1974. But even with the help of reconciliation procedures that set the amount of revenues the tax committees were required to raise and created a rule that floor amendments must be germane, the process that produced the 1982 tax bill was far from a model of deliberation. Still, without the budget process, responding adequately to the 1983 fiscal crisis would have been much more difficult.

The primary effect of the budget process has been partially to recreate the sense of limits that had disintegrated within the revenue committees. By itself the budget process does not necessarily create that sense. On balance, however, it does provide a counter force to do, in the words of a tax staff aide, "things . . . that you want to do, but that you could not find a way to justify politically."[45]

Two elements of the budget process work to foster the sense of limits and force members of the revenue committees to make choices. The first is the budget resolution with its accompanying reconciliation provisions. The second is the focus on tax expenditures.

Technically, the first budget resolution in late spring recommends a revenue level for the coming fiscal year and the two succeeding fiscal years. In practice the first resolution has become mandatory because of the reconciliation instructions to the revenue committees that have accompanied it. These instructions mandate the revenues that must be raised by the tax committees. In 1982, for example, the tax committees were instructed to raise $99.6 billion in additional revenues over a three-year period. This reconciliation sum was set after lengthy negotiations with relevant parties, including the chairmen of the Finance and Ways and Means committees. Senator Dole used this mandated level to force his committee to produce the 1982 bill.

Tax legislation that violates the autumn revenue floor of the second budget resolution is subject to a point of order in the House and Senate. Depending on where the floor is set, the tax committees may have difficult choices to make, at least for the coming fiscal year. Tuition tax credits, state and local gasoline tax deductions, and the Kemp-Roth tax bill were all at one time or another excluded from revenue bills because they would have violated the second budget resolution. In 1981 and 1982, however, the second budget resolution was in effect discarded by Congress, and other aspects of the budget process helped encourage more responsible tax policy making.

The revenue floor can force members to make specific trade-offs between one tax expenditure and another or between a direct expenditure and a tax expenditure, as was the case with tuition tax credits. In 1979, for example, the Senate Finance Committee passed legislation requiring foreigners who buy real estate in the United States to pay capital gains taxes on their profits from real estate investments. American farmers had urged that Congress pass such legislation to make foreigners pay the same capital gains taxes as U.S. citizens. A primary impetus for passage was that the bill would raise $75 million in new taxes and would thus provide room for $75 million worth of new tax expenditures without violating the budget resolution.[46]

Unlike the spending side of the budget, revenue targets and floors are not subdivided by functional category in the budget resolutions. The resolution sets an aggregate revenue figure to be met by the tax committees. The budget committee reports accompanying the budget resolution list major sources of revenues and discuss how revenue targets and floors are to be reached. Yet, as former Senate Finance Committee Chairman Long insisted on several occasions, only the aggregate figure in the resolution is binding, not the report. The report, however, frequently influences the revenue decisions of the tax committees.

The tax committees always take the aggregate figure seriously, and to the degree that it is restrictive, they are forced to make decisions in a context of choice. But revenue levels are not always restrictive, and there are ways to manipulate the process so that the committees technically adhere to the revenue floor while violating the spirit of the budget process. Bills have been altered to meet the revenue floor by moving effective dates to minimize estimated losses for the fiscal year to which the budget resolution applies. The budget process does not control revenue losses in the out years, that is, years after the fiscal year addressed by the budget resolution. Although this loophole lessens budget control on the revenue side, Congress's recent practice of presenting budgets in a multiyear context along with reconciliation exposes this subterfuge to some degree.

The focus on tax expenditures constitutes another opportunity for control of the tax policy process. The provisions of the Congressional Budget and Impoundment Control Act provide a countervailing, if not overwhelming, force to the tendency of members of Congress to say yes to requests that may seem reasonable when isolated from other considerations.

Specifically, the Budget Act defines and gives statutory status to the term "tax expenditures" and requires reporting of these expenditures. Attention given to these tax preferences and knowledge about them have increased as a direct result of the Budget Act. The president's budget must estimate revenue losses from existing and proposed tax expenditures as well as direct expenditures.

The revenue committees are required to provide a five-year estimate of the cost of new tax expenditures and to include a comparison of the figures in the legislation with those in the most recent budget resolution. These reporting requirements call attention to the view that tax credits, deductions, and other preferences are the functional equivalent of spending programs, are costly, and affect budget totals. Some information and some structure are now available for members concerned about the growth and equity of tax expenditures and their effect on revenues. Tax expenditures could, however, be treated more like direct expenditures in both legislative and budget processes. Deductions for home mortgages might be included as an expenditure allocated to the commerce and housing function in the budget resolution. Congress would consequently be encouraged to examine such tax expenditures in the context of other spending in corresponding functional or substantive areas.

Along with other congressional reforms, the Budget Act has contributed to the loss of autonomy of the revenue committees. But unlike the other reforms, it has provided a new source of control. By itself the budget process cannot impose responsibility on tax policy making, but it has tipped the balance a little more in that direction than would otherwise be the case.

Conclusion

The process of making tax policy lacks adequate structure to permit responsible lawmaking. One major, but not exclusive, source of the difficulty is the congressional reforms that weakened the Committee on Ways and Means and dismantled the controls built into tax policy making. Contributing to the problem are three related developments: the absence of commonly held ideas to provide coherence to tax policy making and help translate individual preferences into stable collective choices, the bypassing of normal legislative channels, and the increasing use of the tax system for nontax purposes. Even the countervailing force of the Budget Act, which does impose some responsibility on tax policy making, is insufficient to alter the situation greatly.

With the devaluation of legislative process, the arena of tax policy making is highly manipulable and exploitable. In the absence of political parties or other bases on which to aggregate choices, decision making is ad hoc and individualistic. Building consensus in such an environment would have proved difficult even without the reforms; decentralization and democratization have made the task an elusive one. With the use of tax expenditures to solve a myriad of national policy problems, the disintegration of the tax policy process has wider implications for policy making in Congress.

It is incorrect to charge that the reforms caused all the difficulty. With or without structure, political will to enact responsible legislation is necessary. At the same time, as the Budget Act demonstrates, structure can force attention to certain aspects of legislation. Structure can also help ensure that predictable, careful procedures, such as detailed committee consideration of proposals, are followed. Specifically, members should be able to pay serious attention to the equity and efficiency of the tax code and its ability to raise revenues consistent with other elements of fiscal policy.

For Congress to remain a democratic body, not every member needs to have a say in every provision at every stage of the tax policy process. Nonarbitrary rules and procedures that facilitate deliberation, help aggregate choices, allow leaders to be responsible, and hold members accountable are what is needed. As V. O. Key explained many years ago, too much choice is no choice at all.

Notes

1. James Madison, *Federalist* No. 10.
2. John Manley, *The Politics of Finance: The House Committee on Ways and Means* (Boston: Little, Brown, 1970).
3. Equity refers to horizontal equity (people with the same income pay the same amount of tax) and vertical equity (people with higher incomes pay at a higher rate than those with lower incomes). Efficiency refers to a comparison of the activity stimulated by a tax provision and the revenue lost by that provision.
4. This section is based primarily on Manley, *Politics of Finance*; Richard Fenno, *Congressmen in Committees* (Boston: Little, Brown, 1973); and Lawrence C. Pierce, *The Politics of Fiscal Policy Formation* (Pacific Palisades, Calif.: Goodyear Publishing Company, 1971).
5. Manley's term is "responsible" rather than "reliable." This term is used frequently by Manley to describe Ways and Means members. It means that they were cautious team players who took a "professional approach to legislation" (p. 70) and looked after the political needs of the House as a whole. Because this chapter uses the word "responsible" with

a different denotation, "reliable" is substituted for Manley's term.

6. Virtually any tax proposal can be defended by appealing to the principle of equity, which is frequently meant more broadly than a strict application of horizontal or vertical equity.

7. John F. Witte, "Incremental Theory and Income Tax Policy: The Problem of Too Much, Not Too Little, Change" (Paper prepared for the American Political Science Association annual meeting, Denver, 1982). Witte documents the growth of tax expenditures over time; see especially table 2.

8. One exception to this statement was the work of the Joint Economic Committee, which as early as 1971 called attention to the fact that certain tax provisions act as subsidies and are equivalent to direct spending.

9. Manley, *Politics of Finance*; see also Charles O. Jones, "Joseph G. Cannon and Howard W. Smith: An Essay on the Limits of Leadership in the House of Representatives," *Journal of Politics*, vol. 30 (August 1968), pp. 617–46.

10. The role of Treasury as a restraint on the tax committees has been substantially weakened in recent years, especially since Presidents Carter and Reagan proposed using the tax code to solve a variety of economic and policy problems.

11. Stanley S. Surrey, "Tribute to Dr. Lawrence N. Woodworth: Two Decades of Federal Tax History—View from This Perspective," *National Tax Journal*, vol. 32 (September 1979), pp. 227–39.

12. Quoted in George P. Shultz and Kenneth W. Dam, *Economic Policy Beyond the Headlines* (New York: W. W. Norton, 1977), p. 63.

13. This phrase is David Mayhew's in *Congress: The Electoral Connection* (New Haven, Conn.: Yale University Press, 1974).

14. See, for example, Catherine E. Rudder, "The Reform of the Committee on Ways and Means: Procedural and Substantive Impact, 1975" (Paper prepared for the Southwestern Political Science Association meeting, Dallas, 1976).

15. Thomas J. Reese, "The Politics of Tax Reform," *National Tax Journal*, vol. 32 (September 1979), p. 250.

16. Roger H. Davidson, "Subcommittee Government: New Channels for Policy Making," in Thomas E. Mann and Norman J. Ornstein, eds., *The New Congress* (Washington, D.C.: American Enterprise Institute, 1981), p. 131; and Lawrence C. Dodd, "Congress, the Constitution, and the Crisis of Legitimation," in Dodd and Bruce I. Oppenheimer, eds., *Congress Reconsidered*, 2d ed. (Washington, D.C.: Congressional Quarterly, 1981), p. 411.

17. James L. Sundquist, *The Decline and Resurgence of Congress* (Washington, D.C.: Brookings Institution, 1981), p. 401. In a study comparing the successful passage of legislation implementing the multilateral trade negotiations and the failure of the SALT II treaty in the Senate, I. M. Destler explains the different outcomes of the two matters in part by reference to rules and procedures in the new Congress: "SALT officials were handi-

capped by the weakness of congressional structures and the fluidity of congressional procedures with which they had to work." In the trade legislation, where closed committee sessions and no floor amendments were allowed because of special provisions in the 1974 Trade Act, "an informal but decisive policy-making process" emerged in contrast to SALT II (Destler, "Trade Consensus, SALT Stalemate: Congress and Foreign Policy in the 1970s," in Mann and Ornstein, *The New Congress*, pp. 355, 357). In short, Congress could best do its job, at least in the realm of trade policy, under the old, closed way of operating.

18. See, for example, Richard E. Cohen, "The Business Lobby Discovers That in Unity There Is Strength," *National Journal*, June 28, 1980, pp. 1050–55.

19. Stanley S. Surrey, "Our Troubled Tax Policy," *Tax Notes* (February 2, 1981), p. 179.

20. Reese, "Politics of Tax Reform," pp. 248–54.

21. Thomas J. Reese, *The Politics of Taxation* (Westport, Conn.: Greenwood Press, 1980), p. 194.

22. Article I, section 7, clause 1 of the Constitution requires that "all bills for raising revenue shall originate in the House of Representatives; but the Senate may propose or concur with amendments as on other bills." In 1980, as in 1981, the Senate began work on the tax bill before the House to pressure the House into action. This strategy was successful in 1981 but not in 1980. The 1982 bill, discussed below, was attached to a relatively obscure bill that had already passed the House. Nineteen members of the House have challenged the constitutionality of the 1982 bill in federal court.

23. *Washington Post*, August 2, 1981.

24. Press release, House Democrats, August 1981.

25. Democratic Study Group, "The Tax Cut—Part I," *Fact Sheet*, U.S. House of Representatives, July 26, 1981; *Tax Incentive Act of 1981*, Report of the Committee on Ways and Means, U.S. House of Representatives, July 24, 1981.

26. Kemp-Roth designated the primary sponsors of the original marginal rate tax cut bill: Representative Jack Kemp (Republican, New York) and Senator William Roth (Republican, Delaware).

27. Benjamin A. Okner, "Distributional Aspects of Tax Reform during the Past Fifteen Years," *National Tax Journal*, vol. 32 (March 1979), pp. 11–27.

28. *Washington Post*, August 2, 1981.

29. William Greider, "The Education of David Stockman," *The Atlantic*, December 1981, pp. 27–54.

30. *Washington Post*, June 19, 1981.

31. *Washington Post*, November 12, 1981.

32. This rule existed because the tax bill was a reconciliation bill under the provisions of the Congressional Budget and Impoundment Control Act of 1974.

33. *Wall Street Journal,* July 14, 1982; see also *New York Times,* August 15, 1982.

34. *Tax Equity and Fiscal Responsibility Act of 1982,* Conference Report to accompany H.R. 4961.

35. Stanley Surrey, "The Congress and the Tax Lobbyist: How Special Tax Provisions Get Enacted," *Harvard Law Review,* vol. 70 (May 1957), pp. 1145–82.

36. U.S. Senate, Subcommittee on Taxation and Debt Management Generally of the Committee on Finance, Joint Staff, "Background and Issues Relating to Carryover Basis," 1979.

37. The following observation by the widely respected ranking minority member of Ways and Means is instructive: "We need a tax philosophy. It's distressing to me to find the extent to which we respond to specific pressures—the hostile voices of the moment—and how little we have our eye on some overall goal for our tax system." Barber Conable, "Changing Tax Policy in a Changing Congress," *Tax Review,* vol. 41 (February 1980), p. 9.

38. *Congressional Record,* 96th Congress, 2d session, August 19, 1980, pp. H7197–218.

39. Ibid., p. H7202.

40. Richard Corrigan observes, for example, "The making of energy policy is falling into the hands of the tax collectors," in "Taxing Energy," *National Journal,* April 24, 1982, p. 732.

41. Richard E. Wagner, *The Tax Expenditure Budget: An Exercise in Fiscal Impressionism,* Government Finance Brief No. 29 (Washington, D.C.: Tax Foundation, 1979).

42. Nonna Noto, "Growth in Tax Expenditures Relative to the Federal Budget since 1974," analysis prepared by the Congressional Research Service for Senator Max Baucus, reported in *Congressional Record,* 97th Congress, 1st session, March 5, 1981, pp. S1811–21. See also Witte, "Incremental Theory"; and Congressional Budget Office, *Tax Expenditures: Budget Control Options and Five-Year Budget Projections for Fiscal Years 1983– 1987,* November 1982.

43. CBO, *Tax Expenditures.*

44. E. E. Schattschneider, *The Semi-Sovereign People: A Realist's View of Democracy in America* (New York: Holt, Rinehart and Winston, 1960), p. 30.

45. Quoted in Allen Schick, *Congress and Money: Budgeting, Spending, and Taxing* (Washington, D.C.: The Urban Institute, 1980), p. 557.

46. *Washington Post,* December 7, 1979.

8

Making Regulatory Policy

Mark V. Nadel

In discussing such areas of economic policy as taxation and the budgetary process, there is a reasonably clear notion of what is encompassed by the discussion. Regulation, however, is broader in scope and thus more elusive. Congressional consideration of regulation includes such disparate activities as government control of airline tariffs and routes, minority set-aside programs that give designated groups preferential entry to various markets, and air quality standards. How then to define regulation? In one sense, we do not have to. It can be said of regulation what Justice Potter Stewart said of pornography, "I know it when I see it."

Nonetheless, to limit the discussion, it is necessary to arrive at a common conception of what is meant by the term "regulation." James Q. Wilson argued that "there is a politics of regulation. To citizens, such a statement will appear self-evident, even trivial; to scholars studying the subject, it is controversial."[1] One reason the statement is not self-evident is that there simply is no *coherent* type of policy called "regulatory." Regulation can be defined as political control over the conduct of individuals and institutions in markets to require them to change their behavior in ways they would not do otherwise. In this sense almost every domestic policy involves regulation. The full scope of regulatory policy can be seen in three basic issues.

The first issue is conceptual: What is the proper government involvement in a particular market? Regulatory debate in Congress often deals with the propriety of government intervention. As economists debate the issue, it concerns questions of efficiency and social cost. Politicians are more concerned with normative positions and with the interests of their constituencies.

I have benefited from the comments of Daniel Bensing, James Thurber, and Susan Tolchin on an earlier draft of this chapter. The responsibility for facts and interpretations is, of course, my own.

Second, regulatory issues concern the distribution of political power. Who should have responsibility for rules for hazardous waste disposal, the federal government or the states? Should independent regulatory agencies be subject to review procedures of the Office of Management and Budget? Does legislative intervention improperly shift ultimate authority for executing the law to the legislative branch?

But these two issues are usually subordinate to a third, underlying issue—the distribution through political means of the costs of economic activity. Changing the mixture of costs and benefits in a market is always fraught with controversy; it was at the heart of the debate over airline and trucking deregulation, and it is also prominent in environmental debates. Legislation to hold firms responsible for the costs of their externalities may be economically efficient for society, but it also evokes attempts by firms to avoid those costs.

Congressional consideration of regulatory policy is thus ultimately concerned with the shifting of economic costs through political means. Different kinds of coalitions are associated with different types of issues, but political initiative or reaction stems from the authoritative allocation of costs.

Is there, then, a common political process that can be labeled regulatory policy? I would argue that no useful generalizations can be drawn by considering regulation as a unified policy type. Wilson is correct in asserting that there is a politics of regulation, but he also points out that different political patterns are associated with the different types of regulation.

Regulatory politics is shaped by regulatory policy. The notion that the political process is conditioned by the policy it deals with is well established in the literature of political science. It is futile, however, to categorize regulation as a type of policy that is distinct from distributive, redistributive, or constituency policy since regulation itself affects the distribution and redistribution of wealth and power.[2] The policy-making dynamics in Congress does not change when the policy under consideration is regulatory. Rather, the goals and distributional consequences of a particular regulatory policy determine the shape of politics. A particular policy goal may be achieved by regulation, subsidy, or taxation. The policy process will depend on that goal and its underlying distributional consequences rather than on the particular policy instrument that is chosen. To call a policy regulatory describes only a technique of achieving policy goals—that is, the imposition of an authoritative command or compelling incentive for an individual or entity to alter its behavior from what it would otherwise be.

But to call a policy regulatory really does not tell very much about the political or institutional forces creating and implementing that policy. Thus no macrotheory of regulatory policy making is possible. Useful generalizations can be drawn, but rather than a "single bullet" theory of regulation, we can detect several important themes in the way Congress uses regulation to achieve policy goals.

First, the distinction that is frequently drawn between economic and social regulation is reflected in differences in congressional behavior. Economic regulation concerns entry into markets, conditions of service, and price. Social regulation is broader and far less neat in terms of politics, public perceptions, and economic theory. Social regulation includes the regulation of externalities in situations where people are affected in the aggregate and involuntarily—for example, environmental regulation. It also includes regulation of products and conditions posing particular risk to individuals, such as regulation of consumer product safety and workers' safety. Finally, there is social policy regulation, such as civil rights and access for the handicapped. In both economic and social regulation, politics is conditioned by the distributional consequences of the policy.

Second, Congress lacks an orderly or analytical focus for making regulatory policy. Regulation is not treated as economic policy or analyzed for its financial or social implications, although economic regulatory policy is much more influenced by analysis, information, and economic theory than social regulation is. Congress tends to lurch from one extreme of regulatory policy to another. Having been unable to obtain consensus on broad principles of regulation, Congress has increasingly intervened in narrow disputes involving particular industries.

Third, regulatory policy making has been volatile because it responds to shifting constellations of interest groups and ideologies— not just business but consumer and environmental interests as well. Every interest gets its day in court, but the verdict keeps changing.

This chapter examines congressional policy making for economic and social regulation and procedural regulatory reform. The first section discusses what Congress does when it makes regulatory policy, in particular, the forms of regulatory policy making; the second section addresses the major structures through which regulatory policy is filtered, the committee system and political parties; the third section examines the political dynamics of regulatory policy making in Congress; the fourth section analyzes the role of information and ideology; and the final section, on procedural reform, considers the themes, problems, and issues faced by Congress as it tries to alter the regulatory-policy-making procedures of administrative agencies.

Institutional Powers of Congress

Regulatory policy making in Congress spans the full range of legislative powers and responsibilities, including the creation or termination of agencies, oversight, hearings, the issuance of reports, and the confirmation process.

The Rise and Demise of Agencies. In the past a major focus of regulatory policy making was the creation of agencies. With the exception of the Environmental Protection Agency (EPA), which was created by reorganization, all the major regulatory agencies (or their predecessors) were created by Congress. These agencies were manifestations of the particular regulatory philosophies and purposes that guided congressional majorities at the time they were created.

There has been dispute, however, about who benefited and whose purposes were served by various regulatory agencies. Both the historian Gabriel Kolko[3] and the economist George Stigler[4] have argued that regulation was designed at the outset to benefit the industries being regulated. Stigler argues that industry has a much greater per capita stake in regulation than the public at large and will thus devote the requisite time and resources to get what it wants from Congress; Kolko advances a more conspiratorial view.

These views have been widely challenged by historians who have shown that there was active business opposition to early regulatory agencies in the face of general public support.[5] Moreover, as Paul Quirk has argued, even agencies that subsequently protected and benefited regulated firms were created in the expectation that they would serve broader public interests.[6] Indeed, the creation of new agencies and the expansion of responsibilities of existing ones in the heyday of consumerism in the late 1960s and the early 1970s was opposed by the bulk of the business community.[7]

Since 1964 Congress has created the Equal Employment Opportunity Commission, the National Transportation Safety Board, the Occupational Safety and Health Administration (OSHA), the Consumer Product Safety Commission (CPSC), the Federal Energy Administration, the Mine Safety and Health Administration, and the Federal Election Commission, among others. In each of these cases, Congress responded to perceived problems by creating an agency.

Contrary to common assumptions about the longevity and growth of agencies, when the political climate shifted in the late 1970s, congressional authority was manifested in threats to eliminate or dismember agencies that had only recently been created or enhanced. While Congress debated "sunset" legislation for several years without resolution, it exercised direct control over certain regulatory agencies through major changes, or the threat of changes, in their jurisdiction and authority. The change in fortune of the Federal Trade Commission (FTC) and the CPSC illustrates the rapidly changed political environment in which regulatory policy is made.

The legislation establishing the Consumer Product Safety Commission was passed during the peak of consumerism in 1972 and reflected the temper of the times. The report of the House Interstate and Foreign Commerce Committee on the bill confidently noted, "This legislation proposes that the Federal government assume a major role in protecting consumers from unreasonable risks of death, injury or serious or frequent illness associated with the use of exposure to consumer products."[8]

The bill passed Congress handily, but not without some controversy and political struggle. That struggle was illustrative of regulatory politics in Congress a decade ago. The debate in Congress did not focus on whether there should be an assertive federal role (nobody took seriously the few business claims to the contrary). Rather, it concerned two other political issues. There was a fight over where the agency should be housed; congressional Democrats rejected an attempt by the Nixon administration to consolidate product safety functions within the Food and Drug Administration. Regardless of claims about the adequacy of the FDA and the scope of its responsibilities, the Democratic Congress did not want to entrust a new consumer protection program to the Republican administration, which consumer advocates considered unfriendly to their cause.

A more substantive jurisdictional battle took place over the products to be considered "consumer products." In addition to drugs, which were already covered by the FDA, the act specifically excluded motor vehicles and tobacco from CPSC jurisdiction. Although motor vehicles were covered by other legislation, the tobacco industry had little trouble averting a threat that the new agency would consider its products unsafe. The primary battle and eventual compromises in Congress were not over whether a new federal agency should be given new regulatory powers[9] but over the products to be covered by what was perceived to be a potentially aggressive agency.

The CPSC quickly got into trouble with both its former supporters and its adversaries. In a 1976 report the House Interstate and Foreign Commerce Committee criticized the commission for not regulating with sufficient vigor.[10] The affected industries, however, had their own complaints. Although the agency was reauthorized in 1978, there was serious discussion about abolishing it and transferring its functions to other agencies. Growing congressional concern about regulatory intrusiveness was manifested in a 1978 amendment endorsing voluntary standards over the mandatory standards that had been the original mission of the agency.

In 1981 the CPSC faced the unhappy circumstance of being the first regulatory agency up for reauthorization during the Reagan presidency. Despite widespread sentiment that its performance had greatly improved, there was still considerable industry unhappiness over what many firms considered unreasonableness and overstepping of bounds. Some industry groups were critical of the CPSC's involvement with OSHA and the EPA in attempting to regulate carcinogens. The Reagan administration announced that it favored abolishing the agency. The CPSC survived but in a form that manifested the prevailing drive to clip the wings of federal regulation. The two-year reauthorization directed the CPSC to rely on voluntary rather than mandatory standards when feasible, required detailed cost-benefit analysis of proposed mandatory standards, and provided for a legislative veto of regulations.

An even more rapid turnabout occurred in the case of the Federal Trade Commission. After being excoriated (and given public attention for the first time in more than thirty years) by the first "Nader's raiders" report, the FTC under new leadership (starting with Caspar Weinberger, who was chairman for seven months) rationalized its priorities, became more assertive in antitrust and consumer protection issues, and brought in young, activist lawyers. Indicating confidence and approval in the new direction at FTC, the House and Senate commerce committees pushed through legislation to bolster the power and reach of the commission. The Magnuson-Moss Act clarified the authority of the FTC to promulgate regulations applicable to trade practices in an entire industry rather than case by case. Reflecting the heyday of consumer activism, the act encouraged public participation in rule-making proceedings and made the FTC the first regulatory agency to have statutory authority to reimburse individuals and groups who would otherwise be unable to participate. But it was to be a short-lived triumph for consumer activists.

The turnabout for the FTC in Congress began almost immediately. A major problem lay in the targets of FTC investigations and rule makings. When the CPSC was created, industries whose products posed safety issues knew that they might be targeted for scrutiny and some, such as cigarette manufacturers, managed to escape the reach of the CPSC altogether. Everything was fair game for the FTC, however, because there were issues of competition or unfair trade practices in all industries. Under Chairman Michael Pertschuk, who had been instrumental in drafting the Magnuson-Moss Act in his previous position as chief counsel of the Senate Commerce Committee, the FTC lost no time in going after some of the most politically powerful industries in the nation—life insurance, the legal, medical, and other professions, automobiles, and pharmaceuticals. But the commission's inquiry into television commercials aimed at children was its downfall. A lobbying coalition of more than three dozen companies and trade associations was arrayed against the commission in Congress on this proceeding alone, and soon just about every industry affected by the commission was furiously, and successfully, seeking relief in Congress.

There were two main congressional responses to what was perceived as a new burst of activism (although defenders of the FTC argued that it was only doing what was mandated by Congress in 1974). First, as discussed later in this chapter, Congress voided certain rules through various means. Second, in response to an extensive lobbying campaign by the U.S. Chamber of Commerce and other business interests, Congress asserted greater control over FTC decisions.

In 1977, just three years after passage of the Magnuson-Moss Act and while there was still a Democratic majority in both houses of Congress, the FTC budget was held hostage to a move by the House of Representatives to impose a legislative veto on FTC rules. The FTC was funded by continuing resolutions and special appropriations until 1980, when a compromise was reached and the FTC Improvements Act, containing a legislative veto of FTC regulations, was enacted. During the debate over the FTC legislation, attempts were made by various industries to gain exemptions from FTC actions. Although only one antitrust case was scrapped by Congress, the authority of the commission in other major proceedings, such as children's advertising and insurance, was substantially limited.

One explanation of these rapid changes in their fortunes is that the CPSC and the FTC became runaway regulators and far exceeded congressional intent. A close examination of the record, however, shows that the regulators were prodded by Congress to be activist and acted under explicit instructions in certain matters. The children's advertising proceeding was expressly requested by the FTC's House and Senate appropriations subcommittees, the latter as late as 1977—when the roof was beginning to fall in.[11] Even before the Reagan era, Congress showed itself to be a fickle master of regulatory agencies. It turned on the FTC as soon as the fruits of the Magnuson-Moss Act led to extensive complaints from important business interests. This is not to suggest, however, that regulatory policy in this area was solely a response to interest group politics. A recent study points to changes in the membership of the Senate Commerce Committee as being most responsible for the changed political circumstances of the FTC.[12] The period of greatest FTC activism coincided with the leadership of the Senate Commerce Committee's Subcommittee on Consumer Affairs (the FTC's oversight subcommittee) by liberal members. After the 1976 election, however, there was a nearly complete turnover in that subcommittee, which was then chaired by Senator Wendell Ford (Democrat, Kentucky). Ford had a less interventionist orientation toward consumer protection, and he later became a leading critic of the FTC. The FTC largely followed the preferences of its proconsumer protection oversight subcommittee before 1977, but it was pulled up short when it continued that policy in a political environment changed by the new composition of its Senate oversight committee. In short, the FTC first responded to the policy preferences of its authorizing committee and then was forced to adapt to the new preferences of a new majority.

A fundamental reason for the CPSC's problems was related to the political dynamics of its creation. When it was created, "industry" was an abstraction; later several industries became targets of regulation. Former bystanders became opponents with a new stake in the outcome, and as a result the outcome was very different from what it had been a decade earlier.

Moreover, the political environment had undergone a sea change by 1980, and the claims of business, which were unheeded before 1977, suddenly gained legitimacy (and, of course, more votes in a Republican Senate). Agencies that had previously symbolized necessary consumer protection came to be regarded as the problem rather than the solution. This changed perception gave greater legitimacy to critics of the FTC. In 1973 lobbying efforts by General Mills would have been construed as unseemly pressure by peddlers of junk food; five years later its lobbying coalition could picture itself as the defender of free speech and family rights against a big brother bureaucracy. It became easier for congressmen to vote against consumer protection when even reputedly liberal opinion leaders such as the *Washington Post* agreed that regulation had gone too far.

Because Congress lacks a systematic way of screening regulatory matters and digesting theory and data (as discussed later in this chapter), its powers of creating, modifying, and terminating agencies are used to effect major changes in regulatory policy. The results are frequent administrative upheavals.

Oversight. In 1968 John Bibby wrote: "The typical pattern of committee review of regulatory agencies is no review at all for long periods of time."[13] How most regulatory agencies wish that were true today! In a 1977 report the Senate Governmental Affairs Committee found that there had been a dramatic increase in the percentage of committee hearings devoted to oversight. According to the committee, "It might even be said that Congress is now paying more attention to oversight of regulatory agencies than at any time in its history."[14]

Congressional oversight is particularly important with regard to regulatory policy. The goals of regulatory oversight are ensuring compliance with legislative intent, determining the effectiveness of regulatory policies, preventing waste and dishonesty, preventing abuse in the administrative process, advancing broad public concerns, and preventing agencies' usurpation of legislative authority. Although the goals are much the same as in other areas of oversight, there are important differences in the way regulatory oversight has been handled. It is useful to examine the extent to which those goals are pursued: How successful has oversight been?

Despite a substantial increase in oversight hearings, dissatisfaction with the adequacy of oversight persists. One Senate staff member echoed a common sentiment in asserting that "federal agencies and departments appear to exist under an inertia all their own. Modifying or correcting their behavior is very difficult."[15] Most recent studies agree that oversight falls short of its potential.[16] As in most other assessments of political processes, much depends on whose ox is being gored. Morris Ogul points out that an assessment of whether oversight is effective is tied to preferences on substantive policy issues as well as to one's preferred model of the legislative process.[17]

The oversight of regulatory agencies proceeds through numerous techniques that are common to many program areas. These include periodic reauthorization (which is more likely than other methods to be taken seriously by Congress and the agency), hearings, committee and conference reports, investigations by committees or by the General Accounting Office and other congressional support agencies, periodic reporting requirements, the process of confirming nominees to agencies, and legislative casework on behalf of constituents. Oversight also proceeds informally through letters, phone calls, or meetings with regulators by congressmen and their staffs.

At one time, the appropriations process was of limited use in regulatory oversight, but in the last ten years the purse strings— authorizations and appropriations—have become a major lever of congressional control. In a piecemeal move toward sunset policy, most new agencies and programs have been required to come back to Congress for periodic reauthorization. The objectives have been to evaluate new agencies periodically and to put them on a short leash. Moreover, that leash provides an action-forcing mechanism to ensure that authorizing committees continue to shape the course of agencies under their jurisdiction. As discussed in the following section, periodic reauthorization has been the most direct means of congressional influence on the regulatory agencies.

The appropriations process offers another lever for congressional influence. All regulatory agencies are targets of review by Appropriations committees. Their budgets are relatively small, however, and they do not attract the financial scrutiny that big-ticket defense and social programs get. The economic effect of regulatory agencies lies not in their own budgets but in the costs they impose on others or force others to internalize. In the wake of the budgetary assault on regulatory agencies by the Office of Management and Budget during the Reagan administration, the traditional budget-cutting role of the House Appropriations Committee has been rendered moot. Regulatory agencies occasionally receive instructions or prohibitions against spending money on specified programs, but appropriations oversight tends to be sporadic and reactive to controversial issues that are already prominent on the public agenda.[18]

Ad Hoc Rule Making. It is a short step from vigorous oversight to intervention in particular rule-making procedures. Since the change of fortune for consumer protection agencies, Congress has in a number of instances directly overruled or changed proposed regulations or enforcement actions of regulatory agencies. It has done so through prohibitions in appropriations bills, provisions in reauthorizing legislation, or riders to nongermane legislation or by stripping the regulatory agency of jurisdiction over an industry. The soft drink bottling industry, for example, successfully stopped an FTC antitrust suit seeking to break up exclusive distributorships by persuading Congress to pass legislation prohibiting the action. Similarly, the 1981 legislation reauthorizing the CPSC substantially limited its proposed mandatory standard on power lawn mowers.

Industry efforts are not always successful. In 1982 the American Medical Association led a major campaign to prohibit the FTC from applying the antitrust laws to state-licensed professionals such as doctors, lawyers, and accountants. That effort was initially defeated in a parliamentary maneuver only after it was opposed by an exceptionally strong array of groups, including the National Association of Retired Persons, the American Nurses Association, the National Association of Chain Drug Stores, and a group of large corporations concerned about the cost of employee health care and insurance plans.

The frequency of these campaigns demonstrates that Congress is regarded, and regards itself, as an acceptable arena for resolving regulatory decisions affecting particular industries. Even antitrust enforcement actions in progress are not immune from direct congressional intervention.

Although there have been a variety of techniques for congressional intercession in regulatory decisions, the focal point has been debate over the legislative veto—a technique whereby one or both houses of Congress can invalidate a regulation proposed or promulgated by an administrative agency. While Congress has the authority to alter the policies and activities of regulatory agencies through legislation, the legislative veto expands that process and greatly facilitates it. The legislative veto is a device for directly transmitting political pressure on regulatory decision making—with scarcely the pretext that there is any other basis for judging an issue.

This is amply demonstrated by Congress's use of an agency-specific legislative veto to overturn an FTC rule requiring information disclosure by used car dealers. After ten years of consideration, the FTC issued a rule that would have required used car dealers to disclose to consumers the extent of warranty coverage and known major defects. Although the rule was considerably milder than had originally been proposed, both houses of Congress struck it down in May 1982. There was minimal congressional deliberation on the rule but substantial lobbying by the National Automobile Dealers Association (which in the previous election had contributed more than $1 million to the campaigns of congressmen and senators). Although one need not come to a conclusion on whether the used car dealers bought a favorable outcome, the use of the legislative veto in those circumstances certainly makes that a plausible view.

The legislative veto was struck down by the U.S. Supreme Court in June 1983, but troubling policy issues remain for this and other ad hoc forms of policy making. One can expect Congress to devise new means of influencing particular regulatory actions without running afoul of the Court's ban on the veto. Indeed, its lack of a legislative veto might spur Congress to dictate the terms of regulatory policy in great detail and to constrain the rule-making discretion of agencies.

In summary, the techniques of oversight have not been used systematically or analytically. Legislative activity has usually stemmed from the complaints of important constituency groups, such as the American Medical Association and business organizations. When the medical profession attempted to escape the antitrust laws, for example, the issue facing congressmen was not conflict between the principles of professional self-regulation and greater competition but how to respond to the immediate and particular demand of this important group of constituents.

Senate Confirmation of Appointments. Confirmation of presidential nominees to regulatory agencies usually gets into questions of policy—particularly when a nominee is being reappointed or moved up to chairman. But confirmation rarely entails serious consideration of qualifications or policy.[19] The mixture of serious consideration and mindless back-slapping puffery is probably the same in confirmation of regulatory appointments as in those to other agencies. But there are important differences. First, most regulatory agencies are multi-member commissions whose members rarely serve full terms, and there are thus many more opportunities to review agency policy at confirmation hearings. Second, industries and firms affected by particular agency decisions manifest strong interest in the renomination of commissioners or agency heads. The scope of affected interests is much narrower than in the confirmation of an assistant secretary of the Treasury, for example.

The case of Leland Olds is probably the best-known example of use of the confirmation process for policy ends at the behest of a regulated industry. Olds, who was renominated to the Federal Power Commission by President Truman, had pushed for more extensive regulation of natural gas production. The oil and gas industry mounted a substantial campaign against Olds, and he was rejected by the Senate, 53–15.

Congressional Hearings and Reports. The well-publicized congressional hearing is a device for gaining political leverage. It is difficult to say whether hearings have been more or less important in regulation than in other areas of economic policy, but many regulatory controversies are tailor-made for dramatic hearings and for television. Particularly in the areas of occupational safety and health and product safety, the potential to dramatize a problem and put pressure on an agency or Congress is enormous. Michael Pertschuk candidly related that, as chief counsel of the Senate Commerce Committee, he planned hearings on proposed flammable fabrics legislation "to gain access to the media, to evoke public concern and reaction to the pain and suffering caused by child burnings, and to demonstrate the failure of the industry to make any effort in good faith to raise the inadequate voluntary standards of flammability."[20] Hearings can be a crucial element in this kind of economic policy making if they are purposeful and accompanied by extensive background work and if they succeed in influencing the course of action.

Summary. Despite the decades-long debate over the utility and projriety of the independence of the regulatory commissions, when Congress is spurred into action by an issue or by affected interests, it has generally been able to make its views known and its wishes prevail. It does not do so on the basis of an a priori sense of priorities or an established set of criteria. Congress acts issue by issue through the creation of agencies and threats against existing ones by authorization and amendment, legislative veto, hearings, and the confirmation process.

Congressional Structure and Regulation

The structure of Congress refers to the organization of decision making, especially the roles of committees, parties, and the leadership, and institutional relationships between Congress and the executive branch. This section highlights the features of congressional structure that have been particularly important in the development of regulatory policy.

The Committee System. The center stage of congressional policy making is held by the standing committees and subcommittees. Just as the term "regulation" subsumes a variety of policy types and issues, regulatory policy in Congress is handled by a variety of committees. Indeed, there are few committees that do not deal with regulatory policy. For the major regulatory agencies, the committees of jurisdiction are a scattered but manageable list, as shown in table 8–1.

The formal jurisdictional lines do not tell the whole story. Although the authority to report legislation is based on fairly clear lines and oversight relationships are well established, the regulatory policy arena is full of interlopers. The now defunct Senate Antitrust Subcommittee, for example, held hearings and substantially molded the legislative agenda on a variety of regulatory issues ranging from pharmaceuticals to trucking deregulation. Until it adopted a less activist orientation that came with Republican control of the Senate, the Senate Committee on Governmental Affairs handled a grab bag of regulatory issues. Indeed, it was under the auspices of Governmental Affairs that the Senate conducted its most comprehensive study of federal regulation. This committee had jurisdiction over procedural regulatory reform—until forced to share it with the Judiciary Committee.

This scattered jurisdiction has two results. First, by increasing the number of important players in any regulatory issue, it makes

TABLE 8-1
Oversight and Legislative Committees for
Selected Major Regulatory Agencies

Consumer Product Safety Commission
  House Government Operations Committee
    Subcommittee on Commerce, Consumer, and Monetary Affairs
  House Energy and Commerce Committee
    Subcommittee on Health and the Environment
    Subcommittee on Telecommunications, Consumer Protection, and
      Finance
  Senate Commerce, Science, and Transportation Committee
    Subcommittee on Consumer

Environmental Protection Agency
  House Government Operations Committee
    Subcommittee on Environment, Energy, and Natural Resources
  House Energy and Commerce Committee
    Subcommittee on Health and the Environment
  House Science and Technology Committee
    Subcommittee on Natural Resources, Agriculture Research, and
      Environment
  House Small Business Committee
    Subcommittee on Energy, Environment, and Safety Issues Affecting
      Small Business
  Senate Environment and Public Works Committee
    Subcommittee on Environmental Pollution
  Senate Select Small Business Committee

Federal Communications Commission
  House Energy and Commerce Committee
    Subcommittee on Telecommunications, Consumer Protection, and
      Finance
  Senate Commerce, Science, and Transportation Committee

Federal Energy Regulatory Commission
  House Interior and Insular Affairs Committee
    Subcommittee on Mines and Mining
  House Energy and Commerce Committee
    Subcommittee on Energy Conservation and Power
  House Science and Technology Committee
  Senate Energy and Natural Resources Committee
    Subcommittee on Energy Deregulation
    Subcommittee on Energy and Mineral Resources

Federal Trade Commission
  House Banking, Finance, and Urban Affairs Committee
    Subcommittee on Consumer Affairs and Coinage
  House Government Operations Committee

TABLE 8–1   (continued)

Subcommittee on Commerce, Consumer, and Monetary Affairs
House Energy and Commerce Committee
   Subcommittee on Telecommunications, Consumer Protection, and
     Finance
   Subcommittee on Health and the Environment
House Judiciary Committee
   Subcommittee on Monopolies and Commercial Law
House Small Business Committee
   Subcommittee on Antitrust and Restraint of Trade
Senate Banking, Housing, and Urban Affairs Committee
   Subcommittee on Consumer Affairs
Senate Commerce, Science, and Transportation Committee
   Subcommittee on Consumer
Senate Judiciary Committee
Senate Labor and Human Resources Committee
   Subcommittee on Employment and Productivity
Senate Select Small Business Committee
   Subcommittee on Productivity and Competition

Food and Drug Administration
House Energy and Commerce Committee
   Subcommittee on Health and the Environment
Senate Commerce, Science, and Transportation Committee
Senate Labor and Human Resources Committee
   Subcommittee on Health and Scientific Research

Interstate Commerce Commission
House Energy and Commerce Committee
   Subcommittee on Commerce, Transportation, and Tourism
House Judiciary Committee
   Subcommittee on Monopolies and Commercial Law
House Public Works and Transportation Committee
   Subcommittee on Surface Transportation
Senate Commerce, Science, and Transportation Committee
   Subcommittee on Surface Transportation
Senate Judiciary Committee

Occupational Safety and Health Administration
House Education and Labor Committee
   Subcommittee on Health and Safety
House Small Business Committee
   Subcommittee on Energy, Environment, and Safety Issues Affecting
     Small Business
Senate Labor and Human Resources Committee
Senate Small Business Committee

SOURCE: *Congressional Quarterly Almanac, 1982.*

it harder to achieve coherence or come to closure on a policy. Second, it makes for entrepreneurial politics as dozens of subcommittee chairmen have an opportunity to publicize their regulatory goals. The importance of entrepreneurial politics in regulatory policy is explored later in this chapter.

Parties. In considering the role of political parties and partisanship in regulation, the distinction between economic and social regulation is the key factor. Social regulation issues generally mirror the traditional split on the social agenda between Republicans and liberal Democrats, and congressional votes on those issues tend to be party-line votes—that is, a majority of one party is aligned against a majority of the other. Votes on economic regulation, however, generally do not reflect party divisions except for energy regulation, which has been regarded more as a consumer protection issue (by liberals) or as an unwarranted and inefficient subsidy (by conservatives). The differences between the two kinds of regulatory policy can be seen in the 1981 roll call votes on regulatory issues. There were nine contested votes on social regulation issues, broken down by party as shown in table 8–2. One of these nine votes was nearly unanimous. On six of the remaining votes, there was a clear party-line break, and in all cases the Democrats were more likely to take a proregulation position. By contrast, of six votes on telecommunications deregulation legislation that year, only one (on local government authority over cable television rates) was a party vote—and that was just barely so. The other major economic regulation vote in 1981 was on partial deregulation of the intercity bus industry, and that passed 305–83 with no differences by party. Similarly, the airline deregulation votes in 1978 were not on party lines except for modest partisanship on an amendment dealing with the compensation of airline workers dislocated because of deregulation. As noted earlier, votes on energy regulation correspond more to the pattern of votes on social regulation; an amendment to prevent immediate decontrol of oil and natural gas was opposed by Senate Republicans (3–47) while there was an even split (21–21) among Democrats.

Social regulation often arrays the business community against environmental, consumer, and labor interests. Most consumer protection and worker protection legislation and much environmental legislation is formulated in the context of this split, which finds northern Democrats and a few Republicans against the bulk of congressional Republicans and southern Democrats. Economic regulation finds, to a much greater extent, business groups contending against one another, with the major umbrella business organizations sitting out the issue.

Even in social regulation, however, constituency and ideology often determine behavior. Thus Representative John Dingell (Democrat, Michigan) of Detroit, chairman of the House Committee on Energy and Commerce, has manifested one overriding concern regard-

TABLE 8–2

ROLL CALL VOTES ON SOCIAL REGULATORY ISSUES, 1981

Issue	Total	Democrats	Republicans
House of Representatives			
Prohibit EPA from requiring state vehicle emission inspection programs	177–184	58–141	119–43
Limit scope of Mine Safety and Health Administration authority	254–165	88–145	166–20
Grant steel industry three-year delay in meeting clean air standards	322–3	182–1	140–2
Delete provision limiting Department of Energy preparation of environmental impact statements	233–122	161–33	72–89
Prevent the Nuclear Regulatory Commission from issuing operating licenses to nuclear plants before completion of public hearings	90–304	81–139	9–165
Senate			
Retain federal noise control standards for newly manufactured motorcycles	40–55	21–24	19–31
Exempt Mine Safety and Health Administration from 4 percent funding cut	38–54	36–5	2–49
Maintain existing scope of Mine Safety and Health Administration authority	35–63	25–21	10–42
Kill amendment to provide funding at the level in the conference report	59–37	14–30	45–7

NOTE: Does not include routine, uncontested appropriations and authorizations votes.

SOURCE: *Congressional Quarterly Almanac*, 1981.

ing the Clean Air Act—that restrictions on automobile pollution be eased. Conversely, Senator Robert Stafford (Republican, Vermont) has been at odds with the Republican administration over the Clean Air Act and other environmental matters and was strongly supported for reelection in 1982 by national groups such as the Sierra Club and Friends of the Earth.

The exigencies of constituency have often excused members from voting with party.[21] When legislation like the Clean Air Act affects some localities much more than others, party identification is often irrelevant. Particularly in economic deregulation, constituency counts for more than party and ideology. The Republicans may oppose government regulation, but as an aide to Senator John Danforth (Republican, Missouri) noted during the airline deregulation debate:

> Senator Danforth has campaigned against the heavy hand of government regulation, but he was not sent here to deal in abstract exercises. There are 14,000 people in Missouri who work for TWA, and he wants to make sure they and their families are treated fairly.[22]

Executive-Congressional Relations. The old adage "the president proposes, the Congress disposes" has always been a considerable exaggeration. In the case of regulation Congress has initiated much of the social policy. A substantial portion of consumer and environmental legislation had its origins in Congress rather than the executive branch. Automobile safety, truth in lending, and water pollution control were first pushed by members of Congress, usually senators. Nine of the seventeen consumer protection laws enacted from 1962 to 1972 were initiated in Congress before being made part of the president's program. Only three were originally proposed by the president; five were proposed virtually concurrently, or their origin cannot be documented.[23]

There are several institutional reasons for Congress's role as initiator of policy. First, most of the legislation is pushed by members who have defined their role, and are identified by others, as environmentalist or proconsumer. They can afford to be ahead of the president, even one from their own party, on these issues and can act quickly to promote a particular cause. The executive branch is more constrained; even liberal Democratic presidents have been sensitive to the views of the business community. Second, when initiated, regulatory policies were generally new areas of federal responsibility without established bureaucracies whose interest and expertise would lead them to initiate policy.

In regulation, no less than in other policy areas, there is often tension between the president and Congress over custody of policy. That struggle is implicit in the independent commission form of organization. Through the creation of independent agencies and other means, Congress has often tried to stamp its authority directly on the implementation of regulatory policy. The battle for prerogative extends to all phases of regulatory policy implementation. Thus, during the Nixon administration, congressional Democrats opposed the requirement that the Office of Management and Budget approve questionnaires and other data-gathering activities aimed at businesses by regulatory agencies. The Democrats charged that the administration, through the OMB, was improperly restricting regulatory investigations, and they successfully tacked an amendment on the Alaska oil pipeline bill exempting independent agencies from OMB questionnaire and reports clearance and giving that function instead to the General Accounting Office, a legislative branch agency.

The tension over institutional prerogatives has had major implications for regulatory policy, particularly in the move toward economic deregulation. Under the impetus of procompetition chairmen of the Civil Aeronautics Board and the Interstate Commerce Commission appointed by President Carter, deregulation gained momentum while legislation contemplating deregulation of surface and air transportation was being debated in Congress. These agencies were stretching the law to the limit. They were unilaterally deregulating, and they thereby changed the political situation. Previously industries protected by regulation simply opposed any change from the status quo—always an advantage in Congress. With the agencies changing the rules of the game and introducing great uncertainty in the market, opposition to deregulation softened. Some affected firms withdrew their opposition to restore some degree of stability and to have some influence on deregulation when it appeared inevitable.

Regulation as Economic Policy. With few exceptions, Congress has not viewed regulation as basically an economic issue in the context of the national economy. Regulatory policy has been addressed in relation to a specific industry (transportation, banking) or a specific problem (occupational health, product safety). The externalities of regulation and the interrelationships between regulatory laws have not been examined at the time of enactment. In the consideration of some legislation there has been, almost as a moral principle, the prideful assertion that the costs should not be taken into account.

There is no central institutional focus in Congress on the costs or benefits of regulation. When the Senate commissioned a compre-

239

hensive study of regulation, it was the province not of a regulatory authorizing committee or an economics-oriented committee but of the Senate Governmental Affairs Committee. The Joint Economic Committee has looked at various economic effects of regulation, but it has no legislative authority. A 1976 study of federal regulation by the House Interstate and Foreign Commerce (now Commerce and Energy) Committee did not mention the effects of regulation on the economy as a major issue. Senate rules require a regulatory impact evaluation to accompany all bills reported by committees, but that requirement has rarely been taken seriously.

Congress has passed bills with staggering economic implications for industries and localities without demonstrating an awareness that there are *any* economic implications. Perhaps the best-known and most poignant example is section 504 of the Rehabilitation Act of 1973, which authorizes the Department of Transportation to require public transportation systems to provide full access for the handicapped. The rules implementing that legislation were estimated by the Congressional Budget Office to impose costs of $7 billion in 1979 dollars over the next thirty years. Yet section 504 was not the subject of hearings or floor debate in either the House or the Senate. It was adopted through an amendment offered by Representative Charles Vanik (Democrat, Ohio) and accepted without dissent. There is no legislative history to show what Congress had in mind with this provision, and Vanik, when later asked about it, said, "We never had any concept that it would involve such tremendous costs."[24]

Current and proposed oversight arrangements in Congress do little to facilitate a consideration of economic effects. In theory, periodic reauthorization or sunset review of regulatory agencies could rest on an evaluation that weighs efficiency and cost, but the current authorization process offers little hope in that regard. Instead, Congress has attempted to place the burden on the executive branch and independent agencies through legislation that would require analyses of the economic effects of proposed major regulations.[25]

Congress and the Political Dynamics of Regulation

Interest Groups and Coalitions. Regulation proceeds in a swirl of interest group activity that both constrains and provides opportunities for congressional action. But the play of interest groups varies with the mixture of costs and benefits of policies.[26] James Q. Wilson has set forth a framework that is useful in understanding the coalitions formed in Congress around the various kinds of regulatory policies. In Wilson's scheme "majoritarian politics" ensues when both costs and benefits are widely distributed—most people expect to gain, and most also expect to pay. This is not a common type of regulatory politics. It encompasses antitrust policy and perhaps Federal Trade Commission activities.

When a policy will benefit an identifiable and relatively small group at the expense of another small group, costs and benefits are concentrated, and "interest group politics" ensues. This includes all labor legislation, an increasing amount of telecommunications policy, and ocean shipping issues such as cargo preference. On these issues some congressmen have constituency ties to a particular interest, but most face zero-sum choices, in which helping one group displeases another politically important group.

A more common form of regulatory policy is "client politics," in which a small group receives concentrated benefits and the larger society pays the cost, which is spread widely at a low per capita rate. This was the case in transportation politics when the Civil Aeronautics Board and the Interstate Commerce Commission, supported by their congressional authorizing committees, obtained monopoly benefits for the air transport and trucking industries. The thrust of economic regulatory reform has been in the context of client politics—breaking up an embedded system where the protected industry has much to lose by deregulation, society has much to gain, but no consumer has sufficient gain to raise a fuss or pay attention. This leads to an ironic point. The worse the regulation, the harder it is to eliminate in Congress. The worst regulations entail the greatest redistribution of costs from producers to consumers, the greatest concentration of benefits, and the highest cost. This means that to reform the worst regulatory policy entails great costs to beneficiaries, who would lose their concentrated benefits. The threat to those enjoying monopoly profits brings about strong political resistance. The awesomely powerful resistance of the Teamsters Union to transportation deregulation has often been noted. The union and the industry were rich and powerful because they extracted noncompetitive prices in a regulated market. They had a lot to lose (at least in the short run) by deregulation, but because they had gained so much in the past, they had the influence to keep trucking deregulation far less comprehensive than air transport deregulation. Client politics imposes a major constraint on Congress because changing a policy requires that the subgovernment controlling the policy be subdued. This can be done through a change in ideology, as discussed below, or by taking the issue to a rival committee or subcommittee.

Finally, there are policies that confer widespread or universal benefits the cost of which is borne by an identifiable and relatively small segment of society. The benefits to each member of the public are usually quite small (and people are frequently unaware of them) while the costs are concentrated and hence more keenly felt. In the regulatory arena such policies include environmental legislation and much of the consumer protection legislation enacted in the late 1960s and 1970s. In theory, this sort of legislation should never be passed because it imposes costs on small organized groups that have a much greater incentive to oppose the legislation than the beneficiaries have to work for it.[27] Moreover, it is easier to oppose new policies in Congress than to enact them. The way out of this theoretical dilemma is through "entrepreneurial politics," in which individuals, members of Congress, and staff members advance their careers by promoting widely dispersed and poorly organized interests. They reap the rewards of new coalitions. Consumer protection legislation, for example, was originally passed because of "professional consumers" such as Ralph Nader. Although it is not economically rational for individual consumers to devote time and other resources to a cause such as automobile design safety, it is rational for consumer advocates to do so, and they have become producers of consumer protection policies.[28]

Not all consumer or environmental issues are promoted through entrepreneurial politics; interest group coalitions are often active and decisive. During congressional consideration of the Clean Air Act amendments in 1976 and 1977, for example, environmental groups such as the Sierra Club were joined by eastern coal mine owners and the United Mine Workers in their efforts to require scrubbers (complex and expensive devices to remove sulfur from coal fire emissions). The basis for this ad hoc alliance was that the alternative to mandatory scrubbing was an emissions standard that could be met in a number of ways—including the use of low-sulfur coal from the West. Such a standard would have given western coal (produced mainly without union labor) a substantial cost advantage since it could meet the emissions requirement without scrubbing. The environmentalists favored mandatory scrubbing because they regarded it as an effective way to keep environmental quality from deteriorating in the unpolluted West. The alliance was successful and the 1977 Clean Air Act amendments required scrubbing despite the continuing complaints of electric utilities and greater cost to their consumers.[29]

Given the political dynamics in Congress, many areas of regulation are tailor-made for entrepreneurial politics. Particularly in the Senate, where nearly every member of the majority party chairs a subcommittee, a junior senator can use his or her subcommittee as a platform to champion a cause that is not yet in the jurisdiction of

242

more senior members. Early in his Senate career, for example, Abraham Ribicoff (Democrat, Connecticut) used his chairmanship of the Subcommittee on Government Reorganization to hold hearings on automobile safety. The hearings catapulted Nader into prominence and gave Ribicoff leadership of what was then a new policy issue. The fragmented committee structure of Congress facilitates entrepreneurial politics, and the drive of members and staff to exploit popular issues encourages it.

Although policy entrepreneurship in Congress has led to the creation of programs and agencies, it can also be manifested in a retreat from regulation. As a first-term congressman, Elliot Levitas (Democrat, Georgia) quickly seized leadership of the movement to rein in regulators by doggedly promoting the legislative veto.

The Role of Crisis. The task of the policy entrepreneur is aided by a publicly perceived crisis that focuses attention on an issue. The Great Depression reminds us of the powerful role of crisis in economic policy making; less urgent or widespread crises frequently influence regulatory policy making in Congress. The major food and drug laws of 1906, 1938, and 1962 were passed in the wake of crisis or scandal—the most recent being the thalidomide tragedy in 1962. Crisis is not always necessary, nor has it been the precursor of most of the regulatory legislation of the last two decades. But a crisis or scandal can make it unpalatable to oppose regulatory proposals aimed at ensuring that the problem does not recur. Regulation is often perceived in Congress as a simple and obvious response to dramatic problems, and little attention is paid to trade-offs or side effects.

A crisis shapes the political discussion—usually to the advantage of those favoring greater regulatory intervention. Crisis also shapes public perceptions and creates an atmosphere in which certain options will be prominent on the agenda of public issues.

The Role of Information, Ideas, and Ideology

Like other areas of policy, regulation is the outcome of more than interest group politics. It is formulated in the context of a prevailing ideology—a set of beliefs about the proper and economically efficient role of government. There are times when ideology, or a newly powerful counterideology, greatly influences events. It was ideology more than economic interest that paved the way for the environmental and consumer protection movements. Ralph Nader's major accomplishment was gaining acceptance in Congress of the notion that injuries and deaths in automobile accidents were due in part to the design of cars and that manufacturers have a responsibility, which could be mandated by the government, to make their products safe. The environmental movement made the public more aware of environmental degradation and less willing to accept risk. Ideology is less important, however, in economic than in social regulation. The politics of economic regulation depends more on empirical theory, information, and expectations of what will happen if a policy is adopted; normative beliefs are less important than economic efficiency. The remarkably successful deregulation of airlines is an excellent case in point of the influence of economic theory.

Information and Policy Change. Until the early 1960s most observers believed that although air transport was not a natural monopoly, government regulation was more efficient than open competition.[30] The academic, but not the political, turnabout in orientation toward transportation regulation was due in no small part to the publication in 1962 of *Air Transport and Its Regulators* by Richard Caves. Caves concluded that the airline industry's market structure would function reasonably well without economic regulation. Subsequent studies by Douglas and Miller, William Jordan, and Theodore Keeler demonstrated that economic regulation was not only unnecessary but also more costly and less efficient than a market system.[31] By 1974 the economic case for substantial deregulation had been decisively made, and independent economists were nearly unanimous in favoring this shift in policy.

Once the ideology of economic deregulation became dominant, as it did in both Congress and the administration during the Carter presidency, it became easier to block new forms of regulation or the extension of regulation to new technologies than to undo previous regulatory policies. Thus when AT & T put together legislation to establish itself as a perpetual monopoly, it failed dismally because the bill was widely perceived as anticompetitive.

Ideology is not enough, however. The ideology must be given political life through data and an appropriate political forum. The airlines, after all, opposed deregulation; they were well entrenched in a system of clientele politics, and they had a supportive regulatory agency and congressional committees. But through skillful use of data and congressional hearings, it was possible to overcome that opposition.

The hearings on airline regulation by the Senate Administrative Practices Subcommittee chaired by Senator Edward Kennedy (Democrat, Massachusetts) show how intensive research and well-presented data can move economic theory from academic curiosity to political action. In 1974 the Kennedy staff decided to focus on airline regulation as an area where substantial reform could be accomplished. Although the Administrative Practices Subcommittee might seem to be a strange forum for air transport legislation, Senator Kennedy was following the time-honored tradition of using his subcommittee for any purpose by claiming jurisdiction on the slenderest of threads—in this case, administrative procedures in the CAB. In fact, from the start the focus was on substance, not procedure; this was another case in which the loose structure of Congress and the proliferation of subcommittees fostered entrepreneurial politics.

The resulting investigation was one of the most comprehensive and in-depth instances of congressional oversight of an agency and its major program. Staff members and outside consultants led by Stephen Breyer, then a Harvard Law School professor, worked for over one year on background study, hearings, and a final report. The subcommittee's report concluded that air service could be made available at significantly lower prices through competition in the absence of CAB regulation.[32]

Breyer later concluded that the detailed inquiry was an essential element, together with developing a political coalition and a practical reform plan, in implementing deregulation. The hearings served as a catalyst, forcing other congressional and executive actors to focus on the issues while offering them a forum for their views. By providing an opportunity for airlines, which generally opposed deregulation, to present their views, Kennedy's staff was able to study their arguments and to deal more directly with their objections. A careful review of airlines' claims and data on the issue of whether small towns would lose their airline service found that this was not an intractable problem—and hence not a major obstacle to reform. The hearings illustrated issues for the layman and provided material for the press. California, for example, where an unregulated airline flew from Los Angeles to San Francisco at half the price of flights of equivalent length in the East, provided a compelling argument against regulation.[33]

The Limits of Theory and Data. Although economic analysis has a powerful influence in economic deregulation, it has not fared as well in social regulation. Economists have, for example, often advocated a more efficient strategy of pollution control based on economic incentives. There is considerable evidence that a market in air pollution rights would bring about substantial savings while realizing environmental goals. Nonetheless, such approaches have met with opposition or indifference from most members of Congress. It is not

245

a concept that has captured the imagination of those most concerned with environmental issues.

Not only is economic theory of limited effect in considering social regulation in Congress, but there are limitations in the use and effect of data and policy analysis. Michael Levin has pointed out that in enacting the Occupational Safety and Health Act, Congress paid heed to dramatic statistics and cases of occupational hazards but did not analyze the actual causes of occupational injuries or whether direct regulation would work. Nor did Congress consider compliance costs; it simply assumed that they could be readily borne by industry.[34]

The limited willingness of Congress to use data and analysis in the regulatory arena can also be seen in pharmaceutical regulation. When the economist Sam Peltzman suggested to Congress that the requirements of the 1962 drug amendments actually caused more deaths through denial of useful drugs than were saved by keeping dangerous drugs off the market, the response was both to lambaste the author and to ignore the results. From his analysis of this case, David Seidman suggested three hypotheses about the use of analysis in policy making. First, Congress is almost completely impervious to systematic policy analysis, particularly in the short run. Second, the dominant factor in the use of analysis is not whether it is correct or technically competent but which side it supports. Finally, in dealing with risk, there is a bias in favor of protecting specific and visible potential victims, such as those who would suffer severe side effects, and a bias against unknown and perhaps hypothetical victims, such as those denied new drugs but not aware of what they are missing.[35] Seidman's conclusions are more relevant to social than to economic regulation, particularly since the first two hypotheses have largely been contradicted by recent economic deregulation. But they do point the way to a consideration of the differences in the use of information and analysis between the two kinds of regulation.

The Uses of Information. Theory and analysis have less influence in social regulation for three reasons: complexity, urgency, and cost shifting. First, with regard to complexity, the use and understanding of theory and data in transportation deregulation were relatively straightforward. The issue was considered in the context of a belief system supporting the value of competition. More important, the issue was symbolized by a relatively simple comparison of unregulated air fares in California and regulated fares on the east coast. Try as they might, the regulated carriers could not satisfactorily explain why a trip from Washington to Boston should cost twice as much as a trip of the same distance between Los Angeles and San Francisco. That example was simple and dramatic; it neatly summed up the issue. In contrast, something like a market in air pollution rights is too complex to provide a similarly dramatic example. It is not that congressmen cannot readily master the concept. Rather, the issue is too analytical to appeal to the media or to constituents.

In social regulation Congress wrestles with issues that are horrendously complex. Nowhere is this seen more clearly than in environmental legislation, where Congress has to decide not only on broad strategies for control but also on the amounts of emissions allowable before a new source is regulated, percentage reductions in certain pollutants, and technological approaches. This is the most expensive area of regulation, but there is no agreement in Congress about the extent to which cost should be considered in environmental legislation. Congress is called upon to make judgments about the relationships between pollutants and health effects, many of which are not well understood, and about acceptable risk levels where the probability of danger is not known. Moreover, there is probably no other area of major policy making whose subject matter is so foreign to most members and also so expensive and complex. Representative James Broyhill (Republican, North Carolina), who cosponsored a revision of the Clean Air Act with John Dingell, remarked that action was difficult because of the complexity of the program:

> Few members of Congress have the time or inclination to study this mammoth law. . . . Members of Congress and their staffs are not equipped to evaluate computer models or technical specifications for limestone injection multiburners and the number of unanswerable questions such as "what level of protection is necessary to protect public health and welfare?" or "what is the actual air quality in Chicago?" and "what will it be in 1987 under a specific regulatory scenario?"[36]

In complex issues the executive branch usually exercises great influence in setting the legislative agenda. That would have been the case with the reauthorization of the Clean Air Act except that the Reagan administration never submitted a bill to Congress; it sent a vague set of guidelines that did not satisfy anyone. In the absence of concrete White House proposals, the executive branch did not perform its normal function of providing cues to unravel the complexity of the issues. Senator Gary Hart (Democrat, Colorado) complained that the administration's failure to submit a bill put the Senate Environment and Public Works Committee in the position of "trying to legislate from a hodgepodge of official and unofficial documents."[37]

Of course, in the environmental field as well as in other economic policy areas, lack of information is not always an impediment to legislative action. The Dingell-Broyhill bill was originally drafted before the EPA responded to a list of seventy-eight questions to which the House Energy and Commerce Committee needed "understandable" answers to help it draft a "moderate comprehensive bill."[38]

Issues of social regulation are more urgent and far more emotional. They are often posed in terms of rights ("everyone has a right to a safe workplace"), and a consideration of rights tends to be less amenable to analysis than considerations of efficiency. Unfortunately, the discussion rarely proceeds to an examination of how rights can most efficiently be realized. As Seidman notes, attention usually focuses on specific and visible victims, and this crowds out consideration of alternatives or of the adverse side effects that might ensue from a contemplated regulatory action.

Much of the discussion of regulatory reform has focused on achieving a better balance between costs and benefits. Congressmen understand that costs are more readily quantifiable than benefits, but some maintain that analysis is therefore irrelevant. Albert Gore, Jr. (Democrat, Tennessee), for example, said that he was not convinced "that any kind of ethereal academic analysis can adequately value the benefits of lives saved by regulations that prevent the introduction of unsafe drugs, adulterated foods, and that attempt to mitigate insufferable conditions in the workplaces."[39]

In social regulatory issues it is easier to hide or otherwise dismiss the question of cost, and if cost is not perceived to be an issue, analysis is less relevant. There has always been considerable sentiment in Congress that some goals should be achieved regardless of cost. This attitude is reflected in the statement that "we are not about to put a price on human life." Congressmen are squeamish about imposing limits on the achievement of worthy ends or on the provision of benefits to groups that elicit strong sympathies. Even if there had been consideration of the cost of access to public facilities for the handicapped, it is doubtful that many members of Congress would have wanted to argue that specific services were too expensive. It was convenient, therefore, *not* to consider cost.

Procedural Regulatory Reform

Many of the issues outlined in this chapter appear in the debate over procedural reform. Nearly everyone is for regulatory reform in the

248

abstract. Problems arise only when particular reforms are proposed. But the issue will not go away, and important contituents persistently seek redress from the burdens of federal regulation. Because of the difficulty of achieving substantive reforms in major areas such as environmental protection, there has been substantial congressional interest in comprehensive procedural reform. If Congress cannot change environmental policy, at least it can establish procedures that give it the last word on decisions (legislative veto) or keep pressure on the agencies (sunset). When decision costs and uncertainty are high, a procedural policy is an attractive solution that delays the necessity of a decision.

The main procedural reforms debated in Congress since 1978 have contained several basic provisions. First, agencies would be required to prepare economic analyses of major proposed and final rules. Second, they would be required to review the impact of major regulations already in effect. Third, there would be an oversight mechanism to ensure that agencies comply with the first two requirements. Fourth, control over regulatory decisions would be strengthened through the legislative veto and more intensive judicial review. The debate has revolved mainly around two issues that richly illustrate congressional policy making in the regulatory arena—the utility of cost-benefit analysis or other forms of regulatory impact analysis and the institutional roles of Congress, the executive branch, the independent agencies, and the courts. By 1982 the legislation had become so laden with extraneous amendments representing different views that there was little opposition to the House leadership's decision to let it die without a vote at the end of the Ninety-seventh Congress.

Congress and Regulatory Impact Analysis. As noted above, the use of systematic analysis to deal with complex social issues does not characterize congressional decision making. It is somewhat ironic, then, that Congress has placed so much faith in requiring systematic analysis of proposed regulations by agencies. During the hearings and markup of the procedural reform legislation, there was considerable dispute over whether quantitative analysis, particularly cost-benefit analysis, was possible or appropriate for the concerns likely to be addressed in proposed regulations. In the regulatory reform debate there was considerable distaste for the notion of using *any* valuation of human life in regulatory analyses. Senator Thomas Eagleton (Democrat, Missouri) was so incensed at the apparent use of such a valuation by the Federal Aviation Administration that he requested a General Accounting Office survey to determine whether and how federal agencies valued a human life in cost-benefit analysis.

249

GAO found that no agency was so politically naive as to use a value-of-life cost figure to determine whether to save lives.

The regulatory reform bill passed by the Senate placed a burden on agencies to demonstrate that they had considered alternatives and chosen the most cost-effective one. In the end there was no dissent from the proposition that administrative agencies should conduct an analysis of proposed regulations—even if Congress rarely did so. Consumer and environmental groups and their congressional allies argued, however, that the analytic requirements were designed to hamstring health and safety agencies and would prevent needed regulatory action. As a consequence, analysis was not regarded as neutral.

The Institutional Issues. By far the most divisive issues in procedural reform have concerned the institutional prerogatives of Congress, the executive branch, and the federal courts. The controversy has revolved around the role of the Office of Management and Budget, judicial review, and the legislative veto.

As the regulatory reform debate developed, there was increasing tension between many in Congress and the OMB. A little background may be helpful in understanding the situation. To a considerable extent, the format of procedural reform was set by the Carter Administration's Executive Order 12044, which mandated regulatory analyses for proposed and final rules. The Carter administration set up a Regulatory Analysis Review Group to review the analyses, but it lacked the teeth needed to bring recalcitrant agencies into line. The regulatory reform bills reported by Senate and House committees assigned oversight of agency compliance to the GAO, a legislative branch agency.

Shortly after assuming office, President Reagan issued a new executive order, which also called for regulatory analyses (with a much higher burden of proof imposed on regulators) and gave the OMB the authority to hold up regulations if it judged that an agency had not complied with the analysis requirement. Shortly afterward Senator Paul Laxalt (Republican, Nevada) introduced the major regulatory reform bill of the Ninety-seventh Congress. That bill, as later reported by the Judiciary Committee, followed the president's lead by assigning oversight to the OMB.

A good deal of concern arose in Congress about the way in which the OMB was exercising its new authority over the rule-making process. Those who were concerned certainly had no desire to legitimate that power in legislation. The OMB's power over the regulatory process had already been recognized in statute by the Paperwork Reduction Act of 1980, which established the Office of Information and Regulatory Affairs in OMB and gave it the power to review and disapprove agency requests to collect information.

One frequent complaint about regulatory review under President Reagan's executive order was that the interactions between the OMB and the agencies occurred in a "black box." The OMB's reasons for rejecting or seeking changes in agency regulatory analyses were not part of the public record. Even more disturbing to critics were the frequent off-the-record meetings between OMB officials and industry lobbyists, which circumvented the usual procedural safeguards. OMB regulatory officials argued that the process had to be flexible and informal, while critics claimed that it improperly removed rule making from public scrutiny.

A closely related but more fundamental issue was the status of the independent regulatory agencies under the proposed legislation—an issue that has persisted since the 1937 Brownlow Commission report called for greater presidential control of the regulatory process. The Paperwork Reduction Act reflected that concern by allowing the independent agencies to overrule OMB disapproval of their data-gathering requests. The OMB had already demonstrated that it could use its oversight authority to shape policy; extending that authority to the independent agencies through the regulatory reform legislation was perceived as putting the independent agencies under the president's control. Thus the regulatory reform debate focused in part on basic institutional prerogatives. Of course, as is generally true with institutional prerogatives, attitudes depended in considerable measure (but not entirely) on who was president. Having witnessed the none too benign posture of the Reagan administration toward federal regulatory agencies, congressional Democrats were not disposed to compromise the independence of those agencies that were formally outside the presidential orbit.

The role of the courts was also a factor in the regulatory reform debate. In 1979 Senator Dale Bumpers (Democrat, Arkansas) surprised everyone by getting Senate approval for an amendment that would have changed the presumption of validity accorded to regulatory agency finding of facts in federal appeals courts. The courts would have been completely free, under the Bumpers amendment, to take issue with any legal or factual finding by the agencies. Although the amendment was considered without prior hearings, it passed the Senate handily. Upon reflection the Senate backed off somewhat, but an expanded role for the courts in reviewing agency actions was nonetheless a fixture in regulatory reform bills. As jealous as Congress has been in guarding its prerogatives vis-à-vis the executive branch, it has been willing to increase the authority of the judicial branch. The courts' accretion of authority has been at the expense of administrative agencies rather than of Congress.

The Legislative Veto. Although the legislative veto was long used in a variety of circumstances, such as executive branch reorganization, it gained a great deal of attention and roused intense controversy in recent years as a device to control regulatory agencies by enabling Congress to invalidate particular agency rules. The basic feature of the legislative veto was a requirement that no agency rule take effect until the end of a waiting period during which one or both houses of Congress can vote to invalidate it. The veto provisions differed in whether one or both houses are necessary, the role of committees, and other procedural requirements.

From 1975 to 1983, there were numerous attempts to impose a blanket veto for all regulations. During the years that comprehensive regulatory reform was considered by Congress, there were serious attempts to append a blanket legislative veto to that legislation. Finally, in 1981, the Senate passed regulatory legislation with a provision for legislative veto, but the bill did not become law. Pro-veto members of the House pressed their case every time a regulatory agency came up for reauthorization—and succeeded in enacting a legislative veto for the Federal Trade Commission and the Consumer Product Safety Commission.

The legislative veto had implications for the role of Congress in regulatory policy making. In a typical session Congress enacts fewer than 300 public laws, but regulatory agencies issue many more than that number of regulations annually. Although only a small proportion of these are major regulations, it is unreasonable to expect that Congress will methodically and carefully consider the merits and legality of several hundred regulations each year. Instead there would probably be a shift in decision-making authority. Congress would become a court of political appeal, as was demonstrated by the veto of the FTC's used car rule.

The legislative veto raised the constitutional issue of separation of powers and was opposed by most presidents.[40] One sensitive issue that escaped serious debate was the veto's effect on the distribution of power within Congress and on its relationship to the agencies. Since most veto provisions required some committee action, the authority of a committee over the agency it oversees was greatly enhanced. But in its daily dealing with agencies, particularly in the Senate, the committee is its staff; it was the staff that gained greatly magnified leverage over regulatory decisions and that was the increased target of lobbying by affected interests.

The legislative veto has the potential to undermine the deliberative process in agencies. A major purpose of the Administrative Procedures Act is to ensure that administrative decisions are based on a careful review of relevant information and that there is adequate opportunity for the public and affected parties to make their case. The whole thrust of the legislative veto, however, was to ignore that record and render irrelevant the protections built into the administrative process. This was deemed, however, to be a necessary price for the improved political accountability that proponents claimed for the legislative veto. The demise of the legislative veto at the hands of the Supreme Court did not put an end to questions of how Congress, in an age of complex and far-reaching regulation, controls the rules formulated by regulatory agencies. Within weeks after the Court ruled in 1983, legislation was introduced to prevent regulations from taking effect without prior congressional approval. Members of Congress insisted that they would be more guarded in giving agencies regulatory discretion now that the "reserve power" of the veto was no longer available. It may be years before the full implications of the Court's sweeping decision are known, but it is unlikely that Congress will abandon its efforts to influence regulatory actions.

Concluding Assessment

The purpose of this chapter has been to describe and analyze congressional policy making, not to prescribe. Nonetheless, a concluding assessment is in order. There are two major, related problems with regulatory policy making by Congress. First, with the exception of some economic regulatory issues, Congress has not been able to examine issues from a consistent and useful analytical standpoint. This is hardly a novel or controversial conclusion, but it is probably an immutable one. Congress tries to reach agreement, not to arrive at ultimate truth.

Second, Congress has increasingly interceded in regulatory agency proceedings. During the 1979–1980 fight over reauthorizing the FTC, one house or the other or relevant committees voted, after intensive industry lobbying, to terminate virtually all major commission rule makings, investigations, or enforcement cases. This episode was a crisis not only for the FTC but also for Congress, which pulled back only after editorials and television news programs caricatured it as selling out the public interest to big business and to sleazy confidence men. The spectacle of congressmen actively interceding in rule-making proceedings and law enforcement matters at the behest of campaign contributors does great damage to the integrity and credibility of government.

The way out of this problem is not to entreat Congress to be virtuous but rather to remove the temptation. This can be done only by abandoning the legislative veto and by not focusing on particular proceedings during reauthorizations and appropriations. It would be appropriate for Congress to decide that the FTC should prohibit only demonstrably false advertising, not merely unfair advertising. But to come to that standard only for children's advertising at the behest of the affected industry is quite another matter. It might be objected that this argument is naive in that Congress usually focuses on particular cases with regard to subsidies, taxes, and other policies. In the case of regulation, however, congressional intervention supersedes a carefully structured administrative process aimed at giving all affected parties a fair hearing and expert consideration of issues. If holding to this standard means that Congress would yield to an agency's discretion in instances in which the agency has exceeded congressional intent (assuming that there is such a thing), this is less troublesome than giving the appearance that congressional votes are for sale. A concern with broader policy issues would not only improve the reputation of Congress but also permit it to address more fundamental questions of regulatory legislation and oversight, which would ultimately mitigate agencies' excesses.

Notes

1. James Q. Wilson, *The Politics of Regulation* (New York: Basic Books, 1980).

2. Compare Theodore Lowi, "Four Systems of Policy, Politics, and Choice," *Public Administration Review,* vol. 32 (1972), pp. 298–310.

3. Gabriel Kolko, *The Triumph of Conservatism: A Reinterpretation of American History, 1900–1916* (New York: Free Press, 1963).

4. George Stigler, "The Theory of Economic Regulation," *Bell Journal of Economics and Management Science,* vol. 2 (Spring 1971), pp. 3–21.

5. For example, Robert W. Harbeson, "Railroads and Regulation, 1877–1916: Conspiracy or Public Interest?" *Journal of Economic History,* vol. 27 (1967), pp. 230–42.

6. Paul Quirk, *Industry Influence in Federal Regulatory Agencies* (Princeton, N.J.: Princeton University Press, 1981), p. 10.

7. Mark V. Nadel, *The Politics of Consumer Protection* (Indianapolis: Bobbs-Merrill, 1971), pp. 227–32.

8. H.R. Rept. No. 1153, 92d Congress, 2d session, 1972, p. 21.

9. The powers were not entirely new; the CPSC assumed administra-

tion of several existing acts, such as the Flammable Fabrics Act and the Poison Prevention Packaging Act.

10. *Federal Regulation and Regulatory Reform,* 94th Congress, 2d session, 1976, p. 195.

11. House Committee on Appropriations, *Agriculture, Environmental, and Consumer Protection Bill, 1975,* 93d Congress, 2d session, 1974, p. 88; Senate Committee on Appropriations, *Departments of State, Justice, and Commerce, the Judiciary and Related Agencies Appropriation Bill, 1978,* 95th Congress, 1st session, 1977, p. 53. Cited in Michael Pertschuk, *Revolt against Regulation* (Berkeley: University of California Press, 1982), p. 79.

12. Barry R. Weingast and Mark J. Moran, "The Myth of Runaway Bureaucracy: The Case of the FTC," *Regulation* (May/June 1982), pp. 33–38.

13. John Bibby, "Congress' Neglected Function," in Melvin Laird, ed., *Republican Papers* (New York: Praeger, 1968), pp. 477–88.

14. U.S. Senate, Committee on Government Operations, *Study on Federal Regulation,* vol. 2, *Congressional Oversight of Regulatory Agencies,* 95th Congress, 1st session, 1977, p. ix.

15. Ibid., p. 92.

16. For example, Morris Ogul, *Congress Oversees the Bureaucracy: Studies in Legislative Supervision* (Pittsburgh: University of Pittsburgh Press, 1976); *Committee Reform Amendments of 1974, Staff Report of the Select Committee on Committees,* 93d Congress, 2d session, H.R. Rept. 93-916, March 21, 1974.

17. Ogul, *Congress Oversees the Bureaucracy,* p. 5.

18. Senate, Committee on Government Operations, *Congressional Oversight,* p. 38.

19. U.S. Senate, Committee on Government Operations, *Study on Federal Regulation,* vol. 1, *The Regulatory Appointments Process,* 95th Congress, 1st session, 1977, pp. 163–85.

20. Pertschuk, *Revolt against Regulation,* p. 36.

21. John Kingdon, *Congressional Voting Decisions* (New York: Harper and Row, 1973); and R. Douglas Arnold, "The Local Roots of Domestic Policy," in Thomas E. Mann and Norman J. Ornstein, eds., *The New Congress* (Washington, D.C.: American Enterprise Institute, 1981).

22. *National Journal,* July 30, 1977, p. 1193.

23. Nadel, *Politics of Consumer Protection.*

24. Timothy Clark, "Regulation Gone Amok: How Many Billions for Wheelchair Transit?" *Regulation* (March/April 1980), p. 48.

25. See section "Procedural Regulatory Reform" in this chapter.

26. Wilson, "The Politics of Regulation." The categories in this section are drawn from Wilson.

27. See, for example, Mancur Olson, *The Logic of Collective Action* (Cambridge, Mass.: Harvard University Press, 1965).

28. Nadel, *Politics of Consumer Protection.*

29. Bruce Ackerman and William Hassler, "Beyond the New Deal:

Coal and the Clean Air Act," *Yale Law Journal*, vol. 89 (July 1980), pp. 1466–571.

30. For example, Samuel Richmond, *Regulation and Competition in Air Transportation* (New York: Columbia University Press, 1961).

31. George Douglas and James Miller III, *Economic Regulation of Domestic Air Transport: Theory and Policy* (Washington, D.C.: Brookings Institution, 1974); William Jordan, *Airline Regulation in America: Effects and Imperfections* (Baltimore: Johns Hopkins University Press, 1970); and Theodore Keeler, *Airline Regulation and Market Performance* (1972).

32. U.S. Senate, Subcommittee on Administrative Practice and Procedure, Committee on the Judiciary, *Civil Aeronautics Board Practices and Procedures*, 94th Congress, 1st session, 1975.

33. Stephen Breyer, *Regulation and Its Reform* (Cambridge, Mass.: Harvard University Press, 1981).

34. Michael Levin, "Politics and Polarity: The Limits of OSHA Reform," *Regulation* (November/December 1979), pp. 33–36.

35. David Seidman, "The Politics of Policy Analysis," *Regulation* (July/August 1977), pp. 34–35.

36. Quoted in *Inside EPA*, June 25, 1982, p. 14.

37. *National Journal*, February 6, 1982, p. 240.

38. Ibid.

39. U.S. House of Representatives, Subcommittee on Oversight and Investigations, Committee on Energy and Commerce, *Role of OMB in Regulation, Hearing*, 97th Congress, 1st session, 1981, p. 5.

40. The Reagan administration, however, initially took the position that it did not oppose the veto for independent as opposed to executive branch agencies.

9

The Distributive Congress

Allen Schick

The Ninety-seventh Congress (1981–1982) produced only 473 public laws, fewer than were enacted by any Congress during the previous sixty years.[1] If not for the lame-duck session held after the 1982 elections, the Ninety-seventh Congress would have yielded less legislative output than any other Congress in the past century.

It has become commonplace to blame the "paralysis of Congress" for the failure of the national legislature to face pressing issues forthrightly and expeditiously.[2] The breakdown of Congress is often attributed to institutional defects, such as rules and procedures that delay legislation and enable members to impede action on bills and a fragmented committee structure that obscures jurisdictional responsibilities and invites conflict. Yet despite these disabilities, Congress moves at great speed when it wants to do so. The same Ninety-seventh Congress that floundered for nearly two years managed to overcome inertia and a filibuster during the three weeks of the lame-duck session and enact a major highway modernization program along with more than 100 other measures.[3]

Why is Congress sluggish during some periods and energetic during others? Why has the number of public laws enacted by Congress steadily declined in recent years? Why does Congress work harder but produce less? Answers to these and similar questions about the performance of Congress cannot be obtained merely by examining its organization and procedures. Congress is the most open of our national institutions, and it is highly sensitive to changing political conditions. If it has become disorganized and ineffective, the main problems lie outside Capitol Hill and cannot be remedied by internal adjustments alone. Congress will not be restored to vigor simply by strengthening party or committee leaders or by easing the flow of legislation through the House and Senate.[4] Members will not adopt institutional reforms that do not respond to their perceived needs.

The argument of this concluding chapter is that Congress now has difficulty legislating because the role demanded of it by economic conditions is not congruent with the type of legislation encouraged by its organization and behavior. The Congress that functions in the 1980s is a product of the economic conditions that prevailed in the 1950s and 1960s. During the two decades after World War II economic growth was vigorous, and the public sector was programmed for expansion. A growing economy provided bountiful resources to be distributed by Congress through its legislative processes. Congress could distribute benefits to major segments of the population without raising taxes or otherwise disadvantaging political interests. Even during the brief recessions that occurred from time to time, Congress was confident that growth would resume, and it did not curtail federal spending when revenues fell.

But the early postwar congresses were not effectively organized for this distributive role. This chapter will show how Congress, especially the House, inhibited the articulation and satisfaction of demands for public benefits. The House Appropriations Committee, for example, oriented itself to cutting the president's budget; the House Ways and Means Committee quashed demands for tax cuts either by bottling up legislation in committee or by bringing it to the floor under a closed rule. Congress had resources to distribute, but self-imposed constraints limited its capacity to do so. There was thus a mismatch between the capacity of Congress to distribute benefits and pressure on it to behave distributively.

Congress ended this predicament by relaxing its constraints through rule changes and other modifications of its behavior. The salient changes are discussed later in this chapter; for the present it suffices to note that many of the reforms that "democratized" Congress in the late 1960s and early 1970s opened it to increased pressure for benefits from the federal government. Paradoxically, however, at about the time (in the 1970s) that institutional reforms exposed Congress to distributive pressures, economic conditions became less favorable. After the first oil shock (1973), the U.S. economy weakened, and growth was no longer as vigorous or sustained as it had been in the two preceding decades. Congress was still programmed for distribution, but the economy no longer produced sufficient increments to satisfy the demands placed on the legislative process. Accordingly Congress functioned in a manner that did not comport with the nation's economic situation.

The attribution of congressional malaise to economic conditions does not mean that these are the only, or always the most salient, influences on legislative behavior. Congress is open to just about everything on the mind of America, as the pages of the *Congressional Record* frequently attest. Economic issues must compete with a full range of social concerns for congressional attention. Yet in recent years economic matters have dominated the legislative agenda and have been the principal reason for the mismatch between the capacity and the role of Congress.[5]

This chapter develops the theme presented in the preceding paragraphs. The main part of the chapter briefly surveys the distributive role of Congress during the first 150 years of American nationhood and then discusses how Congress adapted to distributive politics after World War II; the last part examines the redistributive environment in which Congress now operates and concludes with a consideration of how the capacity of Congress to function redistributively might be strengthened.

What is meant by distribution and redistribution? Distributive legislation is financed by economic growth; redistributive policies are financed by tax increases, other social costs (such as regulation), or the transfer of funds among public programs. A purely distributive policy makes some interests better off and none worse off. It might be contended that pure distribution is unlikely because even if no one suffers an actual loss, legislation almost always alters the relative status of interests or makes some interests worse off than they would have been without government action. Nevertheless, for purposes of this chapter a policy is deemed to be distributive if no one's absolute condition is adversely affected.

Redistribution transfers resources among interests. Congress can act redistributively even when resources are plentiful, but it is much more likely to do so when important demands cannot be satisfied without disadvantaging some interests. Because it is usually difficult and unpalatable to make redistributive decisions, Congress often redistributes in ways that appear to distribute benefits broadly. The road improvement program enacted in the closing days of the Ninety-seventh Congress illustrates this behavior. The measure was clearly redistributive, for it financed highway repairs out of increases in gas taxes and other levies. But the bill was perceived as distributive by many members who were convinced that it would provide several hundred thousand jobs, stimulate economic recovery, and repair deteriorating roads. As is often the case, this perception was reinforced by the fact that the benefits were concentrated and the costs dispersed. Large federal grants were earmarked for the fifty states, and a relatively small number of jobs were created, but the tax increases were spread among tens of millions of drivers. Truck operators had to pay higher fees, but Congress provided offsetting benefits, such as improved roads and permission to use bigger vehicles on the highways. Moreover, the principal benefits (road repairs and jobs) would be highly visible, while adverse effects on tourism and other consumer spending were too uncertain and invisible to weigh seriously on the minds of congressmen.

The ability of Congress to define redistributive policies in distributive terms is an important determinant of its capacity to legislate. The 1982 highway bill was enacted because Congress transformed it into a jobs bill and thereby into distributive legislation. But Congress has found it increasingly difficult to behave in this manner; hence its legislative output has declined.

The Rise of the Distributive State

Congress is predisposed by its electoral and geographic bases to distribute benefits to constituents. Some members garner electoral support by practicing public parsimony; many more do so by spending public funds. A few members are indifferent to the flow of federal dollars to their states and districts; most actively seek to increase those funds.

Throughout American history distributive politics has been associated with pork-barrel legislation, such as appropriations for rivers and harbors and for other public works. Yet during the nineteenth century pork-barrel practices were confined to a few policy areas and constituted a small portion of the federal budget. Most of the national budget was allocated to defense and to the recurring expenses of government agencies.[6] From the perspective of late twentieth-century America, Congress has been a restrained spender during most of its existence. To be sure, Congress has been seen as profligate when it has added funds for designated projects in members' districts or has voted generous pensions for veterans. In the nineteenth century these were the main areas into which distributive pressures were channeled. One of the reasons why pork-barrel projects loomed so large in congressional behavior was that they were the principal means of distributing benefits to constituents.

The distributive tendencies of Congress were constrained by the prevailing notions of limited government and balanced budgets. The role and scope of the national government were extremely limited; it would not have been deemed legitimate for the government to take on the broader responsibilities that it assumed in the twentieth century. As pointed out in the introduction to this volume, federal spending amounted to 3 percent of GNP on the eve of the Great Depression, a percentage that had not varied much during the preceding 100 years.[7] Not only was the national government small, but it also had a narrow scope. Most public services were financed and administered by state and local governments. Congress could not break out of the policy confines of the government to distribute benefits more broadly.

These external constraints were reinforced by the rules and organization of Congress. Spending policy was controlled by powerful committees—the House Ways and Means and the Senate Finance committees before the Civil War, the House and Senate Appropriations committees after the war—that guarded the treasury against expenditure demands from government agencies as well as from members and committees of Congress. The rules of the House and Senate separated appropriations from legislation; as a result few federal dollars were distributed in substantive measures that bypassed the appropriations process.[8]

In generalizing about more than a century of congressional practice it is important to recognize that there were periods during which the distributive impulse was dominant. The government did incur some deficits in peacetime, real spending did rise over time, and federal responsibilities were enlarged. There were periods during which Congress relaxed its self-imposed constraints to facilitate the enactment of distributive legislation. In the 1880s and 1890s, for example, the House and Senate shifted jurisdiction over many appropriations bills to legislative committees, which were more accommodating to spending demands than the Appropriations committees had been.[9] The House periodically dropped the Holman rule, which permits the Appropriations Committee to report legislation retrenching federal expenditures.[10] Thus in the late nineteenth century, as in other periods, Congress conformed its rules and operations to the expectations and demands placed on it.

A shift toward a less distributive role occurred after World War I (spurred in part by the enormous wartime spending increases and deficits), and Congress once again responded by conforming its organization and behavior to the changed situation. The House and Senate returned full jurisdiction over spending measures to their Appropriations committees and strengthened their rules against the inclusion of expenditures in substantive legislation. Congress also inhibited distributive pressures by barring federal agencies from submitting their spending requests to it and requiring instead that these requests be packaged by the president into an annual budget. The Budget and Accounting Act of 1921 established a presidential budget process that centralized control over federal finances in the executive branch. The result was that distributive pressures on Congress abated.[11]

Toward Distributive Politics. The New Deal, however, paved the way for a protracted era of distributive politics. It not only enlarged the federal government but also altered public expectations and legitimized an active role for the national government in improving the quality of life by providing benefits and services to the American people. Through new programs and increased expenditures, health care could be improved, roads built, land reclaimed. But the fundamental changes wrought by the New Deal did not immediately change either political expectations or the operations of Congress. Roosevelt's One Hundred Days in 1933 constituted a temporary suspension of congressional norms, not a massive swing toward distributive politics. In the wake of the depression and Roosevelt's election mandate, Congress rushed to enact sweeping legislation formulated by the new president's brain trust. After normalcy returned, Congress became less pliant and the president less successful in imposing his will on recalcitrant legislators. Barely one year after his landslide victory at the polls in 1936, Roosevelt convened a special session of Congress to act on "must" legislation. The session adjourned, however, without passing any of the measures demanded by the president. He responded by trying to purge the Democratic party of conservative congressmen, some of whom held key committee posts and were instrumental in blocking his legislation. In this he failed. Not until the postwar era would Congress adapt itself to distributive norms.

The New Deal did not quickly transform Congress because it did not immediately change America. The Keynesian role of government was not widely accepted in the 1930s, nor was the obligation of the government to intervene massively in behalf of the less fortunate. "America," Harry Hopkins wrote in 1937, had become "bored with the poor, the unemployed and the insecure."[12] In *Middletown in Transition,* the great sociological study of Muncie published in the same year, the Lynds found that "Middletown is overwhelmingly living by the values by which it lived in 1925."[13]

The slowness of the New Deal to take root can be attributed to at least two factors. First, new ideas take time to be assimilated, especially when they challenge entrenched values. The New Deal could not immediately uproot more than a century of political ideology about balanced budgets, the limited role of government, and the responsibilities of the individual. Second, the New Deal was not obviously successful to all those who lived through it. The unemployment rate was 17 percent in 1939, and more than 9 million Americans were still out of work. The economy had improved, but not until World War II brought full employment did the nation accept the enlarged role of government as permanent.

Looking back at the past half-century, it can be seen that the enlarged role assigned to the federal government by the New Deal was legitimized after World War II. The war bequeathed a vigorous economy and an opportunity to roll the clock back to a more modest conception of government. The Republicans controlled Congress shortly after the war (1947–1948) and the White House through most of the 1950s. Nevertheless, in the postwar era Congress extended the scope and reach of federal responsibilities. The 1949 Housing Act did more for housing and community development than the Housing Act of 1937 did; the 1950 social security admendments had a more immediate effect on participation rates and benefits than the original 1935 legislation.[14] Congress also added other activities, such as airport and hospital construction and school aid, to the roster of federal responsibilities.

The March of Incrementalism. If the New Deal was revolutionary, the postwar developments were incremental. There was no massive attempt in the 1950s to remake the role of the federal government or to adapt Congress to the government's enlarged distributive responsibilities. Enlargement was piecemeal, program by program, as expenditures were increased in some areas and functions added in others. But the cumulative effect was to create widespread political support for the government's distributive role and expectations that it would continue. By the end of the 1950s, not only were the New Deal programs here to stay, but most were no longer controversial and were expected to grow.

The pace of change experienced in the postwar era came to be known as incrementalism. As described by Wildavsky in *The Politics of the Budgetary Process*, incrementalism was more than a statement that programs and expenditures grow over time; it was also a normative argument that steady growth is desirable because it moderates conflict, stabilizes political roles and expectations, reduces the time that busy officials must invest in policy making, and decreases the probability that important political values will be neglected.[15] Incrementalism is a pattern of distributive politics in which government agencies ask for and Congress provides more money. Continued growth is seen as legitimate, not just as something that occurs because interest groups and spending agencies outwit the president and Congress. Just about everybody behaves in a growth-oriented manner, including those (such as the budget office and the Appropriations committees) whose traditional role was to resist distributive pressures.

Incrementalism is a distributive process. Program expansions are financed by economic growth, not by transferring resources from

263

some uses to others. In the postwar era government was incremental because the economy was incremental. Real GNP grew at an average of 4 percent a year in the 1950s and 1960s. Disposable personal income doubled during those decades; unemployment averaged about 4.5 percent, only slightly above the 4 percent "full employment" level; and inflation (as measured by the GNP deflator) was at a 2.5 percent annual rate.

Economic growth and government growth went hand in hand; the public economy could expand because the private economy was also expanding. In time the federal government became responsible for stimulating and sustaining economic growth through active fiscal policy. When the economy was slack, the government continued to distribute benefits, which were financed out of idle resources. The government's distributive role could expand steadily even when the economy zigzagged.

Economic growth made it possible for the federal government to muddle through one of the enduring ambivalences in American public opinion. During the fifty years in which scientific polling data have been available, most Americans have been of two minds about the size and services of the national government. Since the New Deal a majority has wanted the government to maintain (and in some cases to increase) its services; yet most Americans also favor balanced budgets, lower taxes, and smaller government.[16] The polls suggest that Americans want distributive policies (more services) but would oppose redistributive ones (such as tax increases).

Economic growth made it possible to satisfy both objectives. Government was able to expand not by taking from the disposable incomes of Americans but by reaping the growth dividends of a buoyant economy. Economic growth made everybody into a winner. Government provided more benefits without raising taxes and without shifting productive resources from the private to the public sector. During the 1950s and the first half of the 1960s, spending increases were virtually matched by economic growth; as a consequence, federal outlays were only a slightly higher percentage of GNP in the mid-1960s than they had been in the previous decade.

Adapting Congress to Distributive Politics. Although expansion of programs and expenditures became a regular feature of the legislative and budgetary processes in the postwar era, there was remarkably little change in the organization and machinery of Congress.[17] Congress was able to distribute increasing benefits without formally adopting a more actively distributive posture. Yet Congress did transform itself through a series of small, uncoordinated changes that accumulated into a significant shift in its orientation.

Congress was organized in the 1950s to make controlled and limited increases in government spending. Growth was steady but not spectacular. Most agencies received increases in the 5–10 percent range.[18] These increases were doled out through the appropriations process, which was oriented to guarding the treasury against spending demands. The Appropriations committees had jurisdiction over virtually the entire federal budget. Backdoor spending was limited, and the authorizing committees were generally inactive in pressing for more distribution because most federal programs and agencies had permanent authorizations. Hence most spending demands were channeled through and moderated by the annual appropriations process.

Appropriations hegemony was secured by two features of federal budgeting. First, most appropriations were made to federal agencies that spent the funds on their own operations. The bulk of the money provided by Congress went for the salaries of federal employees, the purchase of equipment and supplies, and other operating expenses. This simple appropriations-expenditure structure enhanced the power of the Appropriations committees, which had an administrative orientation, unlike most authorizing committees, which had more programmatic outlooks. Second, the distributive processes of government were relatively closed. There was little public knowledge of the budget before it was submitted to Congress, and the Bureau of the Budget strictly enforced its rule against the premature release of budgetary information. Agencies were required to defend the president's recommendations, not their original wants, and although there were occasional breaches, this norm was generally adhered to. The closure of the distributive process was reinforced by a lack of outside understanding of budgetary numbers. The authorizing committees often did not know how much money was being provided for the programs in their jurisdiction. The line-item details that cluttered the president's budget and congressional appropriations obscured the program implications of executive and legislative decisions and made it easier to restrain spending without stirring up opposition. Few outside analyses were made of the budget, and there were few budget watchers outside the small circle of participants. The Appropriations committees marked up their bills behind closed doors, and floor amendments were discouraged.

These conditions made it possible to maintain spending discipline in an incremental environment. Agencies and programs normally received higher appropriations than in the previous year but, as

Richard Fenno showed in *The Power of the Purse,* less than the president requested for them.[19] Even though Congress had no process in the postwar era for comparing all the claims made on it to one another or for relating total expenditures to total revenues, federal spending did not vastly outstrip the available resources. The budget-appropriations process restrained distributive pressures by using current expenditures and the president's request as guideposts for determining how much was to be provided for the next year.

This closed system, however, severely restricted the distributive influence of the authorizing committees on which most members of Congress sat. Over time many of these committees thrust themselves into the distributive process by converting existing programs from permanent to temporary authorizations or by establishing new programs on a temporary basis. As they became more involved and expert in distributive matters, these committees began to devise backdoor spending schemes that evaded the annual appropriations process. The authorizing committees were more interested in programs than in agencies; consequently, much of the legislation that they produced was geared to distribute funds to program beneficiaries rather than to the agencies themselves.

The allocative decisions of authorizing committees differed from those typically made by the Appropriations committees, and these differences enhanced the distributive role of Congress. Unlike the Appropriations committees, which provided funds for agencies to spend on their own operations, most authorizing committees were interested in the amount of funds going to program operators and beneficiaries. The former were often state and local governments receiving federal grants or contractors receiving payments for particular services; the latter were usually beneficiaries of federal entitlement programs. Many of the programs designed by authorizing committees in the postwar era provided for federal dollars to be spent outside the federal government, not by the agencies themselves. Even when subsequent appropriations were made to federal agencies, the funds were transferred to and spent by recipients outside the administrative structure of government.

These outsiders did not submit budget requests through the channels maintained by the president's Office of Management and Budget or by the House and Senate Appropriations committees. But although they did not prepare formal budget estimates for the OMB or "justification books" for the Appropriations committees, the outsiders had a vital interest in the outcome of the budget and legislative processes. They participated in these processes through political rather than administrative activities: by monitoring executive and congressional actions; by pressing members and committees for legislation and appropriations; by mobilizing program beneficiaries to express their views; by making contributions to political campaigns; and by other political activities. To conduct these activities successfully, outsiders could not be ignorant of the legislative and fiscal options available to Congress. They could not abide the closed environment within which appropriations and other distributive decisions were made by Congress. To ensure that they were adequately informed of actions that affected their interests, outsiders increased the number of Washington representatives and budget watchers. They prepared and circulated their own analyses of budget and legislative issues, and research organizations published studies on these issues.

As outside interests became more active and influential, Congress reformed itself by becoming more open and more fragmented. A few of the changes have already been mentioned, such as the shift from permanent to temporary authorizations and the growth in backdoor spending that bypassed the annual appropriations process. These changes gave outsiders an additional channel of influence and made them less dependent on the Appropriations committees. The opening up of Congress was achieved through the relaxation of seniority rules, the augmentation of committees' and members' staffs, the rising power of subcommittees, the breakdown of norms of apprenticeship and specialization, the declining role of party leaders, massive increases in floor amendments and roll call votes, and the requirement that committees conduct their business in the open. Whatever the motivation for these and other reforms, their cumulative effect was to give virtually every committee and member a distributive role in Congress. Distributive politics was thereby broadened to include the full array of federal programs and expenditures.

The opening up of Congress occurred during the period when the federal budget was being transformed from a process for financing federal agencies into a political process for providing benefits to interests. It would be futile to try to determine which of these developments was cause and which was effect. Did Congress reform itself in response to the transformation of government, or did organizational changes in Congress lead to changes in the structure of federal programs and the distribution of benefits? Both developments occurred concurrently, the one feeding the other. As Congress became more open, it was more disposed to expand programs and increase the flow of benefits to outside recipients; as an increasing portion of the federal budget was distributed to outsiders, the pressure for congressional reform grew.

The growth of federal dollars to outsiders is difficult to quantify.

According to some counts, as much as 85 percent of the federal budget (including interest payments) is spent by state and local governments, contractors, bondholders, beneficiaries of federal transfer programs, and other outsiders. The outsiders have been remarkably successful in protecting and augmenting their distributive benefits; during the 1960s and 1970s the bulk of domestic spending increases was in programs that distribute federal benefits to them.

Not only do the outsiders want more benefits, they also want a more accommodating Congress and more secure funding. They secured the first objective through congressional reform and changes in the appropriations and budget processes and the second through entitlements, grant formulas, and other devices that mandated federal obligations. As Congress opened itself to distributive pressures, the Appropriations committees (particularly House Appropriations, which had a critical role in guarding the treasury) adopted more favorable attitudes toward expansion of expenditures and programs.[20] They responded in this manner both to ward off further erosion of their jurisdiction and in response to changes in their structure and composition. The House Appropriations Committee was enlarged, mainly by the addition of liberal Democrats; committee members were given greater latitude in selecting subcommittee assignments; markups were held in the open; and members were more vigorous in sponsoring floor amendments. Once the Appropriations committees became spenders, Congress was bereft of an institutional capacity to resist distributive pressures.

Along with the transformation of the appropriations process from a control on spending into a means of distribution, the tax process was transformed from revenue raising into still another means of distributing benefits through legislation. The changes recounted by Catherine Rudder in this book exposed the House Ways and Means Committee to distributive pressures through generalized tax reductions or increases in particular tax expenditures.[21] By the end of the 1970s, the committee could no longer resist these pressures by bottling up legislation or by bringing its bills to the floor under a strictly closed rule.

The second objective led to a vast expansion in entitlement programs and to a steady rise in the portion of the federal budget classified as uncontrollable under existing law. During the 1967–1982 period, uncontrollable spending climbed from less than 60 percent of federal outlays to more than 75 percent. During this period some major entitlements (such as social security) were indexed to the consumer price index or other measures of inflation. As a result their costs were programmed to increase regardless of the performance of the economy or of other claims on the federal budget.

The Pressure for Redistribution

By the mid-1970s the orientation and procedures of Congress comported with the distributive environment in which it operated. But at just about the time that congressional reform ran its course, the economic conditions that gave rise to the distributive state changed from growth to stagnation. The U.S. economy was buffeted by two oil shocks and three recessions in the 1970s. It experienced stagflation (high inflation and high unemployment) and low productivity growth. Real GNP grew about 3 percent a year in the 1970s, not enough to keep down the unemployment rate, which averaged more than 6 percent during the decade. The inflation rate was even higher—about 7.5 percent during the 1970s—while productivity improved at only half the rate of the two preceding decades. Without robust productivity gains, the economy did not deliver sufficient increments to finance the distributive state.

It is important to note that the economy did expand during the turbulent 1970s. The 3 percent annual growth, however, was not sufficient to accommodate the demands on the federal government. Real federal spending grew at an annual average of about 4 percent. The seemingly small difference between economic and budgetary growth led to high deficits and to a shift in resources from the private to the public sector. Budget deficits averaged about 3 percent of GNP during the 1975–1981 years, twice the percentage of the preceding decade; outlays swelled to more than 23 percent of GNP, compared with about 19 percent in the 1955–1964 years.

These data suggest that the first signs of economic adversity did not uproot incremental expectations. The federal government continued to spend as if the economy were (or would again become) as robust as it had been during the growth years. But when recovery proved to be weak and short-lived and inflation and unemployment climbed concurrently, the distributive politics of the postwar era could no longer be sustained.

The age of distribution had ended, but it has been difficult for the American people or the national government to enter the age of redistribution. Incrementalism had its own momentum and could not be reversed when the economy was sluggish. Congress was organized for growth and could not easily adapt to the changed circumstances. The adjustment of Congress to distributive expectations had only recently been completed and could not be quickly undone when the increments vanished.

By the end of the 1970s, Congress was much more vulnerable to distributive pressure than it had been at the start of the decade. Data and analyses of legislative activities and options were widely available; hordes of Washington representatives of trade associations, state and local governments, public interest groups, and businesses patrolled Capitol Hill and vigorously protected their benefits. Authorizing committees were informed of the budgetary consequences of their programs, and they effectively promoted their legislative and program objectives. The Appropriations committees were more favorably disposed toward spending than they had been in the past, and if they were not sufficiently forthcoming with their recommendations, they faced proposals for spending increases on the floor. Members had ample staffs and could venture into any legislative area that interested them or their constituents. Committees or members that wanted to resist distributive pressures could not prevail merely by bottling up legislation; spending often climbed if Congress did nothing. This meant that legislative inaction or deadlock favored higher rather than lower spending. Nor could spending demands be resisted in the secrecy of committee markups or without a floor fight. Those who would speak for cutting benefits had to stand up and be counted in public.

The transformation of the public sector noted earlier also worked against redistributive policies in Congress. Since the bulk of federal expenditures was paid to outside beneficiaries, Congress could not dampen distributive pressures merely by saying no to government agencies. The means of distribution, which once were concentrated in geographically based public works projects, now sprawled across the full landscape of federal responsibilities. In the 1970s members distributed benefits not only by obtaining a new bridge or dam but also by winning bigger benefit checks for constituents, arranging contracts for local businesses and grants for local governments, and providing other direct services to the real spenders of federal dollars. One might not like the term "social pork barrel" applied by David Stockman to the distributive state, but it is a fairly accurate label of the contemporary role of Congress.[22]

Adjusting to Redistributive Pressures. Congress is a self-correcting institution but not always a fast-moving one. Its openness to outside pressure explains why it has periodically adjusted itself to changed circumstances. But Congress might flounder for an extended period before it conforms its organization and behavior to outside conditions. Because a realignment might be perceived by power holders in Congress as injurious to their interests, they can be expected to oppose far-reaching changes.

The most important change has been the establishment of the congressional budget process, but as John Ellwood argues, a distinction has to be drawn between the budget process devised by the 1974 act and the one that has operated since 1980.[23] The original budget process emerged from diverse and sometimes conflicting objectives. As a bundle of compromises, its main objective was not redistribution. Indeed, the formulation of the basic process (but not its enactment into law) before the first oil shock suggests that economic adversity was not the principal motivating force. The early operation of the congressional budget process also suggests that it was not a constraint on distributive politics in Congress. Until 1980 the Budget committees and the budget resolutions they produced generally accommodated the program and spending demands of legislative committees.[24]

The "second" budget process that operated in the 1980–1982 years was a redistributive process. Through the reconciliation procedures described in this book by Naomi Caiden, Congress managed to redistribute resources in 1980, 1981, and 1982. Through reconciliation President Reagan won enactment of more than $100 billion in spending reductions and program curtailments over a three-year period.[25] Reconciliation forced Congress to vote on the president's demands in a single package and thus enabled him to overcome the delays, fragmentation, and evasions that often hobble efforts to redirect legislative policy. Reconciliation also weakened the ability of interest groups to bring pressure to bear on members of Congress and prevented them from obtaining separate votes on many of the cutbacks. But reconciliation has been a very controversial procedure, and it remains to be seen whether it will be a lasting feature of the budget process.

With or without reconciliation the budget process cannot by itself countervail against spending pressure in Congress. The authorizing, appropriating, and tax committees—all of which are oriented to distribution—can outvote and outmaneuver the Budget committees. To prevail, the Budget committees need allies, either within Congress or in other political quarters. They have tried to enlist the Appropriations committees in support of redistributive policies but with only limited and temporary success. If the Budget committees were to wither away (or be abolished), the Appropriations committees might have some incentive to revert to the guardianship role they played before the rise of the distributive state. But as long as the Budget committees are rivals for legislative and fiscal power, the Appropriations committees are likely to perceive distributive politics as the most attractive course of action.

Support for the Budget committees might come from congressional leaders; but in view of the divisions between the two major parties, they are likely to exploit the process for their own political advantages. The party leaders have given strong support to the idea of a budget process, but they have not been willing to tilt substantively in favor of the process when it has been challenged by other strong participants. Ideally the two parties would provide bipartisan cover for the difficult redistributive decisions faced by congressional budget makers, but the parties have been so openly divided on budget policy that it is not possible to obtain their cooperation.

The president is another potential ally of the budget process, but those who have occupied the White House during the past decade have tended to exploit the process for their own advantage. Gerald Ford lambasted the new process as a budget-busting exercise; Jimmy Carter changed his mind about budget policy frequently and expected Congress to accommodate to his latest position; Ronald Reagan used the process to revamp budget policies and priorities in 1981 but abandoned it when it suited his interests in 1983.

Without strong allies the budget process in Congress has become weak at the very time that the need for redistribution is paramount. The Budget committees are redistributive committees in a legislative environment still programmed for distribution. Unless Congress becomes more redistributive or economic improvements obviate the need for redistribution, the budget process will not survive as an effective force on Capitol Hill.

Notes

1. For data on the number of bills enacted by Congress, see Norman J. Ornstein et al., *Vital Statistics on Congress, 1982*, table 6–1 (Washington, D.C.: American Enterprise Institute, 1982), pp. 130–31.

2. See Gregg Easterbrook, "How Congress Collapsed: A Depressing Guide to Governmental Paralysis," *Washington Post*, Outlook section, December 12, 1982.

3. Congress completed action on 106 public laws during the lame-duck session; 145 such laws were enacted during the entire 1981 session of Congress.

4. For proposals to improve congressional operations, see "Draft Report of the Senate Study Group" (cochaired by former Senators James B. Pearson and Abraham A. Ribicoff), April 5, 1983.

5. In 1981, for example, more than 300 of the 483 roll call votes in the Senate pertained to budget and related issues. See Allen Schick, "Legislation, Appropriations, and Budgets" (Congressional Research Service, 1983).

6. In 1883 federal spending totaled $265 million, the same as in 1876. The composition of expenditures did change over time, however. In 1876 interest (largely for Civil War debts) accounted for almost 40 percent of

total spending and veterans' compensation and pensions for slightly more than 10 percent. In 1883 interest costs were about 20 percent of total spending and veterans' programs 25 percent.

7. This statement is based on unpublished data provided by Rudolph G. Penner of the American Enterprise Institute.

8. The separation between legislation and appropriations is still recognized (but not always adhered to) in the rules of the House and Senate. See House Rule XXI and Senate Rule XVI.

9. See Schick, "Legislation," for a study of appropriations practices during the past 200 years.

10. The Holman rule is an exception to the House bar against legislation in appropriations bills. Although Holman is still part of the House rules, it has rarely been applied in recent times.

11. The success of this budget policy can be seen in the decline of federal spending, tax rates, and the deficit in the decade following the Budget and Accounting Act.

12. Quoted in William E. Leuchtenburg, *Franklin D. Roosevelt and the New Deal* (New York: Harper and Row, 1963), p. 274.

13. Robert and Helen Lynd, *Middletown in Transition* (New York: Harcourt, Brace, 1937), p. 489.

14. See Martha Derthick, *Policymaking for Social Security* (Washington, D.C.: Brookings Institution, 1979).

15. Aaron Wildavsky, *The Politics of the Budgetary Process* (Boston: Little, Brown, 1964).

16. See Royce Crocker, "Federal Government Spending and Public Opinion," *Public Budgeting and Finance*, vol. 1 (August 1981), pp. 25–35.

17. The Legislative Reorganization Act of 1946 made a number of significant changes in congressional procedure, but it did not change the distribution of power in Congress. It made Congress more efficient without really changing its orientation.

18. See Richard F. Fenno, *The Power of the Purse: Appropriations Politics in Congress* (Boston: Little, Brown, 1966).

19. Ibid.

20. See Allen Schick, *Congress and Money: Budgeting, Spending, and Taxing* (Washington, D.C.: Urban Institute, 1980), esp. chaps. 10, 11.

21. See chapter 7, "Tax Policy: Structure and Choice."

22. David A. Stockman, "The Social Pork Barrel," *The Public Interest*, no. 39 (Spring 1975), pp. 3–30.

23. See chapter 3, "Budget Control in a Redistributive Environment."

24. See Schick, *Congress and Money*, chap. 8.

25. See Allen Schick, *Reconciliation and the Congressional Budget Process* (Washington, D.C.: American Enterprise Institute, 1981).

Contributors

NAOMI CAIDEN is professor in the School of Administration, California State College at Bernadino. She is coauthor (with Aaron Wildavsky) of *Planning and Budgeting in Poor Countries* and author of a forthcoming study of almost 1,000 years of French budgetary development.

JOHN W. ELLWOOD is associate professor in the Amos Tuck School of Business, Dartmouth College, and is the editor of *Reductions in U.S. Domestic Spending*. He previously served as special assistant to the director, Congressional Budget Office.

JOHN FEREJOHN is a professor of political science at Stanford University and is a senior research fellow at the Hoover Institution. He is the author of *Pork Barrel Politics* and of a number of articles on American political behavior.

LANCE T. LELOUP is professor of political science at the University of Missouri–St. Louis. He is author of *Budgetary Politics* and *The Fiscal Congress*.

MARK V. NADEL is a senior researcher at the Battelle Human Affairs Research Center. He is the author of *The Politics of Consumer Protection* and was involved in regulatory policy while on the staff of the Senate Committee on Governmental Affairs.

ROBERT PASTOR is a faculty research associate in the School of Public Affairs at the University of Maryland. He has written *Congress and the Politics of U.S. Foreign Economic Policy* and has served as a senior staff member on the National Security Council.

ROBERT D. REISCHAUER is the senior vice president of the Urban Institute. He previously was the associate director of the Congressional Budget Office and a senior fellow at the Brookings Institution. Reischauer has written various articles on economic policy.

Catherine E. Rudder is associate director of the American Political Science Association. She has worked for two members of the House Committee on Ways and Means and has written about tax policy since serving as a congressional fellow in 1974–1975.

Allen Schick is professor of public policy in the School of Public Affairs at the University of Maryland and an adjunct scholar at the American Enterprise Institute. He is the author of *Congress and Money: Budgeting, Spending, and Taxing.*

Index

AEI Associates Program

The American Enterprise Institute invites your participation in the competition of ideas through its AEI Associates Program. This program has two objectives: (1) to extend public familiarity with contemporary economic and political issues and (2) to increase research on these issues and disseminate the results to policy makers, the academic community, journalists, and others who help shape public attitudes.

As an Associate you will receive AEI publications at a reduced rate. For the $39 annual fee you will receive

- Subscriptions for two of the following publications:
  Public Opinion, a bimonthly magazine exploring trends and implications of public opinion on social and public policy questions
  Regulation, the bimonthly journal examining all aspects of government regulation of society
  AEI Economist, a monthly newsletter analyzing current economic issues and evaluating future trends
  (For an additional $12 you can receive all three publications.)
- A subscription to the bimonthly *Memorandum*, the newsletter on all AEI activities
- The AEI publications catalog and all supplements
- A 30% discount on all AEI books, pamphlets, monographs, and proceedings.

Your contribution, which in most cases is partly tax deductible, will also ensure that decision makers have the benefit of scholarly research on the practical options to be considered before programs are formulated.

To join the Associates program, send your name and address and a check for $39 ($51 if you wish to receive all three publications) to: Associates Program, American Enterprise Institute, 1150 Seventeenth Street, N.W., Washington, D.C. 20036. Indicate which two publications you wish to receive. If you live outside the United States and Canada, enclose an additional $20 to cover postage. Payable in U.S. currency only.

The New Congress

THOMAS E. MANN AND NORMAN J. ORNSTEIN, editors

Eleven scholars examine the changes that have taken place within Congress and its environment over the past several decades and the consequences of those changes for the policy process. The authors are R. Douglas Arnold, I. M. Destler, Roger H. Davidson, Charles O. Jones, Michael J. Malbin, Thomas E. Mann, Norman J. Ornstein, Nelson W. Polsby, Michael J. Robinson, Allen Schick, and Barbara Sinclair.

"The quality of anything written about the Congress depends heavily on whether the author has reflected on its complexity and respected the need for a reasonable level of precision. Here—overall, at least—the quality is high. . . . [deals] with contemporary changes in congressional politics, practices, and procedures. Its contributors are certifiably knowledgeable about both Congress in general and the particular subjects they cover. . . especially well organized." *Congressional Staff Journal.*

"Eleven thoughtful essays. . . . This excellent book should contribute to a better understanding of congressional actions in the 1980s." *Library Journal.*

"A more timely book cannot be imagined. This is really fascinating stuff about the very engine of popular government and how it works." *Fayetteville Observer-Times.*

400 pp./1981/paper 3416-0 $9.25/cloth 3415-2 $17.25

After the People Vote
Steps in Choosing the President

EDITED BY WALTER BERNS

What if no presidential candidate gets an electoral college majority? What if a presidential candidate dies before the November election? after the November election but before the electoral votes are cast? after the electoral votes are cast but before they are counted? after they are counted but before the winning candidate assumes office?

Questions like these have puzzled even constitutional scholars. The authors of this guide address these matters and others as they explain the workings of the electoral college and the process of presidential selection.

39 pp./1983/paper 3540-X $3.95

How Capitalistic Is the Constitution?

ROBERT A. GOLDWIN
AND WILLIAM A. SCHAMBRA, editors

Is there a deep contradiction between the promises of democratic equality in the Constitution and the material inequalities generated by American capitalism? Or is capitalism not only compatible with but essential for democratic liberty? The controversy over how to understand and to reconcile our political and economic systems is presented in its full political, historical, economic, legal, and philosophic complexity in essays by Walter Dean Burnham, Edward S. Greenberg, Robert Lekachman, Forrest McDonald, Stephen Miller, Marc F. Plattner, and Bernard H. Siegan.

"Provocative."   *Reason.*

172 pp./1981/paper 3478-0 $6.25/cloth 3477-2 $14.25

How Democratic Is the Constitution?

ROBERT A. GOLDWIN
AND WILLIAM A. SCHAMBRA, editors

Some of the authors in this volume accept a version of Charles Beard's thesis, arguing that the Constitution was designed to protect the wealthy by frustrating popular rule, that it is an aristocratic document garbed in democratic rhetoric, or that it is a middle-of-the-road compromise between radical democrats and "accommodating conservatives." Other authors maintain that the Constitution is unqualifiedly democratic, that it was designed to establish a "deliberative democracy," or that its seemingly undemocratic institutions are intended to secure rights for all. The seven essays were written by Walter Berns, Joseph M. Bessette, Ann Stuart Diamond, Wilson Carey McWilliams, Michael Parenti, Gordon S. Wood, and Alfred F. Young.

"A splendid recent compendium of essays."

The Public Interest.

150 pp./1980/paper 3399-7 $5.25/cloth 3400-4 $12.25

The United States Senate:
A Bicameral Perspective

RICHARD F. FENNO, JR.

This study looks at the U.S. Senate in the context of its relationship to the House of Representatives. Comparisons are made of Senate and House campaigns on the basis of dependency on the media, remoteness from constituencies, and emphasis on personal trust and on public policy. The author explores the effect of the six-year term on senators.

Richard F. Fenno, Jr., a visiting scholar at the American Enterprise Institute in 1981–1982, is William J. Kenan Professor of Political Science at the University of Rochester.

"Deserves special note. . . . Fenno has few if any peers among his professional colleagues in his ability to confront the ordinary, the mundane, and even the banal about the Congress and to discover there the veins of meaning and understanding which should have been apparent to all, and to express his insights with a clarity and a straightforwardness so frequently lacking in others."

Congressional Staff Journal.

47 pp./1982/3499-3 $2.95

The Reagan Phenomenon— and Other Speeches on Foreign Policy

JEANE J. KIRKPATRICK

In these speech/essays, Ambassador Kirkpatrick describes, assesses, and articulates the foundations of what she calls "the Reagan phenomenon" as it relates to the liberal tradition, Western values, America's goals, and U.S. foreign policy.

"She is at once informed, incisive, and challenging. . . . in a fresh and vigorous fashion. . . . This is a stimulating and valuable book, the work of an activist and participant that nevertheless has about it the qualities of scholarship and objectivity." *Contemporary Review* (London).

"Lucid, potent speeches. . . . Valuable reading on a number of levels—as a reflection of Kirkpatrick's work and views on foreign affairs; as an indication of the Reagan administration's policies and opinions; and as substantive material for further discussion of international politics." *Booklist.*

"Ambassador Kirkpatrick. . . understands that truth is the main weapon of democracy."

Jean-François Revel, former editor, *L'Express.*

"The best thinking of the clearest mind in foreign policy today." William Safire, columnist, *New York Times.*

230 pp./1983/cloth 1361-9 $14.95

A Note on the Book

This book was edited by
Gertrude Kaplan and Margaret Seawell of the
Publications Staff of the American Enterprise Institute.
The staff also designed the cover and format, with Pat Taylor.
The figures were drawn by Hördur Karlsson.
The text was set in Palatino, a typeface designed by Hermann Zapf.
Hendricks-Miller Typographic Company, of Washington, D.C.,
set the type, and R. R. Donnelley & Sons Company,
of Harrisonburg, Virginia, printed and bound the book,
using paper made by the S. D. Warren Company.